To James & Mary

May God Bless you for you enjoyment of the blessings that can only come thru Christ †

Peace & Grace
Deacon Jodi Mascona

May God bless you as you journey through life.
Betty Arcement

Journeying

on

Holy

Ground

*Christian Strategies to Reach Your Personal,
Professional, and Spiritual Destiny*

*by Billy Arcement, MEd. and
Deacon Jodi Moscona, JD*

Copyright ©2008 Billy Arcement and Jodi Moscona

All rights reserved. No portion of this book may be reproduced in any form without written permission from the copyright holder.

Source of Biblical Quotations

Scripture quotations taken from the New American Standard Bible®, Copyright © 1960, 1962, 1963, 1968, 1971, 1972, 1973, 1975, 1977, 1995 by The Lockman Foundation. Used by permission. (www.Lockman.org)

Scripture quotations marked (NIV®) are taken from the Holy Bible, New International Version®. NIV®. Copyright © 1973, 1978, 1984 by International Bible Society. Used by permission.
All rights reserved worldwide.

Scripture quotations taken from The New American Bible, Copyright © 1983, Thomas Nelson, Inc.
Used by permission. All rights reserved.

For more information, contact:
www.SearchingForSuccess.com
www.Jodimoscona.com

Library of Congress Catalog Number in Publication Data
ISBN: 978-0-9653446-1-6
Printed in the United States of America

I dedicate this book to my beautiful and lovely wife Darlene, certainly a gift to me from God, and our children Brian, Matthew, and Alicia who continue to make both Darlene and me proud because of the way they live their lives.

—Jodi Moscona

This book is dedicated to my best friend and spouse of 46 years, Ernestine. She is "Mimi" to our ten grandchildren—Amber, Carolyn, Katherine and Jack Allen; Paul, Erin and Beth Ann Arcement; Patrick, William and Nicholas Arcement—and the rock upon which we have built our family. I also want to include our children and in-laws, Stacie and her husband John Allen, Corey and his wife Karen, Pat and his wife Monica, and our youngest daughter, Mary, all of whom have brought so much joy into my life.

—Billy Arcement

Acknowledgments

For Our Peer Reviewers:
Always open to constructive criticism, we acknowledge those that have critically reviewed the text of this book: Jason Doise, Tommy Teepel, Barry Harwell, Fr. Scott Dugas, and Steve Ridley. We prospered by their insights and are very appreciative of their time and commitment to help with this project.

For Our Editor:
The job of reading someone else's ideas and blending them into a sensible story can be daunting. We wish to express our sincere appreciation for the many ideas, comments, and insights given to us by our editor, Louise McLaughlin. She helped Billy with his first book, *Searching for Success*, and was brought back for an "encore" performance with this book. Thank you, Louise, for a job well done.

From Jodi:
I would like to acknowledge the personal inspiration for my contributions to this book that I received from my family, who are evidence to me that the principles in the book work. My wife Darlene and children Brian, Matt and Alicia continue to inspire me by their dedication to our family. I would also like to acknowledge Mr. and Mrs. Charles Wiegand. Growing up, they provided an example of family which inspires me even today.

I would also like to acknowledge the support and encouragement of David Lukinovich and all the lawyers and staff of Lukinovich Law without which I might never have completed this project.

From Billy:
Writing a book required external support and internal fortitude to complete. Certainly, for the patience to put up with the many hours of writing required, I want to express my appreciation to my wife Ernestine. I am truly fortunate to be blessed with her love and support and to have her as my partner in life.

I would like to acknowledge the inspiration and education I've received from the writings of great authors I've read, the examples of the many mentors who have provided guidance, and the spiritual growth I've received from 18 years of attending Manresa retreats and the many years of spiritual study provided by the resident Jesuits of Manresa Retreat House.

Table of Contents

Introduction 9

Part I: The Journey with God. 11

    Chapter 1: The Start of the Journey 13

    Chapter 2: Using Our Time for God 23

    Chapter 3: Using Our Talents for God 35

    Chapter 4: Sharing Our Treasures with God. 43

    Chapter 5: God's Love for Us. 47

    Chapter 6: Fear, Faith, and Love 53

    Chapter 7: Creating Vertical Alignment. .57

Part II: The Journey with Family 61

    Chapter 8: We Don't Choose Family. 63

    Chapter 9: Ideas to Build a Lasting Marriage 69

    Chapter 10: Journeying with Your Children 89

Part III: The Journey with Work 127

    Chapter 11: Some Thoughts about Work 129

    Chapter 12: Develop Personal Leadership Skills
                to Enhance Your Career 159

    Chapter 13: Develop Your Ability to Lead Others
                for Greater Career Opportunities 179

Part IV: The Journey to Personal Success..................195

    Chapter 14: Do You Have a Little Stress in Your Life?.........197

    Chapter 15: The Final Leg of the Journey...................205

Part V: A Little Lagniappe 229

    The Journey Home....................................231

    The Spirit of Manresa.................................233

Personal Growth and Self-improvement Reading List 237

About the Authors.......................................239

Introduction

*"Then the Lord said, do not come near here;
remove your sandals from your feet,
for the place on which you are standing is holy ground."*

—Exodus 3:5

*"Are you not aware that you are the temple of God and
that the Spirit of God dwells in you?"*

—1 Corinthians 3:16

These two Scripture passages capture the basic premise upon which this book is written. In the first passage, the Lord of our Universe reminds Moses that the very ground on which he stood was holy because Moses was in the presence of the Lord. In the second passage, St. Paul asks us to acknowledge that our body is a living place where God is always present. Taken together, these passages suggest that our physical presence combined with God's spiritual presence guide us as we journey on holy ground. We want our readers to understand that this connection can guide us in our relationship building with the Creator himself, with our family members, and with those in our work and social environments.

Our goal in writing this book is to help you design a road map to use as a guide for creating a successful journey through the time you spend on earth, and to better prepare you for the eternal life that follows. Keeping God, family, career, and self as the order of importance is as it should be. God must permeate every part of our life, and it is His moral code that dictates how we behave. We should live our life every day in a way that keeps priorities in order, and God in the forefront. Doing so allows God to guide us through the obstacles life places in our path and to help us open the doors to eternity. Our time on earth is just a temporary stopover in the grand scheme of things. We must never forget the permanency of eternity, our ultimate destination. Creating what we call "Christian Strategies" as part of our daily action code helps us walk this journey with God's graces.

Throughout the book we provide suggested "how to" ideas. We don't have all the answers, but we give you the very best we have to offer. We believe the guidelines we present will give you an edge to journey through your life in the right way. These are the paths we've chosen to use on our own personal journey, and we recognize the consequences of not journeying correctly.

We are constantly searching for answers to the difficult questions life poses. If you are on a similar search, we invite you to journey with us. With our Spiritual Leader as our partner, there is little chance we will not be successful. But, like author John Maxwell said in his book, *Thinking for a Change*, perhaps if we don't feel as successful as we'd like to feel, or if we feel our struggles are too difficult to overcome, it may be that we are not *thinking* our way to the top. How we think about God, our family, our work, and ourselves are keys to making our journey successful. But the critical component of all this is to develop and maintain a spiritual connection throughout the process. We encourage you to think about:

- Your *Spiritual Desire* for a relationship with God
- Your *Spiritual Blindness* that may get in the way of establishing that relationship
- Your *Spiritual Blessings* that you've received throughout your life
- Your *Spiritual Understanding* of what it takes to have a strong relationship with God
- Your *Spiritual Death* that occurs when you alienate yourself from God.

As you begin to read our book, we encourage you to make notes in the margins, highlight passages that grab your attention, write questions that need answering, and work through the "Success Challenges" at the end of each of part of our book. Then, go back and re-read portions that pertain to issues that may be surfacing in your life on a regular basis. In some ways, we hope you will view our book as a "Manual on Life," and a core resource to help with your journey.

May God bring blessings into your life as you walk the holy ground He has provided for you to journey towards eternity with Him in the Kingdom.

PART I

The Journey

with

God

CHAPTER 1

The Start of the Journey

The most successful journeys are those that we spend the proper amount of time preparing to take. Proper preparation should be the beginning of every journey through life. Even for a simple task like going to work, we know that we first have to get ready by dressing for the job, leaving our home, and reviewing the route we will take as we set off. Children preparing for school check their backpack, tell Mom and Dad good-bye, and then embark on a walk, bus ride, or car pool. Our vacations require an even greater degree of preparation—making reservations, gathering supplies, wardrobes, planning routes, and other activities lead the list. Our life journey is no different. But how often do we pay the same attention to planning where we are going, how we are going to get there, and what activities will make our journey a better experience?

Start with a Guidebook and a Guide

"Keep this book of the law on your lips. Recite it day and by night, that you may observe carefully all that is written in it; then you will successfully attain your goal."

—Joshua 1:8

This quotation from the book of Joshua in the Hebrew Scriptures provides a direction we should heed in planning our life journey. We can depend upon the Bible as the guidebook for defining and fulfilling our hopes for eternity in God's Kingdom. Add God's unconditional love and the gift of His son, Jesus, and we have a clear path and support mechanism for our journey to eternity.

We recognize the enormity of these two statements. But we share them because we believe this is the way to reach ultimate success in this life and in the next. Let's examine each of them in greater detail.

In 1992, Jodi attended a weekend conference in Mobile, Alabama hosted by one of the biggest multi-level marketing organizations of that time. Rich DeVos, one of the richest men in the world, owner of the Orlando Magic, and 2003 recipient of the American Inspirations Award from the Presidential Prayer Team, was introduced to the group via a video conference. DeVos was an individual that had been an inspiration to Jodi for many years. In announcing the award, the Presidential Prayer Team quoted Mr. DeVos as saying, "The Bible talks a great deal about being wealthy, and about working hard. I think I'm following the admonition of what I've been asked to do: to work hard, do well, and then share out of that."

The event featured individuals who had made millions through sales in this company. Attendees paid good money, traveled a long distance, and gave up an entire weekend to learn the keys to being successful with their business and were anxious to hear how it could be done. Speaker after speaker produced excitement and enthusiasm as they shared their success stories. After the introduction of one of the many speakers, Jodi heard something that initially shocked him and others in the audience. The speaker shared that he was not a preacher, just a business man who had found a way to be successful. Then he held up a Bible and told the crowd that within the covers of this book were the ideas he had used to create his successes. To the speaker, the Bible was his business plan. Initially there was a sprinkle of applause. Then the room erupted once everyone understood the true meaning of the message they had just heard.

Jodi never forgot that night. Until that moment he had never thought of success in those terms. But over time, the same message was shared by other successful business executives within the organization such as John Crow, Larry Winters, Dexter Yeager, Rex Renfro, Ron Puryear, and many others. Today, he's a true believer in this philosophy of success.

The words of the Bible provide us with a moral code—a model for helping us to make ethical decisions; a moral code that gives us solid directions for being successful spiritually, physically, and mentally. In the Hebrew

Scriptures, *Jeremiah 7:23*, God established His covenant with His people. *"I will be your God and you will be my people,"* is a two-part promise made over and over again. God would forever love, sustain, guide, and redeem His people. In return, the people would follow God's rules: ten direct, simply-stated sentences collectively called the Ten Commandments. God further promised to send a redeemer to free mankind from their sin, and reopen the path to the kingdom. We believe in the promises made by God in these scripture passages, and, in particular, we believe that using the moral code established by the Commandments is a great foundation for becoming God's people. Live by the standards of the Commandments, and we will have taken a giant step towards establishing and maintaining the important relationship with God that we discussed earlier. And, just in case you missed it, the word is Commandments, not Suggestions!

While the Hebrew Scriptures are about covenant, the New Testament is about the kingdom—here, now, and yet to come. We have example after example of Jesus telling parables and stories of how to live in God's earthly kingdom and prepare to share His heavenly one. Jesus' life, His stories, and His commitment to follow the will of the Father are perfect codes upon which to model our daily activities. Follow the Commandments, and the teachings of Jesus—the human representative of God—and your journey will be safe, sound, and spiritual.

Establishing the critical relationship we've been discussing starts by placing our unconditional trust in God, his teachings in the Hebrew Scriptures, and the teachings of his son, Jesus. In the Book of *Proverbs 16:3*, God lets us know how to succeed. The passage states,

"Entrust your works to the Lord, and your plans will succeed."

Wow, do you want to succeed? Make these words your mantra!

Planning Our Destinations

Everyone eventually journeys to the same destination—we die and will face the Creator on our judgment day. When each of us reaches that destination, God won't say, "Hey, you made it to death, good work." No, the questions will more likely be, "How did you get here?" or, "How was your journey?"

Life is a journey—a process by which we seek to bring happiness into our life, and into the lives of those we love. But there is a message many miss as they work their way through their journey. They believe success is the attainment of their life's desires; that success is under their control. In truth, the journey is one in which we discover that we are here to fulfill God's will, and we cannot do it with self-will alone. In fact, our charge is to discover God's will for us—His plan for our life. To do this, we need a loving relationship with the Father.

Why do we need such a relationship? Put simply, while we are on earth, this relationship will support us in life's calm days, sustain us in the difficult moments, and help us enjoy the celebration of the moments of achievement.

This journey called life is not a solo act. It's a partnership. To maximize this partnership, we need to develop a "spiritual travel plan" designed to enhance and enrich our spiritual life—a plan that will lead us to a stronger relationship with God.

We're sure by now you've deduced that this book will have a strong spiritual focus. But don't dismiss the focus until you've explored it a bit more. We deliberately aimed our journey in this direction because we believe that, without a strong spiritual foundation, there will always be a missing element in life. No matter how successful one gets, without a solid relationship with God, there is a spiritual void that seeks fulfillment.

Still have doubts? Consider a very public journey that ended in a very undesirable destination. Recall the scandals in the corporate world that have come to light in the last few years. These executives thought nothing of creating fictitious companies to hide expenses, inflating profits, and lining their pockets with the "gold" they siphoned from others in the corporation. They played a shell game that was eventually exposed, with thousands of people losing their jobs and their savings. No matter how you cast these events, they are deceitful, and in essence derived from a series of lies and a clear violation of the "Thou shalt not steal" and "Thou shall have no false gods" commandments provided by God. These executives had it all. They were rich and powerful. However, their grave mistake stemmed from thinking they were in total control of everything. That attitude ultimately led to their downfall and re-classification from executives to convicts.

We also chose the word "journey" to illustrate what many philosophers and teachers have said—that success is a journey, not a destination. Consider a successful marriage. Is this something we achieve on our twenty-fifth or fiftieth wedding anniversary, or is it really the result of the way in which we live our day-to-day married lives? We tend to look at how we might achieve success without realizing that, when we look back on our life, it will be the way in which we lived each day that determined the level of success we achieved.

Activities and Distractions

We can expect that, throughout our journey, opportunities to engage in activities and distractions to our original plan will catch our attention. Sometimes they will be to our advantage, and sometimes to our disadvantage. We want to talk about an inevitable opportunity, following God's will, and a major distraction, temptation by false gods.

The Will to Choose

In deciding whether you want to follow God's plan or exercise your free will and ability to choose, consider the situation of Mary, the mother of Jesus. No matter whether you believe in Mary's role as an intercessor, or whether you just admire her as the mother of Jesus, she plays a prominent role in Scripture. The angel Gabriel visited her and gave her a choice. She could choose the will of God and become the mother of the Savior, or she could refuse, and remain in control. She chose to follow the will of God as is reported in the Gospel of *Luke 1:38*.

"Behold, I am the handmaid of the Lord. May it be done to me according to your word."

For this, as further reported in Luke she is forever called "Blessed."

If we allow God to mold our will by choosing to follow Him, the result will be delight in whatever life brings. We are reminded of how God works in *Isaiah 64:8*.

"But now, O Lord, You are our Father, we are the clay, and You our potter; and all of us are the work of Your hand."

We must understand that whatever happens in our life is the result of our choices. We can choose the will of God, or we can try to make it alone. Before choosing, we hope you read on.

False Gods, Next Exit!

Throughout the Hebrew Scriptures, there are a number of references to the first commandment, putting God above all things. For example, in the books of Exodus and Deuteronomy, it says,

"I the Lord am your God, who brought you out of the land of Egypt, that place of slavery. You shall not have other gods besides me." —Exodus 20:2-3

"Hear O Israel! The Lord is our God, the Lord alone! Therefore you shall love the Lord, your God, with all your heart, and with all your soul and with all your strength." —Deuteronomy 6:4-5

In these early passages God gives us a very important and significant message. He doesn't beat around the bush. God tells us to give our all to Him in the form of a loving relationship, one not diluted with false gods. But in our human frailty, too often we put other "gods" before the Lord. This commandment requires us to look at our lives and, in a very honest way, decide what we hold as most dear—things or God.

Deacon Glenn Harmon is a Catholic evangelist. His ministry, Glenn Harmon Ministries, focuses on bringing the radical Gospel of Jesus Christ to churches nationwide. In his personal story, he reveals that he was a highly successful business man. His work took him around the world, and often he would find himself on the road for prolonged periods of time. His job ranked first at this time of his life. To the outside world, Glenn was very successful. But the inside world of Glenn Harmon was filled with emptiness. At a critical point in his career, he suspected that his company might be engaged in some practices he considered unethical. Glenn had to make a choice. He shares that until this moment in his life, he had put his work before his God. The time had come to choose between God and his very successful career. He quit his job because he felt his heart turn back to God. He had forsaken his relationship with God and that was not working for him. Thus, he was able to give up a life that included a huge salary, an expense account, power, and prestige because he finally realized that his job had become his "god," and that choice was simply not working for him. We must understand, as Glenn finally realized, that God never turns from us. We turn from God. Scripture supports that idea. The questions to ask at this point are: Would you be able to make such a choice? Would you even consider such a choice necessary?

Now you may never have to make a career choice like Glenn's, but other temptations always await us. Let us cite another example. We live in Louisiana, the sportsman's paradise. Hunting, fishing, and other sporting activities are very popular pastimes. When Jodi lived on a golf course, every Sunday morning, the course was full of golfers. He didn't know these individuals and didn't want to judge them. But he often wondered if they were skipping church to play golf.

Likewise, we know many men who go hunting for the entire weekend and do not attend church. When Jodi was in college, he knew someone who was an avid duck hunter. It was not uncommon for his friend to rise at 4 a.m. to sit in the cold, damp weather waiting for the ducks to fly over his duck blind. He often hunted on Sunday morning. By the time the hunt was done, he was too tired to go to church. Jodi also knew other men who brought their kids hunting on Sundays and justified missing church in the name of "quality time with the kids." What is the common thread in each of these stories? In each case someone made a choice to place "gods" over God.

Right Choices, Right God

Both of us have spent a portion of our lives in politics. We've come to understand that the world of politics is a world where many people have false gods. Many elected officials are very egotistical, although we acknowledge that one almost has to be at least a little egotistical to run for office.

Jodi worked for some politicians that truly had the good of the people at the forefront of their careers. On the other hand, he knows many who spent their entire term working and focusing on getting re-elected because they liked their position of power. To these types of elected officials, power and ego are their false gods.

During Billy's twelve-year tenure in public office, he served on his local school board. After three failed attempts to get elected to his local City Council, he was able to sneak into office for the first time by the overwhelming margin of twelve votes. In his three previous failures, he had several opportunities to compromise values as a trade for possible election to office. By placing trust in the Lord, and striving to follow his moral code, he was able to reject, as tempting as they were, such offers. If values are solid, the discomfort of such a decision far outweighs the prestige of winning an election. Values reveal our character. Putting God first is simply a way to prioritize our focus, and in doing so, we will start to imitate the values God represents to us.

While in office, Billy could say with certainty that, if other "gods" ruled his thinking, he could have taken advantage of his position to acquire considerably more power and influence. He thanked God often for keeping him strong, and helping him to remember his priorities and God's commandments. He chose to make decisions, not based upon what would help him get re-elected, but based upon what helped children. With this focus, choosing was easy and, in the end, the standard for all decisions he made during the twelve years he served in public office. Voters validated his actions by re-electing him to office twice. When he left pubic service by his choice, he felt good and clean. In retrospect, he found that the words of the Beatitudes took on a new meaning.

When Jesus saw the crowds, He went up on the mountain; and after He sat down, His disciples came to Him. He opened His mouth and began to teach them, saying,

"*Blessed are the poor in spirit, for theirs is the kingdom of heaven.*

"*Blessed are those who mourn, for they shall be comforted.*

"*Blessed are the gentle, for they shall inherit the earth.*

"*Blessed are those who hunger and thirst for righteousness, for they shall be satisfied.*

"*Blessed are the merciful, for they shall receive mercy.*

"*Blessed are the pure in heart, for they shall see God.*

"*Blessed are the peacemakers, for they shall be called sons of God.*

"*Blessed are those who have been persecuted for the sake of righteousness, for theirs is the kingdom of heaven.*

"*Blessed are you when people insult you and persecute you, and falsely say all kinds of evil against you because of Me.*

"*Rejoice and be glad, for your reward in heaven is great; for in the same way they persecuted the prophets who were before you.*

—Matthew 5:1-12

We share these stories to illustrate how easy it is to put something or someone ahead of God. As we go on our journey in this book, we want you to think about your life and where you've placed your priorities. The instruction from Joshua 1:8 is very clear. It tells us to look to Scripture for our guidance. We believe Scripture helps us to understand the order of priorities we should follow. For us, it's God, family, and then career. And we hope by the time you finish reading this book, you'll feel the same.

Allowing intrusions (false gods) to prevent establishing that all important relationship with our Creator is a major stumbling block to making the God connection we've been discussing. These intrusions might be our work, our sinful desires, our prejudices, or poor lifestyle choices. To set ourselves firmly in the grip of the Lord, we must learn to never let such intrusions interfere with our connectivity. It's a daunting task that demands discipline, determination, and a desire to live God's plan.

So where are you with your journey? Are you feeling lost, or do you sense that you are getting things right? It is important to get an accurate answer to these questions if you are to make the right choices that will lead to the right path on your journey.

Many of the biblical stories and messages direct us to measure the use of our time, talents, and treasures for service to God. As we said earlier, our charge while on earth is to praise, reverence, and serve God in order to earn our place with Him for eternity. Letting false gods get in the way can be a major impediment to achieving the purpose for our creation. But we believe with the proper use of our gifts from God—time, talents, and treasures, we can demonstrate our commitment and desire to spend eternity with Him.

Chapter 2

Using Our Time for God

Our everyday journeys make use of a component that we don't think about, that we just use automatically. Journeys require time: the time we leave, the time it will take to get there, the time we will return. We arrange and rearrange our plans to fit our journeys into the framework of a 24-hour day. We question, occasionally or often, how we will find the time to do all that we need to get done. We probably even examine how to get our life in better balance, with time enough for work, family, play, and solitude. With one eye on the clock or calendar and the other on the tasks at hand, where does our time for God fit?

> *"Then the king, with the queen sitting beside him, asked me, 'How long will your journey take, and when will you get back?' It pleased the king to send me; so I set a time."*
>
> —Nehemiah 2:6 (NIV®)

Let's take a trip down memory lane. Think back to when you had your first meaningful relationship with a member of the opposite sex. When you first set eyes on each other, you may have initially not been impressed, or you may have really fallen for that person. Over time, you cultivated your relationship. The love between you grew, and feelings became deeper. For those of you who plunged into marriage, you know the exhilaration you experienced by finding the "perfect person." In your relationship after marriage, each of you got to know the other at a very deep level. When you hit the jackpot, keeping the vows is a no brainer! Over the years, the love deepens and, in your heart of hearts, you experience the peace and satisfaction that you made the right choice. Being with your spouse seems like a perfect fit.

Experiencing our relationship with God is very much the same process. Just as we would not dream of interacting with our spouse only once a week for a brief hour or so, our relationship with God is much the same. It's not intended to be limited to attending Sunday church services, and then not thinking about God again until the next Sunday. We believe you'll agree that it is hard to develop a relationship with someone if you don't spend time with him or her. It works the same way with God.

Morning Time

We believe the first 30-60 minutes of the day, to a large extent, determine how we will live that day. What we do, and how we act as we begin our day, is critical. If we get up late, stressed out and rushing, if our initial focus is on the worries of yesterday, our entire day can be influenced by these factors. If, on the other hand, we start with quiet prayer, our day has a much greater opportunity to unfold in a more organized and successful pattern. By prayer, we plan our day with God. By prayer, we follow the biblical message of placing God first. By prayer, we lay a solid foundation for a successful journey through life. By prayer, we have the courage to confront what ancient Christian writers have called, "our morning demons."

Author Glenn Bland, in his book, *Success! The Glenn Bland Method*, describes morning time as the "Thirty Golden Minutes." How you spend those thirty minutes will in large part drive your day. We have heard several preachers say, that if you don't have thirty minutes in the morning to pray, then pray for an hour!

By focusing on building our relationship with God, we establish the right priority for our daily time use. Each of us has three elements to our nature—mind, body, and spirit. We are in essence a spirit captured in a physical body, with our mind serving as a connecting bridge between our spiritual and physical natures. While God can communicate with us on any

Chapter 2 — Using Our Time for God

level, we can only approach God through our spirit. How do we do that? We do it by focusing our thoughts on God and utilizing our mind as the bridge to our spiritual nature. Thus, by concentrating our thoughts for the day on God, we are able to capitalize on the blessings He so willingly wants to give us, and make that "spiritual connection" we so desperately need.

In *Matthew 7:7*, God says,

"Ask and it will be given to you. Seek and you will find. Knock and it will be opened to you."

Can it be any simpler? Ask God for the gifts we want, look for those gifts in our surroundings, and knock on the doors of opportunity to find those gifts. Too often, we are like the salesman who showed his product to potential buyers, but never asked for the order. God wants us to ask, and to work to achieve those things He has in store for us. But it requires that we establish that all-important relationship with Him. And, those first few critical moments are when that relationship begins for the day. Making the "quick connection" with God sets the tone. Call it prayer, conversation, meditation, or listening in solitude—it all comes down to making the connection. God is ever present. Remember, He is a 24/7 God. He is constantly inviting us to engage in conversation with Him through our prayers. It's in those moments that God will reveal His hopes and dreams for us. And, if we establish a trust bond, truly believing that He will be our God, we will be God's people; the door to our heart will be opened, and we will hear the message He has specifically designed for us.

A job interview experience that Jodi had points out the importance of protecting this morning time. The fact that he spent an hour in prayer in the morning came up. The prospective boss asked him if he had a huge project and had to work twelve or thirteen hours, and needed to cut out that hour of prayer, would he do it? Jodi told the interviewer that perhaps he didn't understand how valuable praying was to him. That hour allowed Jodi to be infinitely more productive during the day than if he had cut out the prayer time. The interviewer did not understand the value of the "Golden Minutes with God." Jodi was offered the job, but turned it down because he wanted to work with people who would support, not compromise, his values. Because we spend so much of our time at work, it is important to make sure that the environment supports our values.

Jodi also worked for a time as a staff attorney for the FDIC. In that government environment, it was difficult to find people who never looked beyond surface values, or who were willing to talk about spiritual issues. He did not stay at that job for long.

Other successful executives echo the Morning Prayer message. Rose Hudson is CEO and President of the Louisiana Lottery. She understands the need to maintain that connection with God in the early part of the day. Rose told us, "There is an ongoing conversation that begins sometimes before I get out of bed. Sometimes it continues while I'm driving in to work. It's a conversation with God about concerns with my family, my work, my friends, and me." Rose went on to say that she feels these moments give her the wisdom to make the right choices that day. It's these connections that help her to be grateful when things go right, and able to ask God for help when she senses the need.

Lisa Coleman, CEO and President of Westaff, one of the largest staffing services in the country, begins her day by reading and studying the Bible, which she calls "The handbook for all dimensions of life." Lisa says, "I believe very much in prayer. That is our direct connection to God."

Both of these very successful women understand there must be a connection with God. Even conservative commentator Rush Limbaugh makes the God connection. He often tells his audience that he is "on loan from God." While Limbaugh makes this statement in jest, the reality is that we are all here on loan from God for a limited time. But while we are here, it is our task to determine, through the interaction of prayer, what God has planned for us.

A Prayer for Morning

I thank You, good and gracious God, for giving me the gift of this morning. The sounds of my house surround me, and I hear Your voice. I walk in the light of day, and I see Your presence. I sip my morning coffee, and I drink in all that You have provided for me. Help me, dear Friend, to journey through this day knowing that I live it because of Your design. I pray that, as I travel with You, I may reflect Your loving providence to all whose lives touch mine. *Amen.*

Day Time

Prayer can occur throughout our day and takes on many forms: reading scripture, formal written prayers, or simply engaging in a conversation with God. We don't believe God ignores prayers, and we know that a loving God is always willing to listen and respond to our petitions. We just need to remember that what gets granted is God's choice, not ours. Here are some ideas for finding prayer time throughout the day.

Silence is golden. As we pray, one most effective method may seem strange to us. This method is to observe silence, for it is only in silence that we can hear His voice. There is actually a lot of discipline involved in silence because our natural tendency is to keep our mind moving rapidly on a myriad of thoughts. Shutting down this activity takes time, patience, and a commitment to communicate from the deep recesses of our heart. God talks when we stop talking. Why challenge God's thinking or interfere with His talking? The following passage and story illustrate how simple it can be to hear God's voice.

So He said, "Go forth and stand on the mountain before the Lord." And behold, the Lord was passing by! And a great and strong wind was rending the mountains and breaking in pieces the rocks before the Lord; but the Lord was not in the wind. And after the wind an earthquake, but the Lord was not in the earthquake. After the earthquake a fire, but the Lord was not in the fire; and after the fire a sound of a gentle blowing.

When Elijah heard it, he wrapped his face in his mantle and went out and stood in the entrance of the cave. And behold, a voice came to him and said, "What are you doing here, Elijah?" —1 Kings 19:11-13

We sometimes think that God's message will come like a booming voice from the heavens, or a brilliant inspiration like a flash of lightning. Such occasions are possible, but if this is all we wait to hear, we might miss the many smaller messages that God sends. A friend tells an amusing story. "I was envious of a lay minister who said she occasionally heard God's voice, an inner voice, when she needed guidance. Well, I thought, I have certainly done many of the same things my friend has done. I have been on retreats, I have attended workshops, I have been part of a prayer group, and I have volunteered to minister to others. How come I haven't heard God's voice? I chewed on this for several days. One afternoon, I was sitting in my favorite easy chair, with about half an hour to rest before I had to start dinner. In a state of total relaxation, not sleeping but not fully awake, I heard, 'You silly lady! I talk to you all the time! But I talk to you in the way I want to talk to you, not in the way you want me to! Remember that holy moment when you shared part of your story with a woman who was going through the same crisis I walked you through? Remember the shiver of blessing that fell over you when she turned to me? I spoke to you through her! The rain that glistened on the spider's web, the one you called your husband and son to see, the one you marveled at? Me again! And the woman who picked up the tab for your coffee in the cafeteria and told you to pass on the blessing. I was there. We talk all the time.' I laughed out loud at myself! I would like to think that I now hear God's voice more often, but I know that sometimes it takes a while for me to get myself out of the way so that the message can break through."

God's gentle blowings, His whispers, surround us. Our silence in the face of earthquakes, winds, and fires opens our ears for God's voice to break through!

Make God your friend. As we develop our prayer habits, keep one point in mind—engaging in prayer is the way to build a friendship with God. We speak to His always-open heart. Speak directly about thoughts, feelings, anguish, love for Him. Your Friend will not ignore your conversation. Like a real-life friend, He may respond in ways we don't understand at that time.

There is a Garth Brooks song about unanswered prayers. In the song, he sees his high school sweetheart many years later. He realized that he had prayed to be with his sweetheart, but that did not work out. Now he understands that God did answer his prayer. He is much happier with his wife and family now than he might have been with the high school sweetheart. He calls it an unanswered prayer. But what we think is that God's answer was "No," because He has something better in mind.

We believe there are no unanswered prayers. It's only that sometimes we get an answer that either we did not expect or did not want. Sometimes we have to wait to know the answer. In either case, we have to continue to have faith that God has our best interest always in mind, and that we should always give thanks because it is our gratitude that evidences our continued faith and love in God.

In *Mark's Gospel* 11:24, God makes it very clear how He feels about prayer. It says,

"I tell you all that you ask for in prayer, believe that you will receive it and it shall be yours."

Now, that sounds relatively simple, but the hard part is to believe we are worthy of receiving. Doubt, mistrust of God, reliance on ourselves, and pride often shield us from belief at the expectation level God has set. With unwavering belief, trust, and humility, we open our ears to hear God's word; our hearts to understand His message; our soul to receive the graces prayer brings into our life.

It is also important to devote enough time to prayer to help us control what St. Paul calls our fleshly nature. Paul says there are things in the world that bring us closer to God, and he warns us about the things that tear us away from God.

Maintain Gratefulness. One of the keys to achieving the daily successes we ask, seek, and knock for is our attitude. God wants us to maintain an attitude of gratefulness and thankfulness. This attitude is fundamental to Christian spirituality. It's this "Attitude of Gratitude" that brings happiness into our life. It's this "Attitude of Gratitude" that helps to make our life less stressful. Even medical science is starting to find a correlation between stress and illness and the attitude with which we face life.

We have friends who attend churches advocating attendance at Sunday morning, Sunday evening, and Wednesday evening services. In addition, they advocate one evening a week in small group Bible study. Church members appear to be happy and willing to devote all this time to God. For them, their reward is a personal peacefulness. This creates an attitude that helps them approach life in a way that often leads to the successful achievement of the goals they've set with the help of God. Success in life is a journey. And, if you are on a journey, and you are happy, joyful, and fully connected with God, then you are succeeding.

A healthy prayer life will help you develop a strong spiritual base that will keep you balanced and focused on the right priorities. Moral ethics in business and in life has its foundation, not in laws, but in a strong spiritual foundation built on the word of God. And a wonderful prayer to meditate on each day and use as a model for how to live our life is:

"Give me the grace to know and follow Jesus. Unite me in such a way to your Son that all who see and know me, see and know Jesus."

Our Father in heaven is a forgiving God. When we use prayer as our conduit to Him, the more likely we are to receive pardon for our failings, and the more readily we become able to forgive others for their failings toward us. Forgiveness begets forgiveness. That's a pretty neat thing we often forget to make a part of our life.

Night Time

At the end of your day, with a careful meditation, go over your day. Be thankful and joyous for the good you achieved, and then, clearing your mind, focus on making tomorrow a better day. Calling on God, in prayerful reflection, helps us move on our journey through a series of successful short steps, all focused on making each day better than the last. Reflection prior to bedtime is a great way to finish a day and set the tone for the next day.

A Prayer for Evening

Loving God, I thank You for all that You have given me today. Help me review my actions for this day. You have been my loving companion, and I have felt Your presence in so many "God moments." (Pause to reflect on these moments.)

I thank You for the people I spent time with, for the place where I live, for food on my table. As I sit in Your presence this evening, please show me where I have missed opportunities to be Your loving follower. (Pause for reflection.)

I am always learning, Lord, and I ask Your forgiveness for my failings. I hope that I can do better the next time. I look forward to tomorrow. I pray especially for (name your requests).

Lord, I put my trust in You to lead me in living Your love and doing Your will. *Amen.*

We always look forward to tomorrow, sometimes with anticipation, sometimes with dread. Emotions can overwhelm us unless we find a way to manage them. In the book, *The Secret*, Jack Canfield tells the story about driving a car at night. Canfield notes that the headlights shine only a couple of hundred feet in front of the car. We need only be concerned about safely maneuvering that short distance. Eventually, in two-hundred feet increments, we reach our destination. Life is like that. Our two-hundred feet of driving are the "now moments" of life. We live in the moment, one day at a time, using today as the foundation for tomorrow, calling to mind the assurance that Jesus gave us in *Matthew* 6:34:

"Therefore, do not worry about tomorrow, for tomorrow will take care of itself."

If we've done nothing else here, we hope we've created a higher awareness of the importance of engaging in daily prayer. And we remind you, as

Mother Teresa was once quoted as telling a priest who complained how busy he was and how difficult finding time to pray was, "Father, if you are too busy to pray, then you are too busy."

Special Times: Retreats and Prayer Sessions

We both serve on a team that conducts retreats. Virtually every religion and spiritual tradition encourages retreat-type activity as part of spiritual development. When we take the time to get away and to break away from our normal schedules, we invite God to come more deeply into our lives. It is at these moments that we often can get a clearer vision of ourselves and the potential we possess.

Besides presenting retreats, we are both involved in a monthly prayer meeting for "Men of Manresa." Manresa, located on the banks of the Mississippi River in Convent, Louisiana, is an incredibly beautiful retreat house. Each year almost 6000 men attend the two and one-half day weekly Manresa retreats. (We'll have a bit more to say about Manresa retreats in the *Lagniappe* part of the book.) We have both been annual retreat attendees for many, many years.

A couple of our friends, Bruce LeBlanc and Bob Furlow, who are also part of the Men of Manresa, invited us to help them organize a monthly prayer session. The intention of setting up the prayer sessions was to keep the spirit of the retreat going in the daily life of attendees. Bruce and Bob recognized, as often happens when one goes through an uplifting event, people leave it with a "high" but eventually fall back into their daily routines. They felt, by offering these monthly prayer sessions, the spiritual uplifting the retreats provide would not as readily diminish.

With a thirty-minute prayer session once a month, and the help of the Holy Spirit, attendees have been able to maintain a higher degree of spirituality in their lives. The spirit of Manresa is steadily strengthened with prayer, and the long-term value of the retreat is greatly enhanced. It's been nothing short of amazing. Our attendees tell us that missing one of these meetings is a real downer. They look forward to the message and time together in prayer. It's powerful in their lives and in ours as well.

Preparing for conducting these monthly prayer sessions has been an equally beneficial event for us. Once a month the four of us, Deacon Bob Furlow, Dr. Bruce LeBlanc, Billy, and Deacon Jodi, get together to plan our message. We began meeting at a local pizza place, and eventually labeled this meeting "Pizza with Jesus." Lively spiritual discussions, sharing, and supporting exchanges help us identify the theme and select the presenters for our next prayer session. We value this friendship and appreciate how these events have helped all of us stay connected to God and accountable to each other. We encourage all of you to form or join a group of like-minded people to share with on a regular basis. The passage from *Matthew 18:20* probably sums up our meetings best, and is actually a thought we've shared quite often to each other.

"Where two or three are gathered in my name, there am I in their midst."

The Fruits of the Spirit

How we use our time determines what our priorities are and what we ultimately accomplish. In Paul's writings to the Galatians, he discusses the proper way to use their freedom. Like the Galatians, we are free to use our time as we wish. In his closing comments of Chapter 5 of these writings, he offers what he calls the fruits of the spirit. As you look through this list, we feel you will agree with us that using time in a manner that supports the spirit is a wise choice.

Love: Extending love to our Creator, and those whose lives we touch, is the charge God gave us. We'd be smart to listen to those ideas.

Joy: How happy we are with joy in our heart. And what better way to stay in this state than to live our life in accordance to the will of God. Loving relationships are the perfect vehicle to drive elation into our heart. We just must watch that we don't have a wreck along the way.

Peace: With such strife and violence around us, maintaining a peaceful heart is a wonderful contrast. We should pray for a peaceful heart and a peaceful world. Mankind seems determined to continuously ignore this idea. Don't be a contributor.

Patience: Be slow to anger, and quick to forgive. Life is trying, and it's easy to feel dumped on. But like Jesus, we must practice patience in all that we do. Just think where we'd be if God were impatient.

Endurance: We might compare life to running a marathon. We endure hardships, heartaches, bruises, and a whole lot of other things. But persistence pays. How would we be positioned to enter the kingdom if Jesus had said, "I've got enough of this. I'm returning to the Father. To heck with these sinful humans!"

Kindness: God is so rich in kindness and mercy. For us, kindness can be as simple an act as being nice to those we meet along the path of life. Don't you love being around people who practice kindness? Do you think people would feel the same about you if you extended kindness to them as well?

Generosity: We'll have more to say about generosity later in the book. Suffice it to say here that we should acknowledge all the wonderful things we've been given in this life and, in thankfulness, should share some of those things whenever we can. We are reminded in Isaiah 32:8 that a generous man devises generous things. In other words, we should devise a strategy or plan for our generosity. Do you have a plan? Be generous with time, talents, and treasures, and your reward in heaven will be great.

Faith: Chapter six covers faith in detail. Think of it as the fuel that drives our engine to eternity. Without it, we cannot move towards God, and we may just find ourselves in an uncomfortable position following our last breath.

The beauty of each of these practices is that there is no law that prohibits their use. No law of man; no law of God. That fact alone should tell us that's a good use of our time and life.

Chapter 3

Using Our Talents for God

Another component that we use in our journeys stems from our talents. It takes many skills to navigate our way through daily life. Perhaps it's learning bus or train schedules. Talents could involve buying and maintaining a car. It takes talent to know which streets to take to get to our destination. If our routine is altered, we have to be skilled at finding other means to complete our journey. We probably use our talents without thinking about the many gifts we have. These talents work to make our life journeys easier. Do we also use them to be of service to God and others?

> *"For by the grace given me I say to every one of you: Do not think of yourself more highly than you ought, but rather think of yourself with sober judgment, in accordance with the measure of faith God has given you."*
>
> —Romans 12:3 (NIV®)

Sometimes the hardest part of our journey through life is acquiring a deep appreciation for the wide-range of talents with which we are gifted by our Creator. Perhaps it's our lack of self-confidence that gets in the way. It may be the discouragement we create in our mind by listening to the criticism freely offered by others. But, in truth, we are all given sufficient talents to journey through life at a success level we desire to achieve. God does not play tricks with us. We won't have a burning desire without the talent and tenacity to pull it off. It's often our lack of belief that holds us back. We must trust God, believe in ourselves, and persist with an unwavering desire for accomplishment. Journeying in this manner is how God wishes us to use the gifts He so generously has given each of us.

Finding Our Talents

When Jodi was in sixth grade, the Mother's Club sponsored a debate. The debate centered on the question, "Should children have to do chores?" Jodi's team took the position that children should not be made to do chores. Toward the end of the debate, the floor was opened for questions from the audience. A mother of a girl in his class asked him this question: "Jodi, if you never do chores, and you grow up, get married, and your wife is in the hospital having a baby, how will you know what to do around the house?" As quickly as she asked the question, he popped back his answer. "I would simply call my mother-in-law." The entire audience burst out laughing in a combination of joyous applause and total surprise at his quick response. No team was ever declared a winner of the debate, but from that day on, all of the parents decided that Jodi was going to be a lawyer when he grew up. And that seed eventually sprouted when he began his legal career.

Now, forty years later, he realizes that it was only the first of many goals sought in his lifetime. He also realizes that, throughout these years, he's had to strive to work with God in identifying goals to pursue. He's learned that we plant the seed, water it with God's blessings, and continue to nurture it. God gives us a choice to follow Him on this journey or take another road. Where we end up on our journey is directly tied to the choices we make.

There are certainly similar events in Billy's life when God led him to use his talents, no matter how questionable he thought they were at the time. Much like Jodi, he had an elementary school experience that forced him to use a talent that ultimately became very important in the future.

Sister Mary Raphael, his seventh grade teacher, was probably the most influential teacher Billy ever had. She was the ultimate encourager. From the beginning of the school year, she constantly searched for unique ways for her students to display their talents. One such incident occurred as she was preparing for the annual Christmas play. Sister Raphael approached Billy to be one of the three kings in the story of the Nativity. In this role, he was required to sing a verse of "We Three Kings of Orient Are." To say he resisted is an understatement. But Sister Raphael finally wore him down, and he reluctantly relented. It was a painful event, but he went through it.

Fast forward to his junior year in high school, and one can begin to see God's plan. The band director at his high school wanted to form an orchestra. He selected some of his band students and, being friends of Billy's, they asked him to join them as their piano player. The band began playing the old standards, but rock and roll was around the corner and they wanted to play that type of music. Following his senior year graduation, the band began to think about making a complete transition from big band music to R & B. That switch required someone to sing. With only one Christmas play behind him, Billy volunteered. Through some miraculous quirk of fate (and lots of hard, hard work by young boys with modest talent), *The Imperials* went on to become one of the most popular bands in south Louisiana. They never advertised and had bookings one to three times per week for the next six years. During this period, they cut a record that soared to number one on local radio stations. Billy is convinced that it took Divine Intervention to help make the transition, and to cover the inadequacy of his singing talent for all those years.

No matter what religion you are, we know you are trying to live your life in a way that is consistent with the teachings of that religion. As Christians, we have used the life of Jesus Christ as a model for our life. The New Testament is really a story of the life of Jesus. In the Bible stories of the New Testament, Jesus often taught in parables or stories that illustrated His points in a way that made them more understandable. One such parable is the story of the talents. In *Matthew 25:15*, He tells the story of a man who, prior to leaving on a journey, called together his servants. To one he gave five talents, to the second he gave two, and to the third he gave one. The servants with five and two each doubled their amount before the master returned. The other man buried his one talent because he was afraid of losing it. When the master returned, he was furious at the servant that had buried his talent. His fury surfaced because the servant did nothing with the talent. Because he did nothing, he lost the talent and gained the wrath of his master. The servants that doubled the talents were rewarded with more.

While this story is about money, the analogy with human talents fits as well. The master told his servant who successfully doubled the talents to "Come share your master's joy." That is how God feels. He blesses us all with gifts or talents, and He expects us to grow them for the betterment of others. God does not want us to waste these gifts. If we do, we are going to lose out in the end. That is what Sister Raphael understood when she pushed Billy to sing. God had a bigger plan than singing one time in a Christmas play.

Talents to Serve Others

We have found that the journey of life is made more rewarding when we focus on others rather than ourselves. Unfortunately, we have a strong sentiment in society today that tends to have a "me" focus. It is all about me rather than serving others. But if we look through *Romans 12:6-8*, we see how God views gifts and talents He has bestowed on us, and how we should use them. It's easy to understand when we read this passage that it's not about "me."

"We have different gifts, according to the grace given us. If a man's gift is prophesying, let him use it in proportion to his faith; if he is serving, let him serve; if it is teaching, let him teach; if it is encouraging, let him encourage; if it is contributing to the needs of others, let him give generously; if it is leadership, let him govern diligently; if it is showing mercy, let him do it cheerfully." (NIV®)

Lisa Coleman gives all the credit to God. "He's given me abilities, but it is my duty to use all those abilities He has given me and do something with that." Through the use of her talents, Lisa has created one of the most successful staffing services in Louisiana. It is her innate ability to model strong leadership abilities that keeps her services growing.

Jodi is a Kiwanian. A few years ago, his club worked to repair playground equipment. Some people were good with their hands and actually did work on the equipment. Others spent time cleaning the park or painting, utilizing their talents in the most effective way.

Currently, Jodi serves as a Deacon at Christ the King Catholic Church and Student Center at Louisiana State University (LSU). During exam week, the center is open around the clock, providing food and drinks for the students so they can study as much as they need to. This takes a tremendous effort on the part of a lot of people. Mostly it involves cooking. There are men and ladies who come in at all hours to cook. We don't know all the talents God has blessed these folks with, but they are certainly using their cooking skills in a way that serves others.

As we journey through life, we are called to find success in the way that develops our gifts and talents. Properly using these talents brings a "happiness high" while wasting them can cause us to wander through life without purpose or promise. The following stories illustrate these points.

Louisiana has many good qualities. But one thing that we are infamous for is our colorful, and sometimes slightly bent, political leaders. One such leader, Edwin Edwards, comes to mind. Without doubt, Edwin was one of the brightest minds to ever occupy the governor's office. He had enormous potential to do well and to use his gifts in the service of others. His popularity is attested to in the fact that he held this office for sixteen years, longer than anyone in our history. He had fame, fortune, power, and prestige. But Edwin liked high-stakes gambling. He was also a high-risk taker in the political arena as well.

While some voters of our state felt Governor Edwards, by his life choices, didn't have his moral compass pointing to "moral north," a majority of voters didn't care because Louisiana appeared to be prosperous under his tenure. During his four terms in office, Edwards was often the subject of corruption investigations. In 1998 he was indicted by the federal government on a number of racketeering charges. In 2001 he was convicted and sent to federal prison for ten years. His risk-taking finally did him in. Many think he will die in prison. It is sad, but his life illustrates that we can appear to be successful, but if we are misusing the talents God has given us, our success is not real. If we lose our moral compass in our journey, we will detour down the wrong path, a path that can lead only to sadness and misfortune.

By contrast, former President Jimmy Carter, while also having critics of his time in office, has achieved notable praise since leaving the presidency. His efforts on behalf of Habitat for Humanity continue to attract world-wide acclaim. He is an example of someone who uses his talents in a way that serves others and builds a better world at the same time. Such actions bring happiness not only to the recipient, but also to the giver.

What talents or gifts has God blessed you with? Honestly assess how you are using those skills. Are you putting them to work for the greater good of your family? Your community? The world?

Talents to Serve God

While we've focused on how we can use talents to serve others, we'd like to encourage you to look for ways to bring your gifts and talents to the service of God. We also want to be clear that our talents and gifts were given to us by God. It is our use of these gifts that becomes our gift to God. And when we begin to view these gifts as our possessions, that is the beginning of disconnecting with the giver. Our charge is to seek an understanding of the plans and to appreciate the fact that God wants only what is best for us. Giving us sufficient talents to bring happiness into our life and the world is His way of extending the generous love He has for each of us. We pay God back by practicing what we call God's Golden Rule—"Doing for others what God has done for us." In *1 Peter 4:10-11*, the apostle reminds us of how we should use our gift and talents.

"As each one has received a special gift, employ it in serving one another as good stewards of the manifold grace of God. Whoever speaks is to do so as one who is speaking the utterances of God; whoever serves is to do so as one who is serving by the strength which God supplies; so that in all things God may be glorified through Jesus Christ, to whom belongs the glory and dominion forever and ever."

One such way to carry out our thanksgiving to God is through the church—the place where God's message is delivered to us. A church relies on its members to fulfill its mission. Some of us are called to be ushers, readers, religious, or Sunday school teachers. Some are called to maintain the actual church building, to engage in helping with church administrative activities, or to assist in the many ministries that the Church carries out.

While we both have realized that we do have talent to participate in the service of others at a political level, we have both reassessed the use of our skills and talents, and have begun to see that they could be effectively deployed in ministry work. Public speaking can be preaching. Long hours spent on electioneering can be used instead on evangelization. Churches have committees just as the legislature has committees. It is clear to us those skills, talents, and gifts can be used in many ways. If we continue to look to Scripture for a clue on how to be successful, we see that we need to put God first by using our skills, talents, and gifts in His service. Using our talents for our own pleasure and enjoyment is fine, but we should also focus our efforts for God's service. Everyone leads a busy life. Time is at a premium. But in spite of our busyness, we find time for hobbies or other activities outside of the church. Is there something wrong with this picture?

Talents Freely Given

It is probably fitting that we close this chapter with a reminder of how we should go about utilizing our talents for service to God and our fellow man. Jesus rebuked the self-righteous who performed works in public for their own personal glory. This is the wrong approach. Matthew 6:1 provides a vivid reminder of this point.

"Beware of practicing your righteousness before men to be noticed by them; otherwise you have no reward with your Father who is in heaven."

Those are strong words, yet sound advice for those seeking to truly understand the idea of serving for the glory of God. If we take the focus off ourselves, we have taken the first step. If we give, seeking nothing in return, we have moved even further. We're talking about creating a generous heart, not a big head.

In our human weakness, we sometimes "don't get it." God sent His son, Jesus, to serve us. Jesus sought no worldly recognition for His actions. He had a purpose, and never lost sight of what He was here to do. He did it willingly and lovingly, staying away from being personally glorified for His actions, and always glorifying the Father. We can find passage after passage in scripture that illustrates how Jesus walked away from situations where His followers wished to bring attention to Him personally for the works he performed. But He never allowed that to happen.

To "get it" we must imitate Jesus. We act in the service of others to give glory to God for the gifts and talents He has bestowed on us. And we must do it in such a way that the limelight is not allowed to shine on us. Following this path on our journey is not always easy, but it is always necessary.

CHAPTER 4

Sharing Our Treasures with God

Our travels through this world carry a price. We need finances for food, shelter, and clothing, to survive comfortably. Earning the financing to live consumes a large part of living, and oftentimes we take our eyes off the real goal of life—finding our path to the kingdom. We need money to survive. We don't believe there are too many folks that would dispute this fact. But we don't want the pursuit of wealth to become our all-consuming activity. Money is good when it enables us to sustain a decent level of living. It's even better when it can be used to help others sustain a decent level of living as well. We will speak to sharing your treasure in this chapter. If we make you a bit uncomfortable with our ideas, then we've accomplished our goal.

> *"Honor the Lord with your wealth, with the first fruits of all your produce; then will your barns be filled with grain, with new wine your vats will overflow."*
>
> —Proverbs 3:9-10

We can both attest that when you turn your finances over to God and trust Him, then the stress and strain that often accompany debt and bills go away. It's not magic. It's just God's law. God openly shares in His Book the law of "Sowing and Reaping." There are countless stories of people who have trusted in God and have been blessed because they followed this law. Don't be misled to believe that this law only applies to money. The law applies in every facet of our life.

Our "Stuff" Gets in the Way

Far too many people in the United States have too much "stuff." Not only do we have too much "stuff," we become attached to our "stuff." We build storage areas for our "stuff." We even rent space to store our "stuff." And, if we are not careful, our "stuff" can displace our focus on God. What we tend to forget is that nothing we have belongs to us. Truly everything that we have belongs to God, the Creator. This idea is best illustrated with a comment we heard from a preacher. He said that he has never officiated at a funeral where there was a U-haul attached to the back of the coffin. Be grateful to God for what you accumulate in this life, but never view it as your possessions. Be ready to part with them because one day you will.

St. Paul says in his First Letter to *Timothy at 6:7*,

"For we brought nothing into this world, and it is certain we can carry nothing out."

In *Deuteronomy 8:18*, we read,

"But remember the Lord your God, for it is he who gives you the ability to produce wealth, and so confirms his covenant, which he swore to your forefathers, as it is today." (NIV®)

As Ye Sow, So Shall Ye Reap

Neither one of us likes hearing examples of the "self-made man or woman." That statement removes the idea of our dependence on God. No one can accomplish anything without the gifts and talents given to him or her by God. When someone forgets this and takes credit for his or her own success, that person is sowing a bad seed, and you know what comes from a bad seed? You guessed it, a bad crop.

In our culture we too often place value on our autonomy and self-reliance. We believe we alone are the source of strength to face the burdens and difficulties life places in our path. Scripture reminds us that our source of strength is not within our own power, but in the power of love that God so graciously gives us. *Psalm 59:18* says,

"O my Strength, it is you to whom I turn, for you, O God, are my stronghold, the God who shows me love."

As we discuss treasure in this section, we want to again make it clear that sowing and reaping are not limited to things or money. In *Galatians 6:7-10*, Paul says,

"Do not be deceived. God cannot be mocked. A man reaps what he sows. The one who sows to please his sinful nature, from that nature will reap destruction: the one who sows to please the Spirit, from the Spirit will reap eternal life. Let us not become weary in doing good, for at the proper time we will reap a harvest if we do not give up. Therefore, as we have opportunity let us do good to all people."

For example, you are waiting in line at any business, and the person in front of you turns around, smiles, and says, "Good morning." Chances are that you will reciprocate the smile and return his or her "Good morning." This type of exchange will generally brighten the moment for both of you. If, on the other hand, the person's behavior is nasty or rude to you or the clerk, you are likely, at that moment, to feel negatively about that individual. That person has sown a bad seed and will get a bad crop in return.

We sow the seeds of our words and actions all of the time. If we are always complaining and acting as if everything is going wrong, we are sowing bad seeds. We should focus on a positive attitude, on saying good things, and on acting in a positive manner. They set us up for good things to happen in our lives. If you are thinking, "That makes sense," then why aren't people nice and friendly all the time? The reason—everyone does not get it. They don't understand the law of sowing and reaping.

When we give of our treasure (time, talent, money) to God, we are assured that we will reap a harvest. Let's be very clear here. We are not suggesting that the only reason you give is to receive. We have to give with a happy heart. We have to be joyous in our giving. We have to give expecting nothing in return. When we approach sharing our treasure this way, then we will experience the satisfaction of a job well done. That, my friend, is how you line your journey through life with successes.

The Idea of Tithing

Another area where we tend to put God behind all else is with our money. Many of us budget how much we can "afford" to give to the church based upon what's left over after we pay our bills. This strategy actually puts God in second place. It's almost like we give to God as an afterthought. But following the words of the Bible requires a different mindset. We are called to give to the Lord first, not after everything else.

The idea of tithing changes the tone of our message a bit, and leads us to focus a bit deeper on the subject of money. While most people equate success with the accumulation of wealth, we urge you to consider a strategy to give away the money that you earn. That's right, *give it away*.

Tithing is a fancy word for sharing your earnings with others you feel are deserving of the gift. Few things in life will bring you greater satisfaction than giving to help others while expecting nothing in return. That's right, *expect nothing in return*.

Many years ago, we both were urged to consider tithing. In researching the concept, we found that tithing involves giving away the first ten percent of your earnings. In a religious environment, many consider it an obligation. Perhaps for you, that percentage is a stretch. When Jodi and his wife decided to try tithing, they started out with a smaller percentage and then worked their way up to the ten percent level. There are many approaches to tithing. A good friend of ours and his wife take a full ten percent of their gross income and put it into a separate checking account, and they use that account for their contribution to their church and other philanthropic activities.

We want to urge you to make as much money as you can so you can start giving more of that money away. But we want to take this thought a bit further. Why not start giving generously *before* you make all that money? That's right; *give it away before you have it*.

Here's what we mean. Give now when it will hurt. Give now when you think the money would be better in your savings account. Give now when you could pay bills with the money. Give now when you could use the money to pay for an enjoyable vacation.

Here's why you do all this—because you must *give* before you can *receive*. That's how the law of sowing and reaping works. Receiving the gifts from life is the result of the seeds you've planted through your generosity to others with time, talent, and treasures.

As early as the book of Genesis we read about giving back to God. In *Genesis 28:22*, we see Jacob promising God that in return for a safe journey,

"I will faithfully return a tenth part to you."

While it may look like Jacob is "cutting a deal" with God, Jacob was actually showing appreciation for God's protection by parting with some of his possessions. Get the giving habit like Jacob and you will find riches you never dreamed existed. That's how it works.

Chapter 5

God's Love for Us

Without fuel, we cannot journey. If we walk, we burn calories; if we travel by motor vehicle, the car, bus, or truck needs gas or diesel. Planes need fuel; trains need electricity. Obtaining the fuel requires action on our part, whether it's buying food or fuel, tickets or tokens. Our life journey requires fuel as well. As we journey through this world into the next, love received from other humans is a precious gift. But more precious is the love God has for us. This love is the love of transition. This love takes us from the abyss to the mountain top where God waits for us. Our journey could never be completed if God's love were not there to fuel us. It is love that helps us navigate through the obstacles and challenges of life. It is love that will sustain us for all eternity.

> *"But I am like an olive tree flourishing in the house of God; I trust in God's unfailing love for ever and ever."*
>
> —Psalm 52:8 (NIV®)

Our Most Precious Gift

Humans tend to be a hard-headed species. God continually tells us to trust in Him, yet we continue to seek autonomy and self-reliance as our trust-builders. This is contrary to what we should do. We do not have enough strength to carry the burdens of life on our shoulders without help. We need the support of our loving Master. What is the source of that strength? There are constant reminders throughout the Gospels providing the answer— God's love. In *John 14: 21*, Jesus gives us the answer.

"He who loves me will be loved by my Father and I will love him and manifest myself to him."

What an incredible gift we have with this love! Most of us never quite grasp the generosity given because our humanness gets in the way. This never-ending stream of love is something even the most powerful and strongest person can seek without apology. Now here is the real benefit of seeking and basking in this abundance of love. The more we dwell and desire to love God, the more we will desire to be possessed with His love. Isn't that how we are? The more we love someone, the more we desire to love that individual. And that's God's way as well.

When Jesus walked His holy ground, He offered the wisdom of the Father to everyone. He said the greatest of all the commandments is to love one another as God loves us. Love lights up our insides, moves us to loving actions, and unites us in such a way that we become one people. Our Creator understands that without love, we falter and fail and would ultimately destroy ourselves. And we can validate this idea by looking at the many atrocities in the history of mankind to understand that all were due to a lack of love for one another, and for God.

As we focus our attention on God's love for us, it's important to understand how compassionately and powerfully we are loved. We are His creation, and He constantly seeks to improve on His work, even as we sometimes simultaneously take actions that undo God's work on us. It is our responsibility to allow ourselves to be molded into the instruments that follow the will of the Creator. When we reach the pinnacle of accepting God's love, our spiritual growth will soar, and our relationship with the Light of this world will shine and glow.

Our Response to the Gift

Are you convinced that God loves you? Have we shared sufficiently how generously we have been loved for you to grasp the significance of this gift? How should we respond? Let's start the examination by thinking deeply about the answer to these questions:

1. How grateful am I that God has chosen to shower me with His abundant love?

2. Do I believe that I am loved unconditionally by God? If so, why? If not, why not?
3. How do I dialog with God (prayer) in order to grow the relationship and foster love?
4. How do I grow in my knowledge about Jesus and the purpose for why He became man and died for us?
5. Is the pattern of my life emulating the life of Christ? If so, how? If not, why not?
6. Am I ashamed of my faith, or do I stand willing to acknowledge the great love I have for my Creator? Explain.
7. How well do I use all the gifts and talents I've been showered with by our Divine Friend?
8. We are forgiven through God's love. How am I grateful for this forgiveness?
9. Is the name of God reverent to me or do I use it in vain far too often?
10. Through the divinity of our creation, we are given a wonderful mind. Am I developing it and using it in the service of God? How?

There are many other questions we should seek to answer as we contemplate how we should respond to the generosity we have been extended in the form of eternal love. Add your own questions to the mix as you work on properly responding to the free-flowing love of our Beloved Companion.

God's Actions and Love

If we were to ask you to describe your image of God, what would your answer be? Do you see God as this "Big Stick Entity" that is waiting for us to "mess up" so He can inflict punishment on us? Do you fear God and distrust Him? These ideas are nowhere near the truth and scripture validates that fact. In *1 John 4:7-8*, it says,

"Beloved, let us love one another because love is God; everyone who loves is begotten of God and has knowledge of God. The man without love has known nothing of God for God is love."

Further in this passage of scripture, verses 18-19, John continues,

"Love has no room for fear; rather perfect love casts out all fear. And since fear has to do with punishment, love is not yet perfect in one who is afraid. We, for our part, love because he first loved."

Do you see God as offering His reward program, like a "Frequent Flier" reward? We hope not, because, again, scripture offers another contradiction.

In *Matthew 5:43-48*, he writes,

"*You have heard the commandment, 'You shall love your countryman but hate your enemy.' My command to you is, 'love your enemies and pray for your persecutors.' This will prove that you are sons of your Heavenly Father, for his sun rises on the bad and the good, he rains on the just and the unjust. If you love those who love you, what merit is there in that? Do not tax collectors do as much? And if you greet your brothers only, what is so praiseworthy about that? Do not pagans do as much? In a word, you must be made perfect as your heavenly Father is perfect.*"

What a challenge we are given with these words! Loving your enemies is tough. But Jesus said to do so, and He is the messenger for the Father. His words are God's words.

Lastly, do you see God only accepting certain people, like a private country club membership? Don't be caught in this thinking trap because God reaches out to everyone.

In *Luke 15*, the parable of Divine Mercy is discussed. In Verse seven of the parable, Jesus says,

"*I tell you there will likewise be more joy in heaven over one repentant sinner than over ninety-nine righteous people who have no need to repent.*"

This is a very revealing message that the Divine Mercy of God knows no limit. It's open to all who seek to receive it.

In *Mark 1:40-42*, we find another story of the "reaching out" God offers. In this passage, we read the story of the Leper.

"*Suddenly a leper came forward and did him homage, saying to him, 'Sir, if you will to do so, you can cure me.' Jesus stretched out his hand and touched him and said, 'I do will it. Be cured.' Immediately the man's leprosy disappeared.*"

While many turned their faces from lepers, Jesus was moved with compassion. Such examples of the love Jesus had for everyone He encountered should inspire us to open our hearts and minds to those we encounter as well. There are no restrictions on God's love as demonstrated time and time again through the lessons Jesus taught by His exemplary life on earth. Jesus represented the Father on earth and showed us that God's love is available to anyone who seeks it and is willing to follow His teachings.

Our Blind Spot

Within the human eye, there is a point known as the "blind spot." This is the place in the visual field that lacks light-detecting photoreceptor cells on the optic disc of the retina. At this point, the optic nerve passes through the retina, and, since there are no cells to detect light on the optic disc, the eye does not perceive a part of the field of vision. The brain fills in with surrounding detail, and with information from the other eye, so the blind spot remains the area that we do not "see." That is the scientific definition of a blind spot.

We have another blind spot we call the "spiritual" blind spot. Here we become "blind" to our turning away from God's love by falling into the grasp of sin. In simple terms, sin is doing something that is contrary to God's laws. This blind spot, like the one found in the eye, is missing "God-detecting receptors" where our heart and soul meet. We harbor sinful ideals in our heart, and they darken the soul so the light of the world is not visible. The more we fall into the grasp of this downward spiraling activity, the darker our world becomes. It's only when we willingly receive the light of God's forgiveness and love that our blind spot disappears. You see, God especially loves sinners, and it is His willingness to step in and help that saves us from self-destruction.

For us, the hardest first step is admitting that we are sinners. We need to examine where we fall short of acting as God wants us to act. Our struggle is to be honest with God and admit to those sins that are embedded into the deep fibers of our being. We may constantly slight relatives or coworkers. We may be critical of others because of their gender or race. We may engage in malicious gossip. We may be addicted to pornography.

Once we are able to admit our sins, we need to let go and loosen, with the power of the cross, the bondage we created. Admission closes the gap between God and us and opens our heart to His forgiving love. When we reciprocate that love, nothing we do can serve sin. We need to remember as noted in *Exodus 34:6*,

"*The Lord is kind and merciful, slow to anger and rich in kindness.*"

We need to come to terms with the fact that Jesus came onto this earth, suffered and died for our sins. When you think of this tremendous act, how can you not want to reciprocate this offering of love? We are constantly being called by God because, even as sinners, we can help bring redemption to the world. God is looking for willing servants to help other sinners. The apostles were not perfect, yet Jesus took them in and made them messengers to the entire world on His behalf. We are given this same offer. Don't let your blind spot get in the way to the call of Christ. It's an incredible assignment that we are all given that few accept. Don't risk being in the minority.

Earning His Love

In several places throughout this book, we bring in the fact that it's God's will that we are to follow, not our own. We exist because God loves us. We will only get to really experience the magnitude of His love in the eternal kingdom by living fully in the earthly kingdom. We create a wall of pride that gets in the way. It's when we believe that we are in control that we fall for the ancient whisper in the Garden, "You shall be like gods." Our charge is not to resist, but rather to persist in getting closer to God and receiving the abundance of love He has for us. We earn that right by how well we live our life according to His plan.

CHAPTER 6

Fear, Faith, and Love

We face uncertainty in every journey we take. Sometimes the unknown is relatively minor: will traffic be heavy or light? Will it rain on our vacation? What will happen when I get where I am going? At other times, we step out of our surroundings with dread or fear: what will the doctor tell me? Will my interview land me a job? Our interactions with others before we embark on our journeys influence the way we approach our trips. A hug, words of reassurance, decisions on how to address positive and negative events carry us through each trip we take. Using the graces we receive when we respect (fear), believe in (faith) and love God carries us through our journey on earth. We partner in a sense by reciprocating the tremendous gift of love God offers us. Grace is the blanket that warms our soul when we are cold from sin. It's the "energizer bunny" that keeps our motor running when we otherwise might quit and turn our backs on God.

"You guide me along the right path for the sake of your name. Even when I walk through a dark valley, I fear no harm for you are at my side."

—Psalm 23:3-4

The Beginning of Fear

When God created man and woman, fear did not exist. There was a perfect world with all things provided. It was not until sin came on the scene that fear surfaced. You probably recall reading in Genesis what happened after the apple was eaten. When God approached Adam in the garden, He asked, "Where Are You?" Adam finally replied, "I heard You in the garden but I was afraid." That is the first mention of the presence of fear in the Hebrew Scriptures, and it came into existence as part of the human character when disobedience to God's will occurred. This disobedience resulted in the first sin.

In Acts 22:16, we are told,

"Be baptized at once and wash away your sins as you call upon his name."

From this, most Christians believe that, because of the actions in the garden, we are all born with sin that must be washed away with the waters of Baptism. We nonetheless are not born fearful beings. One only has to observe young children maneuvering their way through life. They will jump into a pool of water, step off a high perch, and touch a hot object. Once they feel the pain of these events, fear surfaces. In such instances, that's a good thing.

But the reality of life is that we all go through learned fears. Young children are fearful of the dark. In a wobbly economy, we fear our company shutting down and losing our job. We fear losing a home or car if we cannot meet the payments. With the volatile stock market, there is a constant fear that the bottom will drop out and our entire life savings will be lost. Are these fears legitimate? Certainly we can lose our job, home, car, and investments. But, generally, we educate ourselves to overcome those potential fears and to concern ourselves only with truly fear-producing circumstances.

Turning Fears Into Faith

While fear began in the Garden, there are other examples of scriptural figures exhibiting fear. When Jesus was singled out by Judas and taken away to meet with the Roman authorities, Peter was in the area. When bystanders asked if he was with Jesus, Peter denied knowing Jesus—not once, but three times. Why would Peter deny Jesus, the person he loved and followed? He feared the repercussions of being identified as a follower of Christ.

When Jesus and some of his apostles were in a boat, a violent storm suddenly came up. Scripture says they became fearful, even with Jesus sleeping in the boat. After awakening and calming the sea and winds, Jesus encouraged His apostles to not be fearful and have faith.

Following the death of Jesus, the apostles went into hiding. They were fearful of meeting the same fate that Jesus went through. But the appearance of Jesus to the apostles helped to change their fears into faith.

In each of these three examples, no one kept his focus on Jesus. They had a temporary "lack of faith" which allowed fear to overtake them. Once they restored their faith, fear exited from their hearts.

Throughout the New Testament as we read the stories of the miracles Jesus performed, a common theme is faith.

In *Matthew 10: 29*, we read Jesus' response to the two blind men who sought healing from their blindness. Jesus says,

" . . . *Because of your faith it shall be done to you.*"

It was the unshakable faith of these two blind men that moved Jesus to cure them.

The story of the paralytic at Capernaum in chapter two of Mark's Gospel is another example of how Jesus was moved by faith. Four friends of the paralytic, unable to get close to Jesus, climbed on the roof of the building in which Jesus was teaching and lowered their friend next to Jesus. Jesus recognized how much faith these men had and cured their friend.

Turning Faith Into Love

"Whoever does not love does not know God for God is love"
—1 John 4:8 (NIV®)

"A new command I give you: Love one another. As I have loved you, so you must love one another." —John 13:34 (NIV®)

Jesus says that faith as small as a mustard seed can move mountains. Love as deep as the depths of the universe grows from mustard-seed faith. Thus we are able to move from fear to faith and finally to love. This movement is the critical journey we all must take to become servants of the Father and guests in his home forever.

We should recall that the Father has a long memory for His promises to us and a short memory for our failures to keep our promises to Him. God will wait on us. He stands ready to help even though we are resistant and cold in our relationship. Our Savior, Jesus, was also very tolerant of the apostles. Time and time again, He taught them and waited for the messages to sink in. He never stops loving and patiently waits for us to come to Him. The Father and Jesus, through Their love, are there for us in our most difficult moments and struggles. They are our true friends, and we have an open invitation to come to Them.

Our Divine Leader knows what is best for us and willingly gives it when we seek that knowledge through prayer. Through faith, we make the Father and Jesus our partners on our journey. There is no excuse we can offer for not tapping into this generous fountain of grace and love. We only need to ask, believe, and trust in Them.

Chapter 7

Creating Vertical Alignment

One of the important responsibilities of owning an automobile is to be sure that the steering mechanism is properly aligned. A misaligned car will wear out tires very rapidly and make steering difficult. The car may sway to the left or right as you drive down the highway, and maintaining control in the driving lane can sometimes be very difficult. No one in his right mind would continue to drive a car in this condition. Likewise, we hope that as you journey through the roads of life, you will keep your "steering mechanism" aligned, keeping God, family, and career in their proper order.

> *"Because he loves me," says the Lord, "I will rescue him; I will protect him, for he acknowledges my name."*
>
> —Psalm 91:14 (NIV®)

Getting Priorities Aligned

We hope by now you see that a journey through life, grounded for the greater glory of God, will bring into your life the peace and happiness you seek. By prioritizing our life in the way God wants us to, we remain faithful to His calling for us. The vertical alignment of God, family, and career, keeps our journey on the path that ultimately leads to carrying out God's will.

Our wish is that you will keep God first in your life. We are certain that your God wants you to come to know and understand Him better. By keeping this perspective, you will find greater value in every human you encounter. Scripture tells us that we are created in the image and likeness of God. If I am created in that image and likeness, then it stands to reason that everyone else is also created that way. As Christians, we are asked to model our lives after Jesus Christ. In that vein, we are called to love others in exactly the same way that we want them to love us.

None of this is easy. There is evil in the universe that is constantly striving to distract us from where God wishes our focus to be. One can observe the happenings for just one day and find clear evidence that evil does exist and is quite active. How can we cope with evil all around us, and what can we do to diminish the impact evil has on the world? We believe progress can only be made by consistently putting God first and growing our relationship with Him. By doing so, we will come to know Him better and, like a good friend, we will come to enjoy His company. It is this perspective that drives evil away and brings God closer to us.

At a gathering of Christian men for lunch that Jodi attended, the speaker challenged everyone to read the Bible from cover to cover, or, as he put it, "from Genesis to the maps." He took the challenge and set up a reading schedule that would guide him through the Bible in a year. He soon found himself speedreading daily to get through the parts that he had scheduled for that day. Although he read the entire Bible, he did not really get a lot out of it. Some time later, while attending a retreat, he was taught that we should "pray" the Bible. By reading a short passage from scripture, and spending time meditating and contemplating that passage, he was better able to absorb the true meaning of the passage. It was not about speed or getting a certain portion read each day. It was about using the words of scripture to help develop a relationship with God.

There is a place where prayer and spiritual growth have merged with many of the success principles being taught today by some of the greatest teachers of self-development. One such example is a method taught by Bill Harris called Holosync—a meditative technique for personal growth and mind development—much like the meditative techniques taught for centuries by many religions.

Another example of the merging of self-help principles and prayerful techniques is taught by Neville Goddard, one of the quietly dramatic and supremely influential teachers in the New Thought field. Goddard teaches a technique very similar to the daily examine we discussed earlier. In both cases, meditating on what is right for you is the key.

Thomas Green, SJ, in his book, *Opening to God*, says that "Contemplation and meditation are means to an end. They are ways of coming to know the Lord in order that we may truly love Him—not merely in word but in action."

It's important to understand the power prayer puts into our life. As we pray to get to know God better, we must, at the same time, get to know ourselves better. This is not always fun because our picture can be ugly at times. But knowing the powerful and forgiving God, at the most intimate level prayer can deliver to us, eases the pain we feel when we come to recognize our true identity. God's graces, given through prayer, provide strength to face and correct our weaknesses. God's graces and prayers help to surface an awareness of the strengths we have and can use to keep our walk on holy ground in a state of sanctity.

We pray your journey will guide you to the ultimate goal of living in the presence of God for eternity. And once God is first in your life, it's time to continue your walk on His holy ground towards your other areas of focus: family, work, and personal success.

Success Challenges

At the end of each part of this book, we will pose a series of questions that expand your thought process on the information presented in that section. We believe in asking questions that are challenging, thought-provoking and sometimes downright hard to answer. But it is in stretching ourselves that we grow, and isn't the walk on the holy ground of this earth all about growth?

1. Carefully examine your prayer life. Is it sporadic? Is it powerful? Does it exist at all? Do I feel the connection between God and me when I pray? Do I believe prayers are answered?
2. How do my actions/habits follow the moral code of God laid out in His commandments?
3. Do you regularly read scripture? If not, can you commit to spending a few minutes each day to contemplate the word of God given to us through Scripture?

4. How much do I trust God will watch over me? Do I feel if it is to be, it's solely up to me? Or, am I willing to place my total trust in God's love and commitment to me?
5. What "gods" have I let get in the way of making a total commitment to placing "God" first in my life?
6. What choices have I made that have distanced my relationship with God? How can I eliminate such choices from my life to rekindle the relationship?
7. Do I have an attitude of gratefulness about the gifts God has given me?
8. What is the strongest talent I possess? How am I using that talent to serve God?
9. Would I classify myself as a generous person or am I generally reluctant to share my treasures with others? In what ways do I demonstrate this?
10. Without altering your daily lifestyle, record in 15-30 minute increments what activities you do for at least one week but preferably two. Then examine how much time you spend in each sector of your life—God, family, work. Then answer this question: Are my real priorities God, family and work?

PART II

The Journey

with

Family

Chapter 8

We Don't Choose Family

Most of us have had the experience of a family vacation. Imagine going on that same vacation and leaving your family behind. It's not a pleasant thought because, to most of us, our family is a very important and very integral part of our lives. As we move through life's journey, the way in which we interact with our family will, in a very significant way, determine whether or not we make it to our destination. Novelist George Moore summed up our feeling on this point quite well when he said, "A man travels the world in search of what he needs and returns home to find it." Next to the love of God, love of family is the most important thing we can experience as we journey on His holy ground.

> *"But if serving the Lord seems undesirable to you, then choose for yourselves this day whom you will serve, whether the gods your forefathers served beyond the River, or the gods of the Amorites, in whose land you are living. But as for me and my household, we will serve the Lord."*
>
> —Joshua 24:15 (NIV®)

Born into Family

None of us has the luxury of choosing our family. Where we initially land in the structure of human society is totally out of our control. For many years following our birth, we don't even have control of what happens to us. We are almost totally dependent upon our parents or those caring for us for some degree of help. There is no other animal on the face of the earth that is as dependent as we humans are for such a prolonged period of time. This is one of the ironies of being human.

We do eventually reach a stage in our life when we can make choices. It is those choices that create our life. If we eventually have a family of our own, we are again faced with choices.

- We can replicate the type of family atmosphere we grew up in and perpetuate similar circumstances within our own family structure.
- We can build on the foundation of our family and make the choice to improve to a better level of performance.
- We can ignore virtually everything we've been taught or exposed to, and go in an entirely different direction, following a "Learn as you go" plan.

In this day and age, there are so many people who were raised and are being raised in non-traditional family environments. We generally cannot choose what type of family environment we grow up in. Unfortunately, no longer are all households comprised of mom and dad. It might be just mom, just dad, mom and mom, dad and dad, grandparent and child, or any combination thereof. But the type of family you were born into or grew up in does not necessarily dictate what kind of person you will be or can become. Jodi was raised by his great-grandmother. He did not come in contact with his dad until he was twelve years old, and that was only for a short meeting. It was not until he was nearly twenty years old that he really got to know him. Many people would use this situation as an excuse to not succeed. Jodi preferred to view his situation as author Napoleon Hill said—*"Every adversity carries with it the seed of an equivalent or greater benefit."* He took the seeds of adversity and used them to his benefit.

Jack Canfield, co-author of the very successful *Chicken Soup for the Soul* series of books, says that psychologists estimate most families are dysfunctional, and so it's one of those "so what" things. Yes, family environments are influential. But it really comes down to the choices you make with the circumstances life deals you.

In this section, it is our intent to help you make the foundation you now have even stronger. We want family to take on a significance right next to God. In our hierarchy, building the right family relationships ranks right next to establishing our relationship with God. We believe that God should be the focal point around which all family decisions are made. His teachings and moral code are what should guide us through all the troubled waters a family might encounter. While we don't have any choice regarding our family, we always have the choice to involve God in our family.

Unlike us, Jesus had His family chosen before He was born. His mother, Mary, was picked by God to bring Jesus into the world. She accepted the choice God requested of her. While we don't have many stories of the family life Jesus led prior to beginning His "public life," we nonetheless believe that it was a very typical lifestyle of the Jewish family structure of the times. Jesus followed the craft of His father Joseph and worked as a carpenter. He was obedient to His parents and was, by all accounts, a good son. He is described in Scripture as a child who "grew in wisdom and knowledge" over the years. Jesus, although fully divine and fully human, always kept His Heavenly Father's will in the forefront.

The Traditional vs the "Reality" Family Structure

Today, people are re-marrying at record rates and the result is that a new family structure—the blend of two families—is rapidly increasing. There are my children, your children, and our children. All these factors have created a dynamic not even conceptualized just fifty years ago. Add to that mix the same sex "marriage" controversy trying to get a legal foothold in today's society, and the entire definition of family and marriage has taken a dramatic turn.

Where does all this leave us? Let's answer that question with a question. If the family organization is in a state of disarray, isn't it time that every effort be put forth to return a sense of balance and order to the family structure?

We don't believe it was a coincidence that Jesus performed his first miracle at a wedding—a family celebration in Cana. The story is told in John 2:1-10.

On the third day a wedding took place at Cana in Galilee. Jesus' mother was there, and Jesus and his disciples had also been invited to the wedding. When the wine was gone, Jesus' mother said to him, "They have no more wine." "Dear woman, why do you involve me?" Jesus replied, "My time has not yet come." His mother said to the servants, "Do whatever he tells you."

Nearby stood six stone water jars, the kind used by the Jews for ceremonial washing, each holding from twenty to thirty gallons. Jesus said to the servants, "Fill the jars with water"; so they filled them to the brim. Then he told them, "Now draw some out and take it to the master of the banquet."

They did so, and the master of the banquet tasted the water that had been turned into wine. He did not realize where it had come from, though the servants who had drawn the water knew. Then he called the bridegroom aside and said, "Everyone brings out the choice wine first and then the cheaper wine after the guests have had too much to drink; but you have saved the best till now." (NIV®)

To us, this is a sign of the importance that Jesus placed on marriage and on obedience to family. Although He mildly protested that "his time had not come," He nonetheless fulfilled His mother's wish. As Christians, we should place a huge importance on marriage and the traditional family makeup as well.

We don't know if there will ever be a complete return to what was once the traditional family design. Our guess is that this will not happen anytime soon. In the meantime, what is one to do? Let's try to answer that question as we move into an important component of a successful family structure—*commitment*.

Understanding the Word "Commitment"

In the marriage vows, the bride and groom make a public commitment to each other. They pledge to love and honor each other all the days of their life. They promise to be together in good times and in bad times. They promise to stay together in sickness and in health, until death separates them. Those are serious promises not to be uttered frivolously. As a whole, these promises create the foundation upon which every component of family and marriage are built. And, like a good house, the construction of your marriage and family household begins with a solid foundation.

Four days prior to writing this passage, Billy and his wife Ernestine celebrated their forty-fifth wedding anniversary. Jodi and his wife Darlene have been married for twenty-eight years. Have we experienced both good and bad times in those years? Has there been sickness? Have we remained true to each other? The answer is "Yes" to all of these questions. Yet there are others who made a similar public commitment whose marriage has not survived. Certainly, we do not place ourselves above any of these individuals. But what is the difference? We believe the difference is that we have made a commitment, and we have chosen to honor every facet of it, no matter the circumstances we faced.

In cases where marriages have not worked out, usually one partner makes the choice to break his or her commitment, changes his or her mind and, no matter what the other partner wishes to do, decides to break up the marriage. It's like a couple taking a journey together, getting in the car, and after traveling awhile, one individual pushes the other out of the car and goes on without his or her partner. The partner did not want to get pushed out of the car, but had no choice. This may seem like a tough comparison, but the truth is that breaking up a marriage can have far worse effects.

During our interview with Lisa Coleman, she said, "With the busy life my husband and I have, we must plan time together. Otherwise, it will not happen." Rose Hudson echoed Lisa's comments. Her husband is executive counsel to the lieutenant governor and, like her, leads a very busy life. They plan trips together and sometimes just sit in their backyard listening to the birds. "We honor each other with our presence," Rose says.

As an attorney, Jodi has spent many hours in court. Although he doesn't practice family law or represent individuals seeking a divorce, he has often seen couples parade in with their witnesses testifying that they have lived separate and apart and want a divorce. Many times only one partner pushes for the divorce, disregarding the feelings of the other. We acknowledge that often one partner makes a sincere effort to reconcile differences to salvage the partnership. However, in spite of their effort, the partnership is eventually dissolved by divorce. We further acknowledge that, in spite of our best intentions and careful evaluation, the wrong choice of a mate can occur. It is sad that society has placed so little value on marriage that, legally, all a person has to do is move out for a period of time, run into court, and get granted a divorce.

Recently Jodi had the opportunity, as part of his diaconate ministry, to counsel a couple seeking a divorce. The man did not want a divorce. The woman had walked out. She blamed the entire matter on a perceived mental illness that the man has. The weird thing is that he had this condition before they got married, and it had been treated. The marriage vows do say, "In sickness and in health." What happened to that vow? We have seen this blame game all too often. It appears to be a convenient and easy way out of a difficult but not impossible situation. These couples don't seem to understand that one person does not make up a partnership!

If we think about our relationship with God and the partnership He has established with us, this is the model around which we should seek to build a marriage and family structure. God has infinite and unconditional love for us. He is a forgiving God. He is a God who only wants us to be happy in His love. Think about a marriage relationship that takes on this tone. Think about a family molded around those principles. If both partners would emulate to each other God's model of love, could divorce ever occur? If parents related to their children as God relates to us, would that not create a solid method to form a family?

Certainly, we are not God and divine perfection is not a human condition. But it's the model that we can use as a guide to make our marriage and family environment work. If we always remember that God never gives up on us, then we can work to assume the same posture with our partner and our children.

One last point here, when choosing a mate, the greater the spiritual compatibility between partners, the greater the potential for a lasting relationship. St. Paul tells us in *2 Corinthians 6:14*,

"Do not be yoked together with unbelievers." (NIV®)

He goes on to teach that you should find things in common with those you work with, hang around with, and marry. When children are involved, the more spirituality you can help introduce into their moral code, the greater the chances that your children will become models for others as well. Isn't that what we are charged to do as parents—be models for others and help to create models others can emulate?

Chapter 9

Ideas to Build a Lasting Marriage

The journey through this world is very lonely without family. We are creatures that need love and support to become our best "us." Through marriage, we are granted the privilege of spending our life with someone who can be both a lover and a supporter, as God loves and supports us. This makes marriage the same type of relationship God offers us. Does that make marriage a Godly thing? We answer, "Yes," to this question.

> *"Anyone who divorces his wife and marries another woman commits adultery, and the man who marries a divorced woman commits adultery."*
>
> —Luke 16:18 (NIV®)

This chapter is not intended to present a magical process by which you can solve all marital or family issues. At best, it's probably a good guide to start you thinking about your commitment, and what can be done to strengthen your partnership with your spouse. We cannot do all the work for you. Sometimes it's the struggles that provide strength. We expect you to work at fulfilling your commitments just as we have worked to share the best information we can on how to get it done right.

There is no doubt that it's by the grace of God that marriages last and that families flourish. It is in fact part of His plan. In the scripture quote from

Luke above, Jesus says very strong words about the obligations of marriage. His words, spoken on behalf of His Father, appear to us that God wants marriages to work. And, as we have alluded to, God should never be left out of the equation when things go bad in a marital relationship. God should always be the "go to" we seek in both the good and troubled times.

We both understand that marriage can be challenging, but we both feel that couples should exhaust every option available to them to keep their marriage intact. That is why making the choice to marry someone is such a critically important decision. Making the wrong choice on the front end can be the kiss of death for a relationship on the back end.

To help you face the challenges of family and martial partnerships, here are a few ideas we've discovered to help make your promises last. Take time to discuss these ideas with your partner, and assess where you are in your relationship-building efforts. Consider this a journey towards learning, not self-criticism.

Make God a Part of the Partnership

Our friends, Jim and Naomi Rhode from Phoenix, AZ, are a great example of incorporating God into their partnership. Their dedication to God, and to each other, enables them to value each other higher than themselves, and to do all this for the greater glory of God. Naomi says, "Knowing that God compares marriage to Christ and the Church, (the Church being 'The Bride of Christ') places an incredibly high value, goal, and commitment to marriage." This is the glue that has kept them bonded to each other and to God and family.

Such a marital loyalty reinforces what we've said before. With God as your partner, the odds of keeping the marriage intact go up dramatically. Too often we've seen couples, unlike the Rhodes, who, over time, make the choice to exclude God and, when troubles surface, the scramble is on. How strong is your partnership with God in your marriage?

While you often hear that half of all marriages fail, those statistics can be very misleading because some in those numbers have been married more than once. For example, Jodi's mom was married four times, his sister five times, and his dad three times. You can see how situations like this skew the statistics.

Actually, we have read in a University of Chicago study that only one in five first-time marriages end in divorce. And when the wedding takes place in a church, the statistic is one in ten ending in divorce. Further, when the couple worships together, the number is one in fifty ending in divorce. This statistic clearly shows that attending church services together each week, spending time in daily prayer and, on occasion, praying together, are some ways families maintain their close relationship with God, and in turn remain true to their marital commitment. The important thing here is that both partners are engaged with God and maintain that relationship as a core component of their marital pledges. Growing this relationship with God opens the doors to our understanding of His will for us, and how He provides the strength to carry out our daily tasks for His greater glory. Have you consciously introduced God in your marriage? Have you consciously introduced God to your children?

God wants us to succeed. By including God in your marriage, you open doors to receive His blessings and spiritual insights to keep yourself, and everyone in your family, walking down the right path of life. God has a plan for everyone, and it is our charge to understand and follow that plan. This is not an easy task, but a necessary one if we are to keep our partnership working and our journey moving in God's direction.

"When you pass through the water, I will be with you; in the rivers you shall not drown. When you walk through fire you shall not be burned." —Isaiah 43:2

Show Me the Money

Of all the issues that cause tensions in a family, money is usually at the top. Most arguments in the home are about money. This is why it is important that there be no misunderstandings on how money is spent, saved, or used. Conflicts can arise when one partner makes more money than the other or if only one person works. Ideally, neither of these situations will cause conflict if both remember that their vow is to serve each other first. When one has a service mindset in a marriage, there is no "counting" what you get versus what I get. Partnerships are not always equal, and those with the right mindset fully understand and appreciate this fact.

In some families, income is not always a common pool both partners equally access. Additionally, the one who ends up controlling and doling out money, if he or she is not careful, can take on the mindset of controller. Such thinking can lead to a feeling of being more powerful. And that surge, in the long run, is not a healthy marital situation. Sometimes in the allocation process, one partner loses a bit and, on other occasions, the other partner loses a bit. But that is the give and take one goes through with a service mindset. It's not about keeping score. It's about being fair.

Major financial decisions such as buying a car, house, fishing boat, or a costly home appliance, should be discussed in light of the current financial status, before the decision to buy takes place. Future schooling cost for your children should also be a topic of discussion and discernment. Taking the time to talk these things out, and weighing the long-term consequences of the decision, can save a lot of stress and heartache.

The second component of home finances is who controls the day-to-day spending of income. Jointly understanding the obligatory daily and monthly distributions of the income generated by both partners is the starting point. When food, utilities, taxes, etc. are totaled, the "left over" monies then become part of the discretionary spending and saving plans for each month. This is where personal discipline and the cooperative spirit of both partners are most important ingredients.

Let's go back to the idea of serving each other again. If we truly want to operate from this mindset, the compromise and bargaining for individual allocations are more easily rectified. If, on the other hand, one partner is more self-serving, the odds of a conflict increase dramatically.

We do believe that each partner should have some personal funds to spend as they wish or save for a rainy day. This promotes financial independence important to personal self-esteem or sense of worth. For one partner to be held subservient by the other, and not allowed some freedom to spend an allocated amount each month on his or her own, can eventually lead to resentment and conflict. Remember, it's a partnership of equals.

One last issue—credit cards. The best advice we can offer here is to minimize them. Only charge what you must, and pay them off as quickly as possible. Both partners should know exactly how much is charged on a credit card each month, and there should be an agreement regarding the total acceptable charges the family can withstand. Having "secret" credit card debt has ruined many families. Recently someone shared with us that his wife had amassed almost $50,000 debt on credit cards without his knowledge. This was a major disaster for the family, and, ultimately, along with other factors, led to a divorce.

If this seems like a complex issue to you, you're right. We could devote much more space to this subject. The important bottom line here (pun intended) is that couples cannot remain silent regarding household finances. There must be dialog and agreement regarding cash flow. If a resolution on this matter cannot be reached, seek professional help. Otherwise, there will be trouble that can produce very serious repercussions.

"*Of what use is money in the hand of a fool, since he has no desire to get wisdom?*" —Proverbs 17:16 (NIV®)

Cultivate Your Marital Field

Louisiana has a large agricultural component to its economy. For a farmer to successfully grow a crop, he must cultivate the land, and prepare it for planting. After the seeds are in the ground, more cultivation of the soil is needed when fertilizer is added, and as part of a weed control program. It's a well-thought-out strategy designed to produce a healthy crop with the highest potential market value.

Marriage is very much like growing a successful crop. Couples must cultivate their relationship in such a way that the "seeds" planted on their wedding day can germinate properly and grow a strong, healthy marriage. Here are some examples of the marital fertilizer couples need to spread over the land of their marriage to insure proper growth of their marital crop.

Be appreciative of each other. When you were courting your future spouse, you probably lavished attention over him or her, constantly expressing your love and appreciation. Once couples are married, and a few years past by, the exchange of appreciation sometimes lessens. Keep the fire of appreciation and love burning. It's the source of warmth that is sorely needed for a marriage to prosper and succeed.

Raymond and Virgie Naquin were the perfect example of a couple with a deep appreciation for each other. If you observed them, it was evident that there was immense love flowing between their hearts. This was not a public display, but the reality of what existed between them each and every day they were together. Billy remembers seeing this appreciative relationship as a child. Raymond always spoke lovingly to Virgie, and she reciprocated in a like manner. He held doors open for her and helped carry packages into the house. His eyes sparkled when he looked into Virgie's eyes. One could feel the love that flowed between them. Over the many years Billy was around the Naquins, he never saw a different picture. The example of their relationship remains with him today, many years later, and became an invaluable lesson for him when he married and began to raise his family.

Jim and Naomi first met when she was twelve and he was fourteen.

It was love at first sight. They genuinely like each other, share common interests, have a deep faith and love of God, and truly love and respect each other. And one senses the same feelings are present today when one is around Jim and Naomi.

Avoid a nagging personality. No one appreciates a person who is constantly nagging or complaining about everything. Have you ever seen a statue erected to a critic? A nag is the kind of person who will turn out the light at the end of a tunnel. Nagging wears one down and will create a feeling of resentment towards a spouse. We are not suggesting that couples should never bring up a point about something that needs improvement. What we are suggesting is that you don't engage in constant bickering about a subject. Fighting and nagging constantly is a destructive habit couples should avoid. If there is an issue that concerns you that much, it is best to seek professional counseling to help resolve the matter.

We wish to make it clear, although in *Proverbs 25:24* it says, *"It is better to dwell in a corner of the housetop than in a roomy house with a quarrelsome woman,"* we believe possessing a nagging personality is not confined just to the female species. We know men who can be a pain in the rear to live with and who, by all accounts, can be every bit as difficult to live with as any woman might be. Our point—nobody enjoys being around such a personality—*period!*

One final thought—parents who constantly engage in a bickering behavior will impact their children. Your kids do not enjoy seeing you fight. It's stressful, and it can have a lasting impact on their thought processes and ability to relate to others. Get issues resolved in an amicable way and everyone wins. Let some things fester unresolved, and only pain and heartaches result.

Don't seek dominance. In *Ephesians 5:22-31* Scripture provides a perspective of the husband/wife relationship.

"Wives, submit to your husbands as to the Lord. For the husband is the head of the wife as Christ is the head of the church, his body of which he is the Savior. Now as the church submits to Christ, so also wives should submit to their husbands in everything.

Husbands, love your wives, just as Christ loved the church and gave himself up for her to make her holy, cleansing her by the washing with water through the word and to present her to himself as a radiant church, without stain or wrinkle or any other blemish, but holy and blameless. In this same way, husbands ought to love their wives as their own bodies. He who loves his wife loves himself.

After all, no one ever hated his own body, but he feeds and cares for it, just as Christ does the church for we are members of his body. For this reason a man will leave his father and mother and be united to his wife, and the two will become one flesh." (NIV®)

    We understand that times have changed since this passage of scripture was written. However, we don't think that "submission," as noted in this passage, means dominance. We recognize that in past years, the husband was the breadwinner because mom stayed at home to raise the children. With the high cost of living today, in many cases, both parents must work. Women are also rapidly moving up the economic ladder and getting very high-paying jobs. In such instances, mom may even be the breadwinner. But a husband or wife making more money is not synonymous with the right to feel superior, or the desire to dominate the household on all matters. That is why we stress the equality of the relationship as critical to the success of the relationship.

    If you carefully read the passage from Ephesians, you will see the equality stance taken. The passage really speaks to establishing roles and responsibilities. It is a passage that defines the respectful relationship a man should have with his wife. And, the clearer a husband and wife can be on who assumes what role, and who accepts what responsibility, the stronger the relationship bond will become.

    Understandably, the potential for one partner to have a more dominant personality is real. If you feel you are the one with this characteristic, raise your awareness of situations where you tend to dominate. Look for opportunities to let your spouse take the lead in such situations. Yes, we're talking about a little humility here. Jesus was the perfect example of humility. Let Him be your mentor on how to be humble while letting your partner shine. Here is a prayer you might use as a reminder of this point.

    "Jesus, meek and humble of heart, make my heart like unto Thine."

    Don't get confused with this suggestion on dominance. We are not advocating pity or a condescending attitude. Your feeling must be one of genuine love and appreciation for what your spouse can contribute. It's all about negotiation, not domination. It's all about sharing credit for a job well done, not seeking glory. Jesus was a great role model of how to relate. He never sought dominance, although He clearly could have dominated. He constantly displayed love for others, service, and commitment to the will of His Father. Use the lessons taught by the way Jesus lived his life as part of your schooling in building successful relationships. Try it. You'll like it!

Talk to Me

In the 1950's, R&B singer Little Willie John had a hit song entitled, *Talk to Me*. The first verse goes like this:
"*Talk to me, talk to me, I love the things you say.*
Talk to me, talk to me, in your own sweet, gentle way."
Sometimes, as time passes, couples begin to drift and find they have less and less in common. Conversations become limited and meaningless. To avoid this syndrome, couples must make a concerted effort to improve their communication skills. Learning to be comfortable expressing your feelings, particularly on sensitive issues, can be difficult without a commitment to the openness a successful marriage needs. Like the song, you've got to love the things your spouse says in such a manner that you are open to whatever he or she expresses. And conveying a sensitive message to your spouse must be done in a sweet, gentle way.

In the communication process, a message is not really heard until it is understood. Think about your choice of words and seek clarification of your message. Once you've said what you need to say, and your spouse is clear about your message, the next important step is for you to *listen* to his or her response. It is this phase of the communication process that causes the most difficulty. Most people by their nature are not good listeners. We prefer to be good talkers. Focus on your spouse and strive to absorb the meaning of every word. Listen in a way that shows you want to hear what he or she is saying. Respond genuinely and let your response show the love you feel for your spouse. Conversation on difficult topics is not about who wins or who provides the most eloquent commentary. It's about resolving the issue to the mutual benefit of both partners.

In *Matthew 17:5*, God tells us to listen to His son. He makes the act of listening an act of love. When we listen intently, we give ourselves totally to that person. Listening is the highest form of prayer we can engage in with God. It's also the highest form of love we can demonstrate to our spouse.

Let's take the idea of conversation a step further. We encourage you to follow the advice offered in *Ephesians 4:29*. It was sound when it was written, and it still is a good piece of wisdom today.

"*Do not let any unwholesome talk come out of your mouths, but only what is helpful for building others up according to their needs, that it may benefit those who listen.*" (NIV®)

Here are some ideas we'd like to share on how to become a more effective communicator. They apply in virtually every conversational situation, and are part of the communication seminar Billy offers his clients. Use them on the job and in social settings. Use them to make communication between you and your spouse operate at the purest level possible, so every conversation ends with the feeling of the last words of Little Willie John's song which are, "I love you so."

You are responsible for information provided to the receiver (the person to whom you are talking). Think the message through before you present it. The more important the message, the more time you should spend thinking about the words and about how you will deliver the message. (Hey guys, how much time did you spend creating your marriage proposal?) Never forget that, as the sender of the message, you are totally responsible for understanding to take place. There will be no communication if there is no understanding—*period!* Can you see how that last statement is so critical in a marital relationship? Does that statement help you understand why the last disagreement you had with your spouse took place?

We'd like to illustrate this point with an example of the importance of crafting the right words. You might *want* to say something like, "You spend too much time on the cell phone and not enough time talking with me." But if you think through your message, and understand why you want to send it, you might realize that, 1) you have something exciting or worrisome that you want to talk over with your spouse; 2) you really value your spouse's input and exchange of ideas, 3) each of you dedicates much of the day interacting with others and you feel the need for special time with your spouse, 4) any or all of the preceding, or other reasons not mentioned. Once you have articulated these thoughts in your own mind, you might say, "I have something that I want to talk to you about because it's important for me to get your input. Can we take about twenty minutes to chat without interruption?" Then, after you have had the talk, reaffirm how much you valued it and suggest that this becomes a regular habit.

Use face-to-face communication whenever possible. Look people in the eye. It's been said that the eyes are the windows to the soul. As you get to know your spouse better, you will be able to "see their soul" through their eyes. That's what intimacy does for you. There is something about connecting with an individual beyond words that helps the message impact go up. It also serves to keep the conversation honest.

Timing is a critical factor in the communication of a message. Time your message well. When you deliver information is probably one of the most critical components of the communication process. A friend of ours normally wakes up at 6 a.m. and hits the floor running. Her husband, on the other hand, rises more slowly at 7 a.m. She would frequently greet him with questions like, "Can you stop by the cleaner's on your way home from work?" Once he pointed out to her that she not only had an hour's head start and two cups of coffee on him, she realized that she first needed to tell him, "Good morning," and let him eat breakfast before discussing the day's agenda. Additionally, be aware of the environment before you pass on a critical piece of information, and be aware of the mood of your spouse, because this can be a deal maker or a deal breaker. Want to greatly enhance your communication process? Watch your timing!

Always get feedback to be sure that your message is properly understood. Clarify with questions. If you can be misunderstood, you will. Never assume your spouse understands. We'd rather see a bit of redundant conversation than a misunderstood message or a marital dog fight take place. For example, you have to join your spouse for a meeting in a location unfamiliar to her or him. You provide detailed directions on how to get to the meeting place. It's a good practice to have your spouse repeat the directions to be sure they are clear. Doing so can eliminate potential delay and a possible argument caused by the frustration of being "lost" for a while.

Keep messages as simple and direct as possible. Don't complicate the message with words that can be misunderstood. Remember, the purpose of communicating is to reach understanding. Keep the vocabulary simple. You just want understanding. We are not suggesting condescending behavior here. This is just a case where simple is best.

Make only one point at the time. Avoid generalities. Be specific. Make your message simple and honest. Those two factors will help you avoid a lot of communication stress. If a couple cannot have honest dialog, resolution will not occur. By discussing one issue at the time, bringing that matter to resolution, then continuing with that strategy until all issues have been resolved, you've just moved on the best path for bringing your communication efforts to a successful close.

We receive about 2000 messages a day and act on approximately 500. By the time everyone comes home from work, sometimes a little quiet is good. By all means talk to your spouse. Just be aware that they may have been bombarded today and need a little winding-down time. Give them a little breathing room before you "unload." This is when the "timing" factor really comes into play.

Research shows that immediately after listening to someone talk we remember 50 percent of what we heard. And, as time passes, our memory of the facts rapidly fades. Those facts alone will get you in trouble with your spouse if you are not listening with the intent of learning. So guys and gals, perk up and pay attention. You might be very glad you did. We might also suggest here that, as you age, using a pen and paper can be a life saver. If some outcome is decided, make sure you follow through. A simple note to yourself can be a great reminder of your commitment.

We tend to respond and pay the most attention to messages that reinforce our self-esteem. It never hurts to build up the self-esteem of your spouse. Everyone appreciates being appreciated. If one spouse notices the other is particularly busy, he or she can volunteer to pick up the groceries, laundry, or help in some other way to save time. When that is done, the giver is showing appreciation, and the receiver should extend a sincere thank you for the help. And guys, be observant of a new outfit or hair-do. Paying your wife a sincere compliment for how she looks is important and clearly a self-esteem booster. In a strong marital relationship, both partners build up each other. It's the loving thing to do. Anytime we can grow the self-esteem of our mate, we should go for it.

Unless people can sell themselves through good communications, they will never advance or get ahead in life. No matter your occupation, you must learn to communicate in a persuasive way to gain advancement and opportunity for growth. Great communicators command respect. Great communication in a marital setting can really save a lot of useless grief.

The most expensive schooling anyone can get is from personal failure. Minimize failure in your life by improving in every form of communication (written and spoken) you use. Whenever there is a breakdown in the communication between you and your spouse, be determined to find out what happened. Learn your lessons well, and don't get caught in a similar trap in the future. Improvement is imperative to creating lasting relationships.

We cannot enlighten anyone beyond our own understanding. Until you put yourself in your receiver's shoes, and adjust your approach to their understanding, *you are only talking to yourself.* We know some couples often feel they are actually only talking to themselves when they engage in conversation with their mate. (We won't get into that debate. We'll only share our thoughts on the point. We know when to stop communicating!)

Before you open your mouth, think carefully what impression you wish to convey. While we encourage honestly in any dialog, we also caution everyone to watch their words. This is sort of Phase Two of the first example shared. Not only do we have to craft precise words to enhance understanding, but we should be aware that our words also create an impression. Saying the wrong thing with the wrong tone of voice can get you in the dog house real quick. Be very clear on the outcome you desire or can live with as a compromise. The more clarity you create on the front end of the conversation in words and tone, the stronger your finish on the back end. Remember, silence can hide your ignorance. But once we speak, we expose ourselves to the opinions of others.

Never stop trying to improve all phases of your communicative abilities—speaking, writing and listening. This is the catch-all advice we'd like to again emphasize in closing our discussion about effective communication. Mastering these skills will set you apart from the competition and help to maximize your achievement potential in any career field. These still remain the most critical skills one can master. And seldom are they more important than in a marital conversation.

The Truth and Only the Truth

We would be remiss if we didn't briefly touch on an aspect of communicating that goes contrary to God's code, and a practice all good Christians should avoid—gossip.

In *James 1:26*, it says,

"If anyone considers himself religious and yet does not keep a tight rein on his tongue, he deceives himself and his religion is worthless." (NIV®)

The book of Proverbs also has much to say about the evil tongue of gossipers and liars. Here are a few examples:

"A wicked man listens to evil lips; a liar pays attention to a malicious tongue" —Proverbs. 17:4 (NIV®)

"Without wood a fire goes down; without gossip a quarrel dies down."
—Proverbs. 26:20 (NIV®)

"Reckless words pierce like a sword . . . " —Proverbs. 12:18 (NIV®)

Thou shalt not bear false witness. Now you know how God really feels about this subject. Remember, this is not a suggestion but a commandment.

Mutual Attraction to Each Other

When you began your courtship, there was a physical attraction in addition to other factors that grabbed your attention. Billy met his wife Ernestine when his band played for a dance in her hometown. They talked at the intermission and, as they say, the rest is history. Certainly in their case, the first impression was what they saw on the outside. As they developed their relationship, they came to love what was on the inside as well.

Attraction needs to be more than skin deep. Yes, we all change physically as we age. Some age better than others. But we owe it to our spouse to strive to maintain our appearance, working to keep ourselves fit and neat looking. We can control our diet, exercise regularly, and keep our bodies healthy looking. No one would say that's a bad thing. If you wish to have longevity as a couple, doing those things is very beneficial.

But the real core components that help create mutual attraction and a lasting relationship are the values each partner uses as life-guidance tools. It is the values each partner internalizes that ultimately build the bond that keeps them together. Honor and respect for each other, honesty in conversations and relationships, moral codes outlined by your religious beliefs, ideas on how to raise children, are some examples of values that should be congruent. Conflicting values are a guaranteed source of tension in a marriage. Therefore, the more congruent you are with your values, the greater the compatibility potential. And, compatibility creates longevity.

Regretfully, some couples are only concerned with physical attractiveness while courting. It's very human to feel this way initially, but it's very important to take a deeper look at the values of the person you are dating. Don't rush into bed and think instant sex translates into instant love. Far too many make this potentially fatal mistake. They don't fully understand that failing to go beyond physical attraction can ultimately cripple the relationship, and add to the divorce statistics.

The following quote from Mark's Gospel about our attraction to God could easily be translated as the way to relate to your spouse. Just replace "the Lord your God" with the name of your spouse and you've just created the "Golden Rule" for mutual attraction.

"Love the Lord your God with all your heart, and with all your soul, and with all your mind, and with all your strength." —Mark 12:30 (NIV®)

It's the Little Things that Count

Thoughtfulness during courtship is something all couples look for and appreciate. However, once the "I do" is in place, that sometimes signals the beginning of the end of thoughtfulness. Little by little, we take each other for granted, and forget to remind each other how much we appreciate the opportunity to spend our life together. Some partners are more romantic than others. For those deficient in this trait, you will have to work harder. It's not an impossible skill to learn. But the one factor to keep in mind is that we are advocating genuineness here. It's important that you feel the need, not the obligation.

In sports, there is a saying, "Perfect practice makes perfect." In the case of love, perfect your thoughtfulness by practicing it. Every day, seek to find just one thing that you can say to your spouse to demonstrate your thoughtfulness. It can be as simple as a "thank you" for something they may have done for you. It might be guys opening the door of the car for their wife. It's really all about appreciation. We all have the biological need to feel important and loved. When you place a strong emphasis on developing the habit of being appreciative for the love and support of your spouse, you will be practicing perfectly.

Later in this part of the book we'll talk a bit about manners. The essence of what we're discussing here can certainly be placed under the banner of manners. Thoughtfulness is all about exhibiting good manners. Our friend Jill Rigby, author of several best-selling books (See our Book List) on manners is helping to rekindle an awareness of the importance of good manners in the home, school, and workplace. She understands that it's really the little things that count. We hope you agree as well.

"*Finally, all of you, live in harmony with one another; be sympathetic, love as brothers, be compassionate and humble.*" —1 Peter 3:8 (NIV®)

Share Interest

We all have something in which we are keenly interested. Perhaps it's a hobby or cause for which we feel a strong attraction. Hopefully, that keen interest also includes your career choice. But the important component here is that we make a commitment to become genuinely interested in what our spouse does with his or her life. Remember, God first, family second, and then work. Hobbies come only after work commitments. So each spouse, while being sensitive to the other's interests, must realize that if he or she is putting work or hobbies before God and the family, then the priorities are not in the proper alignment.

Career choices may be vastly different, incorporating two distinct mind sets. Take the time to share experiences in your work with your spouse. The spouse listening to that conversation should do so with enthusiasm and a willingness to learn. We're not suggesting that home life be dominated with conversations about work. On the contrary, we advocate that time be focused on other things. But do spend some time sharing positive things or troubling times you may be experiencing in your workplace. We all need support and encouragement, and that is an important role of a spouse. If we are to make our family life important, we have to invest time in each other. This includes supporting each other in career choices and interests.

While hobbies should not come ahead of God or our families, they do provide a way in which couples can express their individuality. And that is a perfectly acceptable arrangement. What we are suggesting is that you at least have an inkling of what goes on with your spouse's hobby. This may be an area of great enthusiasm, perhaps even greater than one's career choice. So long as the hobby does not place a financial burden on the family, or take an inordinate amount of time away from family, we should support our spouse. If he or she has no hobby, it might be important to suggest one be undertaken. We can think of nothing worse than retiring from a long, exciting career with no future step in place. That sudden withdrawal from a life-long love can be fatal. Some people give up a desire to live because they retired from their career and lost such an important part of their life. Hobbies, on the other hand, can provide that safety net, in addition to bringing joy to our heart.

Compromise and Negotiations — Not a Sign of Weakness

Many couples experience conflict in their marital relationship over petty things in addition to an occasional serious incident. Both are tension builders. Whatever the case, it's important for couples to talk things out and seek common ground. If the marriage is strong, no partner is threatened by not "totally winning" every disagreement. Couples that enjoy a strong marriage tend to understand that there is a give and take in a healthy relationship. These couples realize that marriage is not a 50-50 proposition all the time. They realize that for a marriage to be successful, it takes each partner giving 100 percent. So marriage is really a 100-100 proposition. In times of conflict, it sometimes is better to handle a stressful situation by arriving at a solution where each partner gets some of the win. It's called compromise. In a marital relationship, compromise should seek common ground that allows each partner to walk away feeling that something has been won in the process.

In the free encyclopedia, *Wikipedia*, compromise is defined as "*A concept of finding agreement through communication, through a mutual acceptance of terms—often involving variations from an original goal or desire. Both parties consider an outcome of agreement to be more important than the potential gain of particular items.*"

As couples go through marital compromise situations, it's important that both experience a feeling of successful compromise. This cannot be a one-sided effort. If one partner always wins and the other always feels a loss, trouble is brewing, and the road ahead will be rocky at best. Such a situation gives rise to resentment. If resentment builds sufficiently high enough, that ultimately leads to a schism (a fancy word for a split in the relationship). Here are some ground rules you can use to help create a win-win compromise.

- **Remove the emotion from the situation.** Emotionally charged discussions are difficult at best. Check your emotions at the door, and enter the room of compromise with your focus on solving the problem. Remember, you love each other.
- **Be a high-level listener.** We've already discussed the importance of being a good listener in your marital relationship. No situation has a more critical application of good listening skills then when we seek compromise.
- **Because marriage should be focused on serving your mate,** this is a good time to have empathy for the position taken by your spouse. We are not suggesting that you entirely forget your position. However, if the compromise is to be successful, by focusing on what your partner wants, you open yourself to being more receptive to the need expressed, and are more apt to be open to compromise. Statements like, "I'd like to hear your thoughts on my comments," and questions like, "Did I make myself clear enough for you to understand your concern?" show your spouse that you care.
- **Ask clarifying questions.** Using questions can be one of your greatest learning tools. A good question might be, "I don't understand what you mean by that. Can you give me an example?" Your mate, as part of this

process, must be willing to give you an honest answer. Again, we remind you to check your emotions, and only seek clarification. This is not a replay of *The Inquisition*. Use the information gained to help you move towards understanding, and ultimately a successful compromise.

- **Keep the focus on both of you winning something** when the process is done. A win-win solution beats a win-lose effort every time. Remember, you love each other.

By keeping your concentration on what the other person wants, by listening intently to what is said, by staying as emotionally neutral as you are able, and by seeking a win-win decision, both of you will find compromise to be a very livable option. Remember, marriage is all about trust, love, and support of each other. Following these steps keeps those components in the forefront.

We'd like to conclude the discussion in this section by taking the compromise effort to a slightly higher level—to negotiating for a resolution. This technique should be used only when a very serious family situation requires resolution. Such situations need both partners in full agreement. Using negotiation techniques is a great way to resolve such issues.

You may be thinking that negotiating is only for a business situation. *Wrong!* Without going into too much detail about how to successfully negotiate, we feel it is important that married couples understand the general principles of negotiating, and that they rely on this strategy to successfully resolve a stalemate. These are great skills to master that have much use outside of the home as well. We will use the purchase of a new home as the basis for going through the negotiation process, integrating questions with possible answers that can be used to finalize the decision process. We'd suggest that you secure good books or CD's on negotiation techniques to shore up your skills, should this brief discussion peak your interest.

It's most important before the negotiations begin that an appreciation for what each party wants be clearly identified. In the case of a new home, how much square footage do I want? In what neighborhood do I want to live? What styles of architecture do I like? How much can I afford to spend? All these are important questions to answer on paper before the negotiations begin. Both spouses should do this independently of each other so they are free to put their "wish list" on the table. Then, as you go through the negotiations, each question can be addressed, and hopefully compromised to the satisfaction of each partner.

Don't be shy about raising questions that may not have surfaced in the preparation stage. Questions cause one to think deeper about a point, and sometimes the information uncovered is critical to making the final decision. In negotiations, information is king. The more you know, the better decision you can make.

At the same time you are creating the dream list, it's important to note the areas in which you are willing to compromise. For example, you may want a home with 3000 square feet, but could certainly live with a smaller space. That doesn't mean you don't strive to get what you want. It only indicates that you can live with less when a compromise is necessary to move on with an issue. As always, your financial condition must come into play when considering such an investment. Less square footage may become a necessity as you discuss your cash flow and what you can truly afford to build or buy.

Be willing to back your choices with facts. Remember, this is an emotionally neutral process. In some ways, this may sound a bit cold-hearted, but it's a necessary step if this process is to maximize positive results for everyone.

It's important to note the consequences of any decision made. Once you've made a decision as a couple, play devil's advocate on each point. List the good and bad side of the decision. Weigh every possible answer you can think of, and be willing to make adjustments or argue your case about why your choice makes the most sense. Persist with your discussions on points of disagreement. Never look at a situation as hopelessly deadlocked. There is always room to squeeze through the maze of disagreement. Sometimes going back to a point of agreement, and proceeding from there, is a way to unclog the rut of disagreements and start the discussion flowing again.

Continue this process until all outcomes are in agreement. Understand this is an effort to come out with win-win results. It's not about dominance or power. It's about peace and harmony in the household, and both of you feeling pleased with the outcome.

In the case of a home purchase, it's probably wise to have another set of eyes look over your final decisions, unless one of you is very experienced in home construction. Sometimes a neutral mind can see things that emotions cloud. This is probably the most expensive outlay a couple will make. You want to avoid as many pitfalls as you can, because even with all your discussions, both of you may be off base with your thinking. And, this could be very costly in the long term.

It's important throughout the process that a climate of non-confrontation be firmly established. Arguments can lead to an emotional upheaval, and severely stress your relationship. From the start, agree to disagree, but always in a non-confrontational way. A good rule of thumb to use here is to avoid taking any argument to a personal level. Focus on the issue, not on the person, because it's all about being impersonal.

Understand that negotiating is a way of life. We do it all the time although we may not be cognizant of doing it. It is a part of all relationships. Compromise and negotiate your way to the things you both want for your marriage and your future. It's a great way to build a loving and successful relationship and a lifetime of happiness.

"As you are going with your adversary to the magistrate, try hard to be reconciled to him on the way, or he may drag you off to the judge, and the judge turn you over to the officer, and the officer throw you into prison."

—Luke 12:58 (NIV®)

We certainly understand that marital negotiations typically don't reach the point noted in Luke's passage. However, keeping that idea in mind is a great reminder of what a seriously flawed negotiation process can produce.

My Space

Although we're not talking about a website here, there is a similar comparison. No matter how strong the relationship, everyone needs time alone. Even Jesus appreciated a little private time. He often went off alone to pray, and it was in these times that He actually strengthened His relationship with His Father. Like Jesus, as you seek to grow your relationship, allow your spouse to have his or her space. Couples need time away from each other to experience the joy of reuniting, even if the time away is short.

Perhaps one spouse just likes to take a solitary walk early in the morning, while the other needs time to participate in some sporting activity. Regardless of the choice, letting each partner "do their own thing" is an important component of a successful relationship.

However, we'd like to make one thing very clear. We are not recommending that "doing your own thing" includes placing yourself in compromising situations. Places that have members of the opposite sex "looking" and alcohol readily available can easily diminish defenses. Alcohol will impair your judgment and open the door to indiscretions. We can carelessly succumb to temptations and ruin a good relationship rather quickly in such an environment. And that takes us to the last point we want to make on how to build a lasting marital commitment.

Remain Faithful

One of the sacred commitments couples make at their marriage ceremony is to remain faithful to each other. From the beginning of time, we suspect people have been tempted by passion. It's a natural instinct of all animals. But the difference between us and a horse is that humans can think. That is the major defense we can use to avoid compromising our marital promise to remain faithful.

In today's environment, temptations are all around. We see permissive sex in the movies, on TV, and in the workplace. Clothing for women is more revealing and daring. Men flirt and build their male ego by the attention they strive to get from women.

We should never forget that God was so interested in man keeping this promise that He included doing so as part of His Commandments. *Thou shalt not commit adultery* and *Thou shalt not covet thy neighbor's wife* are pretty direct statements from God. He did not skirt around the issue. For us, that's a serious message. Think in terms of the outcome before making a decision that could be deadly to your marriage. A question to consider is, "How would I feel if my spouse did that to me?" If your answer is, "I wouldn't like it," why do you think your spouse would feel differently about you if you wander off the straight and narrow path of marital loyalty?

Sex is a natural part of life. It's a physical act that can be one of the most exhilarating moments couples can experience. But we need to look beyond sex to love, because sex with someone you love is *really* an exhilarating moment.

Don't trade a lifetime of joy and happiness with the one you married for a few minutes of sexual pleasure with someone else. The trade-off is not worth the risk. If you truly love the one you married, you will find the strength to resist temptations. But if you feel the pull, start praying for help. Never forget that God is always on call for us. He's a 24/7 God! God will always listen to your petition and will always be a source of strength in times of weakness. He will intervene on your behalf if you sincerely seek His help. He will remind you of your commitment and the command He shared with us. And who can argue with God's wisdom?

CHAPTER 10

Journeying with Your Children

Today, with the ever increasing secularization of society, it is virtually impossible for a public school system to have the word "God" mentioned in any facet of the education process. Although Billy served as an elected school board member in his community, he agrees with Jodi that having children in Catholic or basic Christian schools is the only way to keep God in education. Jodi's kids went to Catholic school and Billy's grandchildren are fifth generation Catholic school attendees. One of Jodi's friends asked him once how important it was to have his children in a private Christian school. Jodi answered this way, "I don't know if God intended me to be a lawyer or even a deacon, but I do know that God intended me to be a *Dad*. He gave me these kids, and I am certain that being *Dad* is what God wants me to be. So, I think it is my number-one job to make sure that the children that God trusted me with are raised to know and honor God. And the best way to do that is to give them a good Christian education." Certainly, those who cannot afford private education can help their children by enrolling them in a Sunday school program or other church sponsored religious educational opportunities. In the context of the journey that our children will take through life, their education is the fuel. Without fuel, the trip is not possible. Without God, the ultimate destination of this journey will never be reached.

"Therefore, whoever humbles himself like this child is the greatest in the kingdom of heaven."

—Matthew 18:4 (NIV®)

Some Basic Considerations

Raising children is no easy task. Without hesitation, we tell you it is one of the most daunting tasks a person can undertake. And when we choose to have children, we cannot escape the responsibility to provide for them. Unfortunately, there are fathers and mothers who abandon their child. The percentage of children born out of wedlock keeps increasing, and almost daily we read or see TV news reports of abuse to children. But given all this, we strongly feel that once you have a child, there is no choice but to do the best you can to provide the basics of decent living. It's the obligation God places before us and one, if we severely neglect, may result in a rather serious dialog in our judgment before Him. Here are our thoughts on the basics we feel parents should provide their children:

Shelter: While it's certainly nice for children to grow up in a beautiful home, the quality of the building is not nearly as important as the quality of what goes on inside the building. When Billy was growing up, the houses in which he lived were all very cold in the winter and very hot in the summer. The accommodations and appearances were modest at best, and sometimes left a lot to be desired. But when Billy reflects on those years, somehow being raised in such an environment has provided him with a very deep appreciation for the home in which he raised his children, and the one he and his wife now own. If you have a nice home, it is not a reason to feel guilty. We all want to succeed, to move up, and to perhaps live in a better home than our childhood residence. Thus, our children become the beneficiaries of our efforts. But the real point is not to lose focus on the fact that it is not the house but the home that is important. Some people that live in huge houses don't have "homes." Homes are filled with love.

Food: Children need nourishment for their bodies to grow properly. Parents should educate themselves on what foods are best and strive to avoid the "junk food—fast food" syndrome. It's easy to take the drive-thru at McDonald's, but it's not good to make this a daily practice. Obesity in children is out of control and is almost at epidemic levels in this country. As parents, we have the responsibility to be role models to our children, and that includes dietary habits. Educate yourself on proper diets. Keeping your weight and the weight of your children at healthy levels increases the potential for a longer life, and can dramatically decrease medical cost over the years.

Safety: Children deserve to be in safe environments. With households that have both parents working, many children have become part of the after school "latch key" generation. They are home alone waiting for parents to return from work. We will not pass judgment here. All we want to do is stress that it is up to parents to be sure that safety is not compromised in such situations. Teach your children what to do in case a fire breaks out, when visitors come to the door, how to answer the telephone, what to do if they begin to feel very ill, etc. We think you get the idea of your responsibilities here.

Security: Children need a sense of security. They need to feel wanted, loved, appreciated, and comfortable around you. Parents should bring warmth to the hearts of their children. Yes, there are times you must discipline them and raise the fear level a bit, but in the end, children need to know you care. They'll accept, and actually want, discipline. They just don't want rejection.

Clothing: You don't need fancy clothes or the latest trendy fashions. Today, there is a great emphasis on clothing. For parents that cannot afford these expensive garments, this might be a source of concern. Let us ease your conscience. You don't have to buy $150-200 tennis shoes if you don't have the money. Buy stylish shoes you can afford, and teach your children that setting their own course separates them from the crowd. It makes them leaders, not followers. Yes, it takes a lot of psychology and persuasion to satisfy a crying child. They will pressure you to buy the latest fashion garment because their friends wear that type of clothing. But you must persist, and make your children aware of your financial situation. They will understand and, in the long term, come to appreciate the lesson you taught them about being too materialistic.

Before we move very far into this section of the book, we want to remind our readers of how God feels about children. It's really a two-way street of love. On the one hand He commands children to *"Honor thy mother and father."* This is a real boast for the importance of being parents. In God's eyes, parents deserve honor. As parents, we should feel the obligation to carry our out lives in such a manner that being honored would be an easy thing. In many books of Scripture, writers speak to honoring parents and the wrath God has for those who fail to do this. Those passages leave no doubt about what position God has on this message.

Through Jesus, God let his message about children take a more widespread tone.

"*Let the little children come to me and do not hinder them, for the kingdom of heaven belongs to such as these.*" —Matthew 19:14 (NIV®)

Here Jesus equates the innocence of children as the character we must have to enter into the kingdom. These are pretty strong words and advice from a very credible source.

Throughout the rest of this section we will discuss various aspects of being a parent. We've begun with the basics and will build from here. Remember, it's all about the journey.

The First Step in the Journey:
Appreciation

Teach Appreciation

Perhaps some of you grew up in an economically challenged (That's big words for being poor!) household. Such was the case during Billy's childhood. Many families, similarly to his in the small community of Labadieville, Louisiana, struggled to make a decent living. Abundance was lacking. While even finding twelve cents to go to a movie was sometimes challenging, whenever attendance was possible, it was a special event. Doing "without" was a frequent episode in many households, and no stranger to his. But these struggles were not lost in the lessons of life. Experiencing such circumstances has greatly helped him appreciate the good things life subsequently brought. He has come to believe that experiencing a "lack of" can be a good thing. Too many possessions lessen our appreciation for them. And appreciating what one has becomes a very important character builder, one that will certainly not harm the development of your child.

Working to achieve a dream and reaching that destination is a natural high that no drug can duplicate. Being given something without effort can lead to a lack of appreciation. One only has to look at kids opening Christmas presents. They rip open the packaging and move on to the next toy. Sometimes they prefer to play with the box rather than the toy. We are not suggesting that families deliberately deprive children. What we are suggesting is that you take the time to teach your children how to appreciate their good fortune and circumstances. Overindulgence diminishes appreciation and, when we do not appreciate the things life brings, we take a giant step towards becoming a miserable human being.

We have encountered families that give away toys that are not used by their children. It makes sense to share and not be selfish. Teaching your children to give can be the greatest form of appreciation they can learn.

"Each man should give what he has decided in his heart to give, not reluctantly or under compulsion, for God loves a cheerful giver." —2 Corinthians 9:7 (NIV®)

Where are you on the scale of appreciation? What lessons are you teaching your children about appreciation? Do you believe America is the land of opportunity? Are you encouraging the idea that working for an achievement is better than being handed the keys to the castle? Important questions to consider as you work to develop your parenting skills.

Show Appreciation with a Simple "I Love You."

When was the last time you told your children that you loved them? Perhaps you grew up in a home where your parents seldom said those words. If you are among the lucky individuals, you heard those words often from your parents. That is not the case in many households.

When Billy was growing up, he didn't hear his father tell him that he loved him. He never doubted he did, but that feeling was never reaffirmed with words. Perhaps that was the way it was for many parents of this generation. It wasn't until his father was six weeks away from death that he hugged Billy and told him he loved him. Billy was fifty-two years old. It confirmed what he always knew, but even at that age, those words were tremendously emotional, and very important to hear.

Today, we have very busy parents. Most parents work, and oftentimes there is only one parent in the home. To begin our forward journey, why not go over to your children and tell them how much you love them right now. Put the book down and do it. If they are not present, grab them when they hit the door. If they no longer live with you, call or write them. Perhaps they'll be surprised. Hopefully, it will be just another repeat of an often-played out scene. "I love you," are just three little words. But to a child, they are magical and reassuring. We encourage you to carry it one step further. Give them a hug! You'll both be glad you did.

Perhaps a fitting close to this point would be to remind you of the great love Jesus has for us. He suffered and endured a horrible death by crucifixion because He loves us. No greater love has a man than to lay down his life for another. We suspect those who are parents would endure a similar fate for the love of their children.

Appreciate Their Talents

Throughout their school years, encourage your children's participation in extra-curricular activities. These types of activities teach your child leadership and social skills, personal responsibility, teamwork, and how to build relationships—all important for personal and career success. Studying hard and achieving good grades are basic expectations all parents should have for their children. But sometimes parents don't see the important contribution membership in school organizations, athletic teams, and student leadership experiences brings to their child. We are firm in our belief that it was these experiences that laid the foundation for most successes we've experienced since graduating from college.

Encourage your child to run for a class officer or leadership position in a club. If they have any inclination for athletics, let them participate. If they are musically talented, the band or the dance team might be welcomed experiences. Let them join the 4-H club, or some other similar organization. Involvement beyond academics brings balance and rewards that have lifetime benefits.

The final and most important point is that you should be there to support your children when they participate in these types of activities. Go to a football or basketball game. Be in the audience for their band concert or dance team exhibition. Support activities sponsored by school organizations that permit parental involvement. Become their cheerleader, or watch them lead cheers at a sporting event. You will forever keep these memories in your mind, and so will your child. We guarantee it.

Appreciate the Fact That You Were Blessed With Children

Both Lisa Coleman and Rose Hudson feel blessed to have children. Rose finds great delight doing simple things with her children. She shared a story about when she and her children went shopping for a pumpkin. This could have been a quick trip, but she let her children look over the entire stock, not rushing them for a decision. Lisa has a sign on her refrigerator and on a pillow in her bedroom that says, "What you do speaks so loudly, they can't hear what you say." For her, walking the talk is how she builds a solid relationship with her twin daughters.

No matter the trepidations children might bring to parents, they are a blessing from God. The joy children can bring parents clearly outweighs the pain that is sometimes inflicted. The key here is to keep God as the central focus of family life. He is the way and the light to a successful family structure, and the reward is the parental pride and blessed bliss we experience from God's gifts. And children multiply your blessedness when grandchildren enter the picture. So in essence, children are the gift that keeps on giving.

We think this passage from Proverbs 17:6 sums it up quite well.

"Children's children are a crown to the aged, and parents are the pride of their children." (NIV®)

The Second Step of the Journey:
Your Child is a Unique Individual

Let's Talk Sports:

Genetically, there are no two people exactly alike. We are created as unique beings, and what a wonderful gift that is. As parents, we should celebrate how different each child is, and we should encourage our children to celebrate their uniqueness as well.

But rather than celebrating uniqueness, some parents seem determined to create a clone of themselves. This is particularly true of fathers who live vicariously through their sons. They are determined to make their child the athlete they never were. They push and force children to be a perpetual participant in athletic events. Such parents are often blind to the true athleticism possessed by their child. They believe he or she is the most gifted athlete that ever lived. They dream of college scholarships and a professional athletic career. In such circumstances, sports supersede everything.

We don't want to play the role of pessimist on this point. Certainly, we want children to participate in sports *if that is what they want to do*. Children who are blessed with great athletic skills can overcome almost insurmountable odds, and reach the summit of athletic participation. The world is filled with examples of individuals who, through hard work and dedication, became world-class athletes. But understand that the percentage of such children is very low, and the price for glory and fame is very steep. If talent is present, if desire is strong enough, if sacrifice is acceptable, and if this is their dream, then go for it. Just let it be your child's dream, not just yours. We have witnessed too many children "abused" by parents who were determined to turn a sow's ear into a silk purse, more so for their own personal glory than for the welfare of their child. It's a sad exhibition of selfish behavior that only serves to bring misery to children. Be alert and wise enough to recognize if you fit that pattern. If you do, make the commitment to change your behavior. In the long run, your child will thank you.

Athletic competition can be a great character builder. Let it be fun and give it the level of importance it should have. If you're blessed with a real superstar, (a very rare occurrence), encourage and pray that your child gives it his or her best shot. If talent is mediocre (the norm), be realistic, and let the experience be fun. When children are no longer competitive or miserable participating, let them find something else to bring satisfaction to their heart. Never forget it is their life, not yours to live over again. You've had your chance. Let your children have theirs.

Never Compare

This bears repeating—each of us is a unique creation, and your children are no exception. Sometimes parents (out loud and to a child) comment on how one is different from a sibling. And usually, that comparison is done in a negative way. We may say things like "You're not as smart as your sister." "Your brother never talks back to me." "You don't keep your room as neat as your sister and brother."

Thinking in such a manner is quite normal and, in some cases, it may be accurate. The only error here is that you are comparing people, not behavior. When you confront your child for unacceptable behavior, focus your words on the behavior. Don't make it personal. If you ask your child to clean his room, but he neglects, or forgets, to do so, as a parent you have a right to confront the child about this situation. But, in doing so, please do not resort to calling him names like "lazy, good for nothing, irresponsible, etc." Confront the behavior as being unacceptable. It's the behavior that you don't like. It's your child that you love.

Nowhere can we get a better validation of the individual nature of man than to understand how God treats us. Everyone in God's eyes is unique, and on our own individual path. And, as we are judged by God, it is our behavior that He reviews and will remind us about on judgment day.

The Third Step of the Journey:
Teaching Values

Everything Starts With Values

The foundation of character is created by the values we use to guide our daily actions. Values make things right or wrong. Values forge our decision process. Values drive our desire for a career, our choice of mates, and our ultimate contribution to the world. Values create the moral code by which we run our life.

As parents, we are the first influencers of the value-building process. Some research supports the fact that, by age five, many of the values that drive our life are in place. Yes, values can be added or changed, but much of our foundation is determined by what happens to us during these first five critical years of learning.

Children pay attention to our decisions and watch our actions. Then, they begin to emulate what they have observed. That is why what we do as parents is so pivotal in developing the character traits of our children. If they see you throw trash out the window of your car they will probably do the same. If they hear you constantly invoke foul language, those types of words will enter their vocabulary. If they listen to conversations that display prejudice, chances are they will discriminate.

Look within your own character for the lessons you learned from being around your parents. What we've observed is that you either adopted the values they displayed, or upon serious reflection, turned 180 degrees away from what you saw demonstrated. These lessons and choices ultimately became the foundation upon which you built your own values and moral code. Certainly, outside influences also played a role. But acceptance or rejection of these influences is still dictated by the values foundation you learned from your parents.

As part of the mix, never forget that God gave us a moral code by which to live embedded in scripture. If we use the Bible as our guidance document, we will ultimately develop values and moral character that are pleasing to God. It's when people decide their values and moral code supersedes what God created that trouble starts. Homes that are spiritually void miss the opportunity to connect with God in a real way. We are not saying that those who do not believe in God cannot have good values or moral codes. What we are saying is that the relationship with God is greatly enhanced when we bond with Him by adopting His values and moral codes.

As parents we must not shirk our duty to grow a sound value system within the character of our children. That is a solemn responsibility we gain with parenthood. Accepting the task of properly parenting children is an obligation we must satisfy. Never forget that parenting is serious stuff.

Where Have All the Morals Gone?
We are both from the old school—*we believe in morality*. In our lifetime, we've watched the moral character of society rapidly decline to the point where we are deeply concerned that turning things around becomes more and more difficult. It seems moral decadence has become the new norm.

What is particularly disturbing is that this generation of children is witnessing the "new morality." And that makes the job of parenting harder and more serious. Building the right values so that a strong moral character ultimately develops is under attack with our current new moral outlook. It's a real challenge that parents must meet head on.

When the show "The Simpsons" began, Jodi did not let his children watch it. While other parents did, he and his wife did not. The morality was out of line with what they were teaching in their home. Now that their children are adults, and can judge that kind of stuff, they watch those shows and see them as just off-hand humor. As young children, it might have affected their morality. Now, their morality affects the way they look at the show.

Throughout the history of mankind, we have seen declines in societal morality similar to what we are experiencing today. And we have also noted that when the shift becomes too immoral, the society collapses. Where we are on the scale of destruction is difficult to predict. It's important that parents recognize the significant role they can play in halting this slide of morality, and the important role the teachings of God play into this entire process.

We are not prudish. But we recognize that society is off balance. The last stronghold is in the home, and even that institution is wavering. Every day that parents are in front of their children, they must reinforce the values that build strong moral character. This is the most important battle of the new century. Failing to win this war has dire consequences no society can afford to let happen. In Mark 7:20-21, it says,

"What emerges from within a man, that and nothing else is what makes him impure. Wicked designs come from the deep recesses of the heart."

Examining this passage, we can come to appreciate that we are the instigators of our own immorality. Until we clean our hearts, and rid ourselves of the inner wickedness, we will dwell in the darkness of moral deficiencies. How do we cleanse our heart? If you haven't figured it out by now, we'll tell you again—you must place God in your heart and make Him, not immorality, the focus of your most inner being. With our Divine Friend present, there is no room for immoral activity. It's when we shut out the Light of our life that we dwell in darkness. It's no coincidence that as morality declines, so does widespread belief in God.

A Little Ethics, Please

Our personal code of ethics, based upon the values we've adopted, are the rules by which we run our life. They are the guiding principles upon which we build a career, raise our families, and interact with other human beings on a daily basis.

Why not take time to write a personal code of behavior for your family and the way you wish to conduct your professional career? Discuss those ideals with your children. Then, let them formulate their own code. Besides crystallizing their thinking, this document will become a great discipline tool. When they violate their code, you can remind them of their commitment. This reminder helps to keep them on track better than you could without the written code. And here is an added benefit: the code your children develop now can serve them for the rest of their life.

With a clear articulation of a standard by which to live life, parenting becomes consistent. When you help your children do the same, you've provided a life-long benefit that just might help you sleep a bit easier at night.

The Daily Dozen List of Values

Here is a list of what we call our "Daily Dozen List of Values" that all parents should have introduced to their children *before* their first day of school. (We encourage you to add to the list so that all your important values can be taught and passed on to your children.) Each demands continual refinement and improvement, but they are the foundation upon which character building takes place. We've strived to provide sufficient examples under each point to validate the values as sound principles. We feel parents should also possess these important values. (We realize that you cannot teach what you do not know, but now you don't have an excuse . . . you know!)

1. ***A Belief in God:*** This entire book is about traversing on the Holy Ground God gave us because of His continual presence. We shudder to think of what a totally God-less world would look like.

2. Courtesy and Manners: We believe the world of courtesy and manners has shrunk. The foundation is learned in the home. Children responding, "Yea" to an adult rather than, "Yes, Sir" or "Yes, Ma'am" may seem trivial, but in the long term, it does affect respect for adults. Teaching children to speak in a civil manner to their siblings and to their parents provides strong communication skill-building as well as courtesy and manners towards others.

3. Compassion: Jesus was the ultimate in compassion. Our goal should be to strive to emulate His actions. He ate with sinners and tax collectors, cured individuals who were disabled or diseased. These acts were from a compassionate Jesus who, through His death, showed the ultimate compassion for the entire human race.

4. Honesty: We touch on this point in various places throughout our book. Suffice to say that God commands us not to steal. We believe this applies to any activity, from time paid for by your employer to the coveting of goods owned by someone else. Honesty is also important to use as the standard for our dealings with others. Yes, honesty is still the best policy.

5. Strong Self-Worth: What we think about ourselves drives us. What your children think about themselves directly controls the success level they will experience. Feeling good about self builds confidence in our abilities, courage to take the necessary risks in order to climb the ladder of success, and more easily overcome the "no's" life places in our path. Encourage your child to tell you about the good things that happened during the day. Spend time talking about such events as often as you can. These conversations build positive thoughts that support the self-worth feelings.

6. Thriftiness: There is no greater lesson you can teach a child than to learn how to responsibly handle money. Start a savings account very early, and bring them to the bank to make a deposit. Discuss their spending patterns to help them understand how to get the most value from expenditures. Teach them that too much debt is detrimental to their financial security.

7. Continually improving: This term implies "there is no end" to anything undertaken. Constantly striving to make things better is how winners live their life. They examine their performance and look for ways to improve. This is really about self-competition, using past performance as the standard upon which to base improvement. Billy used this idea when he coached his track team. Athletes would always strive to better their previous event mark. It was this self-competition that made the athletes work harder. In the classroom, we are not suggesting that every child should make only "A's." Whatever their grades, whatever their level of performance, there is always the opportunity to grow knowledge and move up the curve a bit. This way of thinking can be the genesis for avoiding complacency and growing in all facets of life. Constantly improving means that one stays unsatisfied with the status quo and keeps looking to create a better world.

8. Self-discipline: This is the push we need when we'd rather rest on our laurels. Those with discipline don't detour from their destiny. Discipline helps one stay on course with God's will. Discipline allows us to better distinguish between good and evil and make the correct choices. Discipline helps us maximize our talents and gifts from God for our greater good and the good of humanity.

9. Positive attitude: This is the fuel for sustaining energy levels sufficiently high enough to bring success into your life. Negativity creates drag in our life much like an ill designed race car would do for a race car driver. Maintaining an uplifting mindset reduces drag and, in fact, lubricates for greater momentum. Norman Vincent Peale, in *The Power of Positive Thinking*, says a positive attitude increases belief in yourself, generates a peaceful mind, surfaces energy, helps to create happiness, reduces worry, grows faith, and helps people like you. Who can argue with those benefits?

10. Service to others: Our life is brightened when we serve our fellow man. Getting involved in a youth group, a church mission, or working with a non-profit organization, are examples of what we can do to serve others. In 1 *Timothy* 3:13, it says,

"Those who have served well gain an excellent standing and great assurance in their faith in Christ Jesus." (NIV®)

Serving others is what Jesus did. Doesn't it make sense that we should seek to emulate His example?

11. Using their talents: The key to internal happiness is to utilize our skills and talents. God provides each of us with sufficient skills and talents to cope with our world. It's our task to identify which talents, when used, make us most happy. Those who have the skills to teach, derive much happiness from sharing their knowledge, and helping others acquire knowledge. Help your children identify their talents, and help them find ways to incorporate these talents in their life.

12. Time Management and Goals: The essence of life management is maximizing our time and creating a vision for our future. We are all given, free of charge and equitably distributed, twenty-four hours each day. Time is the great equalizer. It's what we do with our time that makes inequality appear. Likewise, those individuals who take the time to visualize their future with goals, and take the proper action to make those goals reality, lead the charge towards a successful life. God wants everyone to be successful. He has opened these doors by giving us time to carry out activities and the intellect to set and accomplish those activities.

Love of Country

Our country is like no other place on earth. Travel to other parts of the world, and you will grow more appreciative of what we have. In 1983 Billy took his first trip outside the boundaries of the United States. He was asked to participate in a technical/managerial exchange in China. The group traveled throughout mainland China speaking to economic and government leaders about American business practices. Never had he seen so many people who knew so little about freedom. That trip was an eye-opener. Since that trip, his work has taken him to many other parts of the world. Those experiences have provided Billy with a deep appreciation for the blessings of this great nation. If you know someone who continuously expresses his or her lack of appreciation of the greatness of America, buy that person a one-way ticket to some third-world country, and see how fast he will swim the oceans to return home.

For those of you who grew up in the shadow of World War II, witnessed the Korean conflict, observed the outcome of our involvement in Viet Nam, or carefully monitor events in Iraq today, you understand the tremendous sacrifices soldiers make for our country. You probably know people who fought in one of these battles, or perhaps never returned from those battlefields. How proud we should all be of those soldiers and the personal sacrifices each of them made for the welfare of all American citizens.

This is the home of the free and the brave. But understand that it takes bravery to produce freedom. Don't miss the opportunity to teach your children what made this country great, and to encourage them to keep those fires of freedom burning for their children. Our gut feeling is that we have drifted away from patriotism, and pride in country is almost a forgotten trait of Americans. It's both frightening and sad.

In our lifetime, we have seen the rise of groups like the ACLU, who consistently challenge any reference to God and country in the same statement, rise to power, and influence what happens in our life. With selective legal interferences, the ACLU has managed to remove God from many public places, even though there is clear evidence that the foundation of this great nation rests in the bosom of our Creator. What we must never do is allow such organizations to successfully remove God from our hearts. As Christians, we know we are on the right path, but we must also realize that the Prince of Evil is ever striving to push us off that path. We cannot succumb nor can we afford to let down our guard. Through prayer, persistent resistance to legal challenges, and a never dying faith that the Creator of the Universe will prevail, we will be successful.

May God Bless you and your family and this great country called *America*.

The Fourth Step of the Journey:
Help Children Become Successful in School

Today, more than ever, children must grow skills beyond what they learn in high school. With global competition for jobs now a reality, the career stage is a much bigger place than when we finished high school. In this section, we will share a number of habits to help children increase their successes in school. There are certainly more items we could list, but we both know that these habits, if properly developed and applied, open doors to opportunity, and enhance the potential career successes your children can achieve.

It's important to remember that your support forms the foundation, and your encouragement the momentum to help your children succeed. Your involvement makes all this work. Spend time discussing these points with your children. Help them learn how to use these skills, and do all you can to encourage their implementation and application in daily activities. This is an investment of time that pays lifetime benefits. What better way for parents to help their child! What better way to help yourself!

As the adaptation of Stephen Covey's *Seven Habits of Highly Successful People* has helped millions improve their life, we feel these seven habits, if adapted to the school life of your children, will make them successful both in the classroom and in life.

Become An Effective Communicator:
In an earlier section, we thoroughly reviewed how to improve the communication process between couples. At this point we want to more strongly emphasize how valuable understanding and using the skills of a great communicator can be to your children's successful future.

There are few skills in life that pay more dividends then to be able to speak, write, and read well. You've read those words earlier but they are so critical that we repeat ourselves. Students able to express clear, logical thoughts in classroom discussions make better grades. Encourage your child to participate in extra-curricular activities. This requires using their leadership abilities and relationship-building skills. Both demand good speaking skills. Good diction and proper pronunciation of words separate them from their peers. Enroll them in a speech class. Working hard on this skill will have lifetime rewards.

How does one learn to write well? *Write!* That's it. Sounds simple? At every opportunity, encourage your children to write. Have them start a journal, write articles and stories. The idea is to write. Seek good feedback on the clarity and effectiveness of the writings. Encourage learning this skill. Great writing skills foster creativity, help your children focus their thinking, and build their self-confidence. Most people never learn to write well. Don't let your children be among those numbers. Make them write. And assure they get exposure to this in their school environment as well. If you feel your child is not experiencing the opportunity to grow writing skills in school, speak to the administrators, and encourage them to broaden this offering. Get outside groups to sponsor writing contests, get creative, but be sure your children get to learn writing skills.

The glue that bonds speaking and writing is the first of the 3 R's—reading. Honing this skill improves the skills of speaking and writing. Do all you can to help your children develop the reading habit. Buy them books. Take them to the library. Let them see you read. Use what they read to help develop their success mindset and their general knowledge. Have them set reasonable, but realistic reading goals. One book a month is a good start. That quantity puts them in the upper percentile of books people read in a year. Speak, write, read—three great habits to make your child a winner.

While you are cultivating the habit of reading, don't forget to include good books on spirituality, scripture, prayer, and other topics that provide insight into the life of Jesus, or that help us understand how to build a stronger relationship with the Architect of the Universe. Getting the habit of reading passages from the Bible, and discussing their meaning with your children, is a great way to build a spiritual reservoir of knowledge. Having to express these ideas to others is also great practice in communicating.

To help a bit with growing the reading habit, we list many good books in the "Lagniappe" section of this book as a starter list for you and your children.

Maintain a Positive Attitude

If you recall, we listed this as one of the "Daily Dozen" habits to teach your children. We emphasize this point again because we believe successful students maintain a positive approach to their studies. They plan ahead for assignments, and do the best they can every step of the way. Teach your children that their thoughts influence the results they get. Help them understand that a positive attitude directly correlates to the quality of their successes. Build confidence in their abilities and a strong desire to do well. Both help them climb the mountains of life. A positive attitude also helps develop a strong self-concept. Our performance as we journey through life will take on the view we hold of ourselves. Therefore, to become a winner, one begins with a positive attitude, a strong self-concept, and a belief that one is a winner. You cannot find a successful student who lacks all three traits.

What better place to plant the seed for a positive attitude than to help your children understand what Jesus brought to mankind. By dying on the cross, He freed us from sin. His death opened the doors to eternity and brought hope to mankind. This is not ordinary human hope, but Christian hope for the salvation of all men. Thus, this hope creates within each of us a positive desire for eternity in the kingdom.

Make Learning a Lifetime Pursuit

Too many students feel receiving their high school diploma marks the end of their learning days. Nothing could be further from the truth. Completing high school is the beginning of their learning journey, not the end. Remember that their graduation ceremony is called a Commencement— *the beginning of a new part of their life.* Help your child understand that a commitment to continuously improve his or her mind pays handsome dividends, and is an integral part of a successful life. Students who master this process become the leaders of tomorrow.

Likewise, we encourage you to make learning about Christian doctrines a part of this perpetual pursuit. Study the lessons Jesus taught while He was on earth. This information is an integral part of the knowledge one should learn on life's journey. Application of knowledge gained as part of the journey will pave the way towards a successful transition into the continuous component of eternity.

Clearly Define Your Values

Successful people know what they stand for. Developing a clear vision for your life is the only way to begin a journey of successful activities. As we emphasized earlier, values lay the foundation for our life's mission. Our mission in turn drives goal creation. Achieving goals is how progress is made. But the process begins by having a strong value system. Parents, become clear about what you stand for so you can help your children do the same.

There is no better source of values creation than within the pages of scripture. Following the moral code God laid out for us in scripture is the perfect place to build your value system. God will never lead us astray with His words. Each syllable is designed to provide a key to open the doors to His kingdom. Adhering to the core values God established, and then reinforced through the teachings of His son Jesus, is the only way to cultivate your field of values. What a family legacy that is!

Develop the Habit of Planning Each Day

Nothing beats the satisfaction of fulfilling your daily plans. Identify the most important tasks for each day. Work your plan. Doing so sets you apart from most people who simply react to the events of their day. Focusing on the critical tasks places your energy right where it should be. Students who plan never suffer from a lack of time to do their homework assignments. Study time is in their daily to-do list. Helping your children get into this most important habit will take much stress out of your life, reduce arguments about doing homework, and make the home environment much more pleasant.

Part of each daily plan should include time spent with God. Don't let a day go by without engaging God. Teach your children the value of this important habit by having them see you do this. Begin this journey towards God by teaching you children to pray, and begin as soon as they can speak. This is not something that thrives by using delay tactics.

Everything Counts:
Help your child understand that every action has consequences. Teach your child to appreciate that doing the correct things raises the odds for success. Understand that life is not neutral. All actions cause a reaction. Build an awareness of what works and what doesn't work. With a keener awareness, one can prevent the same mistake from happening twice. Once is forgivable. Twice borders on stupidity.

And let's not forget that Jesus reminded us that every action we take has consequences. That's exactly what He had in mind when He discussed "sowing and reaping" in *Galatians 6:7* where it says,

" . . . *a man will reap only what he sows.*"

When it comes to school assignments, this is an important principle to remember. Studying every day, adequately preparing for a test, is the sowing component. Getting good grades then becomes the reaping component.

This idea, also expressed in one of the scientific laws, *"For every action, there is an equal and opposite reaction,"* is essentially a reaping and sowing idea. Motivational commentator, Earl Nightingale calls it "The Boomerang Principle."

Everyone is Responsible for His or Her Life:
When Billy wrote his first book, *Searching for Success*, he began the process by asking this question: What is one of the most significant issues facing society today? It didn't take long to settle on the idea that far too many people are willing victims and, for the most part, do not want to accept responsibility for their position in life. These folks are content to point fingers and place blame on any number of entities for their plight. They never give one thought about their failure to take personal responsibility. Thus, the genesis of *Searching for Success* centered on lessons to teach people how to take responsibility for their life.

We believe that we reach full maturity when we understand that we are in charge of our life. No one is coming to the rescue—if it is to be, it is up to me, are two important ideas we must process into our thinking. Our time on earth is the real thing. This is not a dress rehearsal. By taking full responsibility for the results of all our actions, we avoid the finger pointing syndrome, and get a better understanding of how to keep acting in a successful manner. When we take charge, we can bask in the glory of success, and we can more quickly learn from our lessons. Taking charge opens our eyes a bit more to observe what happens. When we do this, we experience fewer failures.

Yes, there is even a Scripture passage that discusses personal responsibility. *Galatians 6:5* is very clear on this point.

"Everyone should bear his own responsibility."

The Fifth Step of the Journey:
Helping Children Become Successful at Work

Even Sweat Has Dignity:

One of the many tasks we face as parents is to help prepare our children for the world of work. Unless they're born into the lap of luxury, children will have to earn a living. But even under such circumstances, some effort may be needed to keep that luxury going.

How do you start educating your child about work? Begin early to give small jobs around the home. Teach responsibility, and sharing the load of household burdens. Let children know that a little sweat won't melt them; committing to task completion is a vital part of the world of work.

Normally those who work their brain stand a better chance of making more money than those who work by the sweat of their brow. But it's pleasurable to sweat a little. We grew up having to do things that generated a lot of sweat around our home. Our work today involves using our brain more than our muscles, so an occasional shift to sweating is a welcomed change.

If you don't mind working hard, sweating a lot, and getting your hands dirty, you will always be able to find work and make a living. So, mom, dad—let 'em sweat!

It's interesting that, as noted in Genesis, even God engaged in work.

"By the seventh day God had finished the work he had been doing; so on the seventh day he rested from all his work." —Genesis 2:2 (NIV®)

Jesus worked with His father Joseph as a carpenter from a young child until He began His public ministry at about age thirty. And certainly, we don't want to forget the most important work Jesus did was to teach us how to relate to His father, and to free us from the burden of Original Sin through His death and resurrection.

"My Father is always at his work to this very day, and I, too, am working."
—John 5:17 (NIV®)

Initiative is In

Firms studying the job market are predicting that employers are shifting their focus to attract employees who possess key critical skills needed by their organization. While cost controls are still important, employers are striving to balance this activity while retaining the best and brightest needed to drive their profits up. Employees not possessing critical skills will be more vulnerable to workforce reductions.

Employees who demonstrate initiative by properly preparing themselves become key players in an organization. While that has always been the trend, the importance of doing this has risen sharply in recent years. After firms discovered that a "brain drain" occurred when they forced very experienced older employees to retire, they're now changing their tactics.

What does that mean to you as a parent? From our vantage point, we'd say teach your children to be an observer of what key skills are needed in the industry upon which they've focused their future career. Teach them that initiative is in, and minimally contributing to the welfare of the organization is out.

There are always exceptions, and sometimes one is employed by a bad corporation. But from our work experiences, we still maintain that good workers will always be employed. And if you are a good worker with an exceptional skill base, you will be in demand, and probably never be without work opportunities in front of you.

Jesus, through His disciples, took the initiative to spread His message throughout the world. Look at what that bit of initiative has produced. Teach your child to take a "Jesus initiative."

Some Ideas on Job Success

No matter what career choice your child might make, there are some basic characteristics one must master to be totally successful. Here are six key components of job success, no matter what career choice is made.

   1. *Honesty and Dependability:* No one wants to hire a crook unless your child is applying for a job with organized crime! That career choice aside, organizations want someone honest to the core—no stealing (things or time); my word is my bond! If I tell you I'll do something, I do it. Being willing to step up to the plate in times of need is dependability. Dependable and honest people will always be in demand in the workplace.

2. Responsibility: Workers who understand that their performance is their responsibility are a step ahead of the competition. Taking responsibility to learn all one can about a job, the duties required, and how to improve profits, are traits organizations need in this competitive economy. "I am responsible" are mature words.

3. Solves Problems: Don't go to your employer with problems. Provide solutions. Organizations need people who can assimilate facts and draw smart, correct conclusions. Problem solvers survive. Problem-producers perish.

4. Forms Relationships: Strong workers know how to work well with his or her fellow workers and build personal respectability. They are team players who have equal concern for helping others, as well as helping build their own careers. Relationship-building is the key to opening career options or building business.

5. Being Punctual: Whatever time your work schedule starts, be there. Companies want you to show up on time and ready to work. Habitual patterns of tardiness can quickly result in termination.

6. Self-starter: Managers don't have time to jumpstart workers. They are not battery cables! Organizations want initiative, energy, and enthusiasm from workers. Always be ready to "get up and go." Learn to overcome your own inertia, and you will make progress.

Mastery of these six simple characteristics sets your children apart from a large number of their co-workers. Take a second look at the list, and you'll notice that every one of these characteristics begins to form in the family environment. Help your children get a fast start by teaching and demonstrating these values in the home. You cannot afford to shortchange your children on this important parental responsibility, nor can you trust that they will learn these qualities on their own.

Begin with this short list and build other character-building ideas into your parenting responsibilities. Make these items the subject of talks with your children. Continual emphasis raises the relevancy and importance.

Let's look at the team Jesus assembled. They were dependable, responsible, offered a solution to building a stronger relationship with God, showed up for work, and certainly were self-starters. If these traits were important for the disciples to carry out their work, shouldn't they be something we should pursue as well? And who can doubt the success they achieved?

The Sixth Step of the Journey:
Build Lifetime Relationships with Your Children

Building Bridges

As one travels on the highways and byways of this country, there are bridges that pass over potentially troubling waters to connect roadways. Creating that strong bond with your children serves much the same purpose as a bridge connecting highways. Just like the bridge is a necessary part of a great highway system, your relationship bridge is the connector between you and your children. Happy bridge-building!

We are both blessed to have a very close relationship with all of our children. Have we had our tensions? You bet! There have been disappointments, misunderstandings and everything in-between. But in the end, we work it out. Everyone eventually has to give a little, but the glue that makes this whole thing work is the love that we share, the strong desire by everyone to have a meaningful relationship, and the pull of family. We clearly recognize that some families are not so fortunate.

What does one do if the relationship with his grown children is strained or non-existent? We don't profess to have all the answers, but we'd like to share some ideas to help you focus your thinking. In severe cases, where relationships remain strained, we strongly recommend family counseling.

Parents make mistakes. They say and do things that prove very regrettable. Stop and understand you cannot go back and re-live the childhood of your child. The past is over, and the future is the only thing you can build. But understand that it's never too late to build that relationship bridge, regardless of the tensions and disagreements of the past.

Some parents have guilt pangs. Please don't feel guilty about what you did or didn't do. If you made mistakes, admit them and move on. You can't saw sawdust, so forgive yourself. If, upon deep reflection you feel that you were not always the best parent, apologize to your children. Let them know that you are sorry and want to begin anew. This is not easy, but it is a necessary step to cleanse your soul, and to enable you to start the relationship at a new level. It's important to release tons of guilt from your shoulders.

Bridge-building is best done under the veil of honesty, truthfulness, and genuineness. Don't concern yourself about being vulnerable. Get the air cleared with your children first. Then, if they are married, and there are issues with your son or daughter in-law, you can move to them next. The last step is to meet with both and seek finality of any tensions that might exist. We have come to learn that an open and honest dialog goes a long way toward mending fences. Face to face discussions are the most beneficial forms of problem solving. Share your thoughts with an open heart, listen to the other person's thoughts with an open mind, and listen with open ears. Come ready to resolve differences, not grow them, and you give yourself a greater opportunity for resolution. Again, if you cannot work this out in this manner, we encourage seeking the help of a professional to facilitate your dialog. Do what you must, but don't give up on resolving the relationship.

We suspect one of the most difficult moments any parent could experience would be to not have access to a child or grandchildren. This situation may be due to the relationship breakdown with a child, or with his or her spouse. The agony of such a situation has to be like a living cancer. It eats away at you. Pray for help to find the words, actions, and strength to bring peace back into your life. Knock on their door, and do everything in your power to show up. Persist to resolve the tension. If all else fails, again, we advocate getting professional help. The ideal would be to have your child and the child's spouse to participate in the counseling sessions as well.

It's tough to see your children struggle financially. But if you taught them well as children, keep your money. If they work, let them figure out how to live on their earnings. Handing them money creates an enabling posture that often lacks appreciation for what you've done. If they have children, *help your grandchild.* Purchase clothes, help pay for school—whatever you can afford. It's OK to help when times are hard for your children's family. Just resist becoming an enabler.

This last idea is the most important, yet perhaps the most difficult to accomplish—*practice discernment.* When you discern, you pray for the ability to accept either situation—a strong relationship or no relationship at all. When you can genuinely be comfortable with either, you will be at peace with that decision, and we firmly believe something good will happen. You will get back your child. It's an amazing process that has worked for us in some very difficult and troubling situations. We've prayed for acceptance of whatever outcome occurs, and in every case, our prayer was answered. The outcome we wanted prior to beginning to discern always happens. It's truly unexplainable. Do you think maybe God has something to do with this?

It might be important to remember that our children are not given to us by God to keep. He only loans them to us and, as repayment of the loan, we are charged with the responsibility to teach them to be independent, productive, and, hopefully, God-loving members of society. When we act like our children are our possessions, we risk the buildup of resentment in them, and the risk of a painful experience when they leave as adults. Take the responsibility for raising your children seriously, but at the same time remember the long-term goal for your work as parents is to allow them to take what you've taught with them as they leave.

Jesus, the human representative of God, never wavered in His relationship with His earthly mother and father. He was also always faithful to His heavenly father. But, as He hung on the cross, He gave up His mother and, without hesitation, willingly surrendered Himself to His Heavenly Father.

"Seeing his mother there with the disciple whom he loved, Jesus said to his mother, 'Woman, there is your son.' In turn, he said to the disciple, 'There is your mother.' From that hour onward, the disciple took her into his care."

—John 19:26-27

"Father, into your hands I commend my spirit."   —Luke 23:46

The Seventh Step of the Journey:
Helping Your Children Avoid Addictions

It's difficult to perceive of a more dire circumstance than to learn that your child is suffering from a drug addiction. Addiction to drugs is nothing new to society. But it's becoming an increasingly larger component of family life. The addiction to prescription drugs is rising and introducing a new component to this war. To not let this monster overcome your family, you must be vigilant 24/7 for any signs of different behavior caused by an addiction. (We might add that this also includes alcohol addiction as well.)

Our families were blessed with not having to face this monster. We began to discuss the dangers of addiction to drugs with our children while they were very young. We encouraged them to be responsible. We asked them to tell us if anyone offered them drugs—and they did.

We were very lucky, in spite of having examples of genetic predispositions to addictive behaviors in our family. We had no blueprint. Many times all we had was instinct and our own personal values. We share the following parenting tips not to place accolades at our feet. Rather, we're hopeful they will enable you to develop more insights to prevent use of drugs, or excessive alcohol use within your own family.

Our Lucky Insights
- We advocated an open discussion on all issues facing our children. Our door was always open to talk about any subject.
- We made every effort to have a conversation about what was going on in their life every day.
- We stressed the destruction drugs and alcohol brings to one's life.
- We got to know their close friends and their parents.
- We took a very strong interest in the development of their character. Our philosophy of life is heavily blanketed with a strong spiritual belief. We emphasized this by encouraging personal prayer and regular attendance at Sunday service. No one ever slept in on Sunday morning.
- We encouraged participation in sports and extra-curricular activities. Staying busy lessens the time to think about and become involved with drugs or alcohol.
- We encouraged them to become leaders and take responsibility for their actions.
- We hugged, kissed, and told our children that we loved them quite often.
- We strived for consistency in our discipline. There were rules that everyone had to follow. When discipline was necessary, it was followed with a hug, kiss, and an explanation of why we did what we did. We asked for a commitment to not repeat the behavior in the future. If they failed again, we took the same approach. There was always accountability for their actions.
- We encouraged and expected our children to do their very best at all they undertook. However, the results were never as important as the effort.
- We stressed the importance of family and support of each other.
- We strived to emphasize the positive, while acknowledging that life doesn't always go the way we'd like it to go. We encouraged persistence to reach goals.
- We supported them even when they failed at one of life's challenges.

- We walked the talk by not using drugs or alcohol ourselves.
- We prayed a lot.

There aren't many places in scripture where the word addiction is used. Here are two passages that make very valid points on addiction:

"Everything is permissible for me"—but not everything is beneficial. "Everything is permissible for me"—but I will not be mastered by anything.
—1 Corinthians 6:12 (NIV®)

"They promise them freedom, while they themselves are slaves of depravity—for a man is a slave to whatever has mastered him."
—2 Peter 2:19 (NIV®)

The Eighth Step of the Journey: *Being a Responsible Father and Mother*

"From everyone who has been given much, much will be demanded;
And from the one who has been entrusted with much, much more will be asked." —Luke 12:48 (NIV®)

For us, the privilege of being parents constitutes being given much, much more. And the result of that previous gift from God means we have to take the responsibility of being parents very seriously. Parents who understand their role know that their needs are subordinate to the needs of children. We are the adults, and children need our knowledge, experience, financial support, and love. As God so ably put it, "The greatest of these is love." There is no room for "selfish" in the same breath as one discusses parenting. Bringing children into the world is the personification of responsibility, and not something to build our ego.

A Few Thoughts on Fatherhood

We are blessed with a total of seven children between us. Raising them was not easy, and we certainly could not have done it alone. The help and support of our spouse was critically important. Without a unified front, our results could be dramatically different. It's impossible to overstate how much we both appreciate the love, support, and wisdom our spouse brought to the family.

Let's make it very clear from the beginning—fathers have a responsibility to promote the spiritual growth of the family. In far too many cases, fathers relegate this duty to their wife. If creating a relationship with God is a prime responsibility we are charged to carry out on earth, why would a loving father not want his children to experience such a relationship?

Throughout this book, we discuss how to build that relationship bridge with God. In this instance, God expects parents (father not excluded) to build followers. We suspect parents who neglect this duty will have tough questions to answer at the Pearly Gates.

Understand that children are watching and mimicking what you do. If they see you valuing your relationship with God, that will impact the way they establish their personal relationship with God. So, like Jesus, become great teachers of the will of our Heavenly Father. It's not only a duty, but an obligation we are charged to carry out.

When we become parents, we take one or a combination of two paths. We mimic the parenting style of our own parents for things that we feel they did properly, or we acknowledge their shortcomings, profit from our observations, and hopefully improve on how they did things. Couple those choices with external forces, such as advice from friends and family, ideas we glean from books, and advice from experts, and you have the process by which we educate ourselves to raise children. On top of this, parenting requires constant evaluation of our performance because children don't come with an instruction manual.

It takes years to see if the sacrifices, prodding, pushing, fussing, loving, and everything else you did for the welfare of your children worked. With our children now all grown and on their own, we find ourselves evaluating if the values we strived to instill have taken root. We did not start out, nor did we wish, to create clones of ourselves. Each child is a composite of our genes, and his own person. And we like it that way. There were basic core values that we consistently and constantly emphasized. They are now the checklist by which we gauge our success as parents.

Each child is different, and brings his or her own special gifts to the world. Sometimes children hurt. Sometimes they make you burst with pride. Emotions run the gamut. But we know of nothing more satisfying than holding your child in your arms.

We are dismayed and very disappointed in men who refuse to be fathers. Some use children as a status symbol of their manhood, yet contribute nothing but sperm to their creation. There is nothing manly about an absent father. Some, while present, abuse their children physically and even sexually. There is nothing manly about physically overpowering a child, or scarring them for life to satisfy a sick sexual desire. Some, through their own selfishness, fail to provide financial support. They drink or drug away monies needed to raise their children. They divorce and fail to provide monies for child support. There is nothing manly about deadbeat dads.

One of the saddest things going on in our society is the failure of men to accept the responsibilities that come with parenting. Children need the discipline that sometimes only a father can provide. God has given us a blueprint and it is this: the man is the head of the family, and the mother is the head of the children. Together they can form an invincible team.

God expects men to be loyal to their families just as Jesus was loyal to His earthly family (the entire human race); so loyal that He died for us. The man of the family must be willing to die for his family. It is a tough assignment, but if a man is going to expect his wife to respect him, he has to put his wife and children first, even above himself. If a man does this, then his family will respect him, and his position as disciplinarian is legitimized. In both our families, the wife has always been the head of the children. Our children knew to respect their mother because if they didn't, she looked to dad to discipline them. It has worked well for us.

Each year this nation celebrates Father's Day. It's a fitting tribute to those who have earned the title, "Father." We want to take this moment to congratulate all fathers who have stood by their children and diligently worked to help them become responsible adults.

In the end, we will be judged by the way we lived our life. Part of that legacy rests in the character of our children. The question—Will you pass or fail this part of the judgment?

To close this section, we'd like to share a poem Billy composed on a recent Father's Day celebration. We hope you find value and lessons in the words. They are shared in the true spirit of love and service for you.

On Being a Father

As a father of children, you should keep nothing in reserve.
It's your job to provide your children what they deserve.
Fathers must serve as mentors, comforters, providers, and a source of love.
All this takes much help from our spouse and from the Lord above.

Don't get caught up in the "I'm the boss syndrome."
In the end, children will venture where they want to roam.

All you can do is offer wisdom and insight.
And pray like heck with all your might.

There are times when you'll wonder, "How will I get it done?"
The pressures of fatherhood can keep you on the run.
But in the end the pride, joy, and happiness children can bring
Will make all your troubles seem like a small thing.

For there is no greater role that one can play
Than being a father to your children every day.
Keep in mind that even when you don't have a clue
They'll melt your heart with a simple, "I love you."

I'm thankful every day that I've been blessed
With children that didn't leave me in a mess
Each in their own special way
Have truly made my Father's Day.

A Few Thoughts on Motherhood

In many families where fathers are absent, the mother has to assume the responsibility of being the head of the family. There is a different relationship between mother and child than between father and child. And that's a good thing, because together father and mother can bring a synergistic and balanced approach to raising children. Either parent alone has a much more daunting task to fill the void made by the missing spouse.

With a vast number of households having two working parents, mothers sometimes experience guilt because they are not always available for their children. The demands of work might keep her out late each day. The rush to get to work limits time with children in the morning. It's a vicious cycle for which there is no easy solution. If you are part of such a household, then it is even more important that the roles and responsibilities be clearly defined and carried out. Men, you cannot expect your wife to work all day, clean the house alone, take care of the children alone when she returns from work, and cook the meals. This is where the balancing act is important. Couples need to list all the household duties and agree to an equal distribution of tasks. It's important that once duties are divided, each spouse does his or her part. These are not activities that should be left undone, or relegated to your spouse if you don't complete a task. A great way to overcome the repetitiveness factor is to alternate chores on a weekly basis. This eliminates boredom and provides an even more balanced approach to keeping the household moving. (Re-read the part on negotiations in the last chapter of helpful ideas on developing your individual task list.)

While the love a father extends to his children is certainly special, the love bond between a mother and child is also very very special. Children love their dad but they loooove their mom. Watch a sporting event, and what does the athlete say? It's certainly never, "Hi, Dad!" Sorry, guys. You know we're right on that point!

We suspect this special kind of love for moms is earned by the months of carrying their child in the womb. It's a laborious effort, culminated with the painful birthing process. It's that ability we can admire in women as being unique to them, and worthy of the special bond between mother and child.

The first President of the United States, George Washington, makes this point very well. Here is what he said about his mother: "My mother was the most beautiful woman I ever saw. All I am I owe to my mother. I attribute all my success in life to the moral, intellectual and physical education I received from her."

Jesus, in His human form, respected, loved and was obedient to His mother Mary. She helped Him grow in wisdom and knowledge in His childhood years. We suspect Jesus, like George Washington, thought his mother was the most beautiful woman he had ever seen.

Some Admiring Words for Mom

We don't want to shortchange mothers by not including some poetry in their honor. Here are a few thoughts especially for moms.

Three Verses about a Mother and Child
by Billy Arcement

I watched as you gazed into her eyes
It was the trusting gaze of a child without doubts
Without doubts a child understands that it's not about lies.

A young boy cries from his fall
He looks up and sees his mother's concern
That look of love soon soothes all.

Children have a sense of motherhood
They understand the love bond mom provides
It's security and reality understood.

A Little Dose of Reality

We found this humorous (yet all too often true) story about motherhood. There was no author listed so we regret not being able to properly credit the person who composed it. Enjoy!

"Mom and Dad were watching TV when Mom said, 'I'm tired, and it's getting late. I think I'll go to bed.' She went to the kitchen to make sandwiches for the next day's lunches. She rinsed out the popcorn bowls, took meat out of the freezer for supper the following evening, checked the cereal box levels, filled the sugar container, put spoons and bowls on the table and started the coffee pot for brewing the next morning. She then put some wet clothes in the dryer, put a load of clothes into the washer, ironed a shirt and secured a loose button. She picked up the game pieces left on the table and put the telephone book back into the drawer.

"She watered the plants, emptied a wastebasket and hung up a towel to dry. She yawned and stretched and headed for the bedroom. She stopped by the desk and wrote a note to the teacher, counted out some cash for the field trip, and pulled a textbook out from hiding under the chair. She signed a birthday card for a friend, addressed and stamped the envelope and wrote a quick note for the grocery store. She put both near her purse. Mom then washed her face with 3-in-1 cleanser, put on her Night Solution and age fighting moisturizer, brushed and flossed her teeth and filed her nails.

"Dad called out, 'I thought you were going to bed.' 'I'm on my way,' she said. She put some water into the dog's dish and put the cat outside, then made sure the doors were locked. She looked in on the kids and turned out their bedside lamps, hung up a shirt, threw some dirty socks into the hamper, and had a brief conversation with the one up still doing homework. In her own room, she set the alarm, laid out clothing for the next day, straightened up the shoe rack. She added three things to her six most important things to do list. She said her prayers, and visualized the accomplishment of her goals.

"About that time, Dad turned off the TV and announced to no one in particular. 'I'm going to bed.' And he did . . . without another thought.

"Anything extraordinary here? Wonder why women live longer? 'Cause we are made for the long haul . . . (And we can't die sooner; we still have things to do!)"

The Ninth Step of the Journey:
Forgetting and Forgiveness

Billy spent the last four years of his teaching and coaching career working with legendary Donaldsonville High School coach, Floyd Boutte. Coach Boutte led Donaldsonville High School football teams to a number of state playoff games, and won the state championship in 1954. All of Coach Boutte's teams were noted for their hard-nosed competitive spirit. He was a hero and a very well respected individual in our community.

Coach Boutte had a very simplistic approach to coaching football—tackle and block well. He also took a very simplistic approach to teaching kids more about life than how to tackle or block in a football game. No matter now irritated he got during practice, he never let that irritation go beyond the practice time. He would shout at a player with such intensity, there were days when Billy thought Coach Boutte might have a heart attack. But as the team returned to the dressing room following practice, coach would walk with that player, all the while talking and teaching. By the time both reached the dressing room, all was forgiven, and coach Boutte never brought up the incident again. Each day was a new day for every player on his team. Forgiveness didn't mean he forgot the mistake made by a player. It just meant that he did not throw that momentary failure in someone's face every day for the rest of the season.

This story has great value to parents. We get angry at our children and, all too often, we keep slamming them with their mistake. We never let up. Why not learn a lesson from Coach Boutte—forgive and move on. Use the situation as a teaching tool, but don't keep reminding your child about a mistake. You don't have to forget, but you must forgive.

Forgiveness Has a Godly Quality

We'd like to take this discussion on forgiveness a bit further. For those of you who have a belief in God, you know that forgiveness should be His middle name. God is constantly offering forgiveness for our transgressions. He offers unconditional love and a willingness to forgive. The ultimate act by God, that displays His love for us and His willingness to forgive, was sending Jesus to die for our sins.

God understands that without forgiveness, we cannot have a relationship with Him or with anyone on earth. For us to have friends, we must be willing to forgive. For us to maintain a relationship with our spouse, we must forgive. For us to be loving parents, we must be willing to forgive.

In *John 8:1-11* we find the story of the woman who was caught in adultery. The Law of Moses called for her to be stoned to death. Jesus was confronted by the Pharisees to seek His opinion in order to trap Him. After some moments of reflection on the persistent questioning of the Pharisees, Jesus said,

"Let the man among you who has no sin be the first to cast a stone." One by one, the audience drifted away until only Jesus and the women were left alone. He asked her, *"Has no one condemned you?"* She said, *"No one, sir."* Then Jesus said, *"Nor do I condemn you. You may go. But from now on, avoid this sin."*

This is a great story about forgiveness because we can very easily relate to the events that transpired. We are all guilty of transgressions for which we have been forgiven. And we should extend this same courtesy to those who commit transgressions against us. If God can forgive, why can't we, as mere mortals, do the same to our fellow man? On this point it's probably good to remember the words of the prayer Jesus taught us: " . . . *and forgive us our trespasses as we forgive those who trespass against us."*

Sadly, there are many incidents within families where siblings don't speak or where children don't speak to their parents. What a shame either party cannot extend the hand of forgiveness and renew the relationship. The burden of being an unforgiving person is immense, and does more harm, mentally and physiologically, to the person harboring the hate than to the person to whom it is directed.

If there is someone with whom you are now in an unforgiving state, why not try this exercise. It's not easy but it is very powerful. Here is a very important exercise you can use to bring forgiveness to your heart and lift the burden from your soul.

- As vividly as you can, picture in your mind's eye the face of the person you wish to forgive, positioned about one foot in front of your face. Bring all the clarity you can to this visualization. See the face of the person staring right at you.
- Once you have the picture solidly in front of you, muster all the emotion and sincerity you can, and say these three words— *I Love You.*
- If you've followed these steps precisely, an instant peace will overcome you, and the hatred once in your heart will melt away.

Once you complete this exercise, and you sense the power it brings forth, your heart will soften, and you will have great difficulty ever feeling that hateful towards another human again.

Billy can personally attest to the incredible power of this exercise. He used it many years ago with amazing results. When he had completed the steps of the forgiving process just described, he literally felt the hate drain from his body onto the floor, and was instantly at peace. Never again did he feel about that person the way he felt prior to doing the exercise. It didn't change his opinion of the person's morality, but he no longer played the role of judge and jury regarding his ethical antics. With this exercise, Billy transferred the judgment to God, and his heart was at peace with the situation.

He has shared this story with audiences throughout the United States, and has had people give him testimony regarding how powerfully it worked for them as well. We pray this exercise will offer you the same results if you are now harboring any malice towards a friend, foe, or family member.

We'd like to close this point with one of the most challenging readings found in all of scripture. Matthew 5:38-46 says this about forgiveness:

"You have heard that it was said, 'Eye for eye, and tooth for tooth.' But I tell you, do not resist an evil person. If someone strikes you on the right cheek, turn to him the other also. And, if someone wants to sue you and take your tunic, let him have your cloak as well. If someone forces you to go one mile, go with him two miles. Give to the one who asks you, and do not turn away from the one who wants to borrow from you.

You have heard that it was said, 'Love your neighbor and hate your enemy.' But I tell you: Love your enemies and pray for those who persecute you that you may be sons of your Father in heaven. He causes his sun to rise on the evil and the good and sends rain on the righteous and the unrighteous. If you love those who love you, what reward will you get? Are not even the tax collectors doing that?" (NIV®)

What a challenge God puts before us.

The Last Step in the Journey:
Moving Your Family Life Closer to God

We hope by now you've sensed that it is not our intent to preach to you or to promote any specific religion. We're sorry if we've come off that way. It's just that we both have strong personal beliefs and want to share them with you. We also want you to understand that you have the freedom to accept or reject our ideas. Our goal is certainly to have you adapt our message into your lifestyle. And we cannot think of a more important message than to build God into your family structure. In sharing some thoughts on this God-relationship throughout the book, we pray that our words will touch you in a way that lightens the burdens of life and brings contentment to your soul.

We ask you to consider your current relationship with God. Do you believe there is a God? If you do, what kind of God do you believe exists? Throughout the book we openly share our views on this relationship because, to both of us, God is most important in our life.

We believe God touches our individual soul in such a way that we can achieve the purpose for which we were created. He has planted, in the depths of our heart, a dream that is waiting to spring forth. To find that dream, we must first be willing to listen. Sometimes we are too busy talking to God instead of listening to the words He is sending to us.

Our journey towards God requires that we trust Him to provide us with insights to find and live out our purpose. But we must listen to develop that trust. Our journey requires that we share the special gifts God has given us with the world. But, we must listen to maximize those gifts in such a way that our presence makes a difference. Our journey requires us to be grateful for what we have—no matter how meager those circumstances might be. When we take on an attitude of gratitude, we transform ourselves into this pile of positive energy.

A relationship with God is a very personal thing. All we ask is that you work on the relationship. If you truly seek to build your friendship with God, we can promise that life will take on a new meaning. We can promise that you will be happier and able to better cope with the struggles that confront you.

Once you find your personal relationship with God, remember that the family that prays together stays together. This might be an old worn out statement, but it is fundamental to developing a strong bond that holds families together. The addition of God to the union acts as a glue to hold a marriage together and, as parents, we are charged with the responsibility to be our children's first teachers about God. If we make God a part of our family life, we can lean on Him when necessary for that extra bit of wisdom, knowledge, and understanding in fulfilling our role within the family.

God is a willing friend. He waits for us to come to Him. All we have to do is reach out to Him, and to make Him a part of our lives. Are you willing to take that step of the journey? If so, we remind you that in our vertical alignment, God comes first, and family comes second. After family comes *work*, the topic of Part III and the next step on our journey.

Success Challenges

1. What is the single most important lesson you feel you should teach your children? How much time do you spend teaching this lesson?
2. How do you strive to help your children retain their individuality apart from their siblings?
3. List the ways that you teach your children to appreciate the freedom and opportunities this great nation offers them. Are they growing in their patriotism?
4. Are you creating an atmosphere in your home that supports the value of education? The value of establishing strong work skills? The value of family? The value of a strong relationship with God?
5. How aware are you about potential addictions your child may have acquired? What about their friends? What about parents of their friends? What about your friends?
6. Spend time with your spouse discussing the various aspects of your parenting responsibilities. Be open and honest with each other. Resolve to not take any comment personally, but look at it as an opening to journey in a better direction. Repeat this on an annual basis and the results will astound you.
7. Is there anyone that you need to forgive? Don't carry the burden of a grudge in your heart. Make the commitment to forgive just like God does for you.
8. Talk to your children about your parenting style. Listen to what they say and be willing to admit when they are right by changing. Children have brains, too!

PART III

The Journey

with

Work

Chapter 11

Some Thoughts about Work

Part of the journey of life involves our commitment to engage in some type of work. Few escape having to work, and frankly, those that do not have to contribute to the betterment of our world through work, miss some of the most potentially gratifying times we can spend on earth. There is something enriching in accomplishment. And when we engage in meaningful, productive work, we enrich others as we enrich ourselves. The search we should be on while journeying through life is to find work that satisfies our personal character while providing for our families and improving conditions in the world. What a wonderful place it is when we get it right. That message holds true for employer and employee. Therefore, in this part we will address a number of ways to find satisfaction with your work, ways to remove unhappiness from your workplace activities, and to help you grow professionally. We will also look at the workplace for non-profits and service industries.

" . . . *complete the work required of you* . . . "

—Exodus 5:13 (NIV®)

As we assess how we use our time, it is quite evident that we spend a large portion of our waking hours in some type of work activity. If how we use our time is a gauge of our priorities, work time quickly jumps to the top of the list. If we are to keep God as our first priority, placing such a huge emphasis on time use and work might appear to be a huge problem in our efforts to experience a successful journey through life. But that is not necessarily so.

The Bible is full of references to work. Paul tells us in his second letter to the Thessalonians (3:10) that any man who does not work shall not eat. In other places Paul instructs people to do good work. Even Jesus engaged in meaningful work with His father Joseph until He began His public life. At that point, Jesus began to engage in the "real work" for which He came on earth—to demonstrate how to move closer to God, and to demonstrate God's commitment to man by sending His Son to die for our sins. Can there be any better example of giving 100 percent to your job?

Work in and of itself is not bad. However, when we put our work before our God, and before our family, we take the risk of making our work a "god." And this violates the way God expects us to set priorities, as stated in the first Commandment given directly to the people of Israel on Mount Sinai, "You shall have no other gods before me." . . .

Letting our career obligations dominate our life will produce stress in our home environment. Occasionally taking work home because we are excited about our work, or have an unusual deadline to meet, is one thing. But when this work pattern becomes a daily trend, family relationships will suffer.

When Billy was a teacher and coach, he worked an average of 80-100 hours each week developing lesson plans, reviewing the material he was to present to his students, grading papers, and coaching sports. Frankly, it was a test of the love his wife Ernestine had for him. As he recalls those years, he was not fair with his time allocation to her. And having some workaholic tendencies didn't help the situation. Today, he makes a conscious effort to dedicate time for family activities; otherwise, the workaholic tendencies will take over. The same thing is true for Jodi who went to law school at night while working full time in the day. It's easy to fall into the "wrong priority" trap, but only continuous consciousness can bring us back on the right priority path.

Understanding how our job or career fits into our life is very important. Bringing that understanding to you is the objective of this section of our book. We want you to maintain the right priorities, while fulfilling your work responsibilities. But we realize that some work requires unusual times away from family, as in the case of people who work various shifts. We further realize that some careers will require working time at home. As we mentioned earlier, it's being conscious of your time allocation, and reminding yourself what the important priorities are that will keep you properly focused.

Many people who appear to be very successful in their careers are so motivated that they are ruthless in the way they carry out their responsibilities. Some take advantage of people, and use them as pawns in the chess game of life. These individuals seem to forget the saying, "Watch out for the people you step on as you go up the ladder of success, because you will see them again on your way back down." We don't fault ambition, but we take exception to ruthless ambition. We believe that the way you get to the top will in large part determine how long you stay on top. If you got there by taking advantage of others, your stay will be short. If, on the other hand, you display a genuine concern for people in your upward career mobility, there will be no fear of meeting these same people as your stay on top diminishes.

View your work as a career-building opportunity, not a job. Too many people want to collect a good paycheck without providing the necessary effort to earn that pay. Viewing your work as a career, and not a job, gives one an entirely different perspective. Careers offer a future and greater security than a job. A career mentality enables you to see the bigger picture, and ultimately make more significant contributions to your employer, employees, customers, and peers. People with jobs think about the weekend. People with a career think about their future. That is the mindset we want you to use as you view your career destination. Move beyond a job into something that will energize you each day you work. Far too few reach the pinnacle of success where enthusiasm replaces drudgery, where commitment replaces reluctance, and where professionalism replaces casualness. But we know you can overcome these tendencies by keeping your priorities in the right alignment.

"Do nothing out of selfish ambition or vain conceit, but in humility consider others better than yourselves." —Philippians 2:3 (NIV®)

Finding Your True Vocation

We want to start your journey by sharing what we feel is the best definition of the word vocation that we've ever come across. It's found in the book written by Frederick Buechner entitled, *Wishful Thinking*. Buechner considers a vocation as, *"The place God calls you to where your deep gladness and the world's deep hunger meet."*

If you focus on the real meaning of those words for a few moments, you will quickly sense the brilliance of this definition. If we all were working in careers that are our deep gladness, and, at the same time, that work satisfied the deep hunger of the world, do you think there would be unhappiness on the job? Our answer to the question—Never! But the harsh reality is that there is much unhappiness in America's workforce. And that is such a waste of human potential. In a recent conversation with a life-long friend, he revealed that he had spent forty years working at a job he hated. That torture is almost impossible to comprehend, but sadly, it is more the norm than the exception.

We understand that everyone who is employed is not in an organization that is solely in business to make a profit. There are many non-profit and governmental agencies whose existence is not tied to making money. However, the circumstances we discuss in this section of the book can certainly exist in these agencies. For example, it behooves employees at every level of the organization in non-profits or governmental agencies to produce a full day of work for a full day's pay. These workers need to look at cost savings as an important responsibility, because by doing so, more monies can be freed to serve their clients. It's also important for them to have a high degree of customer service, a critically important factor in the for-profit sector as well. We feel if you are a worker or leader in any type of organization, the ideas that follow can be useful for you. Sound business practices have their place, no matter the reason for the existence of an organization.

So, let's begin the journey by getting an understanding of some of the reasons why people are unhappy with their work.

Unhappiness in the Workplace and Some Ways to Cure It

If one listens to the hue and cry of people in the workforce, you will begin to sense an immense dissatisfaction with the career choice they have made. Workers go through a robotic existence routinely getting in their car and driving off to a place they find dull and de-motivating. They go through the paces of the day, all the while looking forward to what they will be doing after work or on the weekend. Clearly, their mind is not on the task at hand. Clearly, their productivity leaves something to be desired. Clearly, this inefficiency is costing American business billions of dollars each year.

Why is there so much unhappiness in a place where we spend about one-half of our waking hours? Here are some reasons workers cite for their unhappiness, and examples of how circumstances can be turned around to create a feeling of personal satisfaction and happiness in a career.

"My employer does not treat me fairly."

That's a broad statement that can cover many fronts. But, in general, workers will make this statement because they want to be treated differently from the way they perceive they are being treated. The range of reasons covers such things as insufficient pay, lesser benefits than other similar companies in their industry, an unfriendly culture, or a lack of appreciation for the quality of the work done. It really comes down to workers looking for a bit more from their work than the job offers, and going to work with a negative mindset.

We understand that some individuals working for local, state or federal governments don't feel appreciated by their agency leadership or the public. Lower pay in this employment sector is always an issue. But some of that is countered by a better benefit package. Individuals in this type of work environment oftentimes must make the choice between money and greater benefits. And, some stay, preferring the long-term benefit of a younger retirement age and long-term healthcare benefits over the immediate benefit of more pay. We believe, like workers in the private sector, public employees have to weigh all the options before them and do what is best for themselves, their families, and their future. Once workers have an appreciation for what is before them, they can better alleviate and dramatically reduce the idea of being treated unfairly. Life doesn't always seem fair and at times it isn't. But facing our reality squarely goes a long way towards tempering our attitude and ability to work through the difficult moments of life.

Perhaps you are familiar with the scripture passage in chapter 20 of Matthew's Gospel about the Laborers in the Vineyard. In this passage Matthew describes the owner of a vineyard hiring workers to bring in his crop. He hires a few workers early in the morning and promises them a day's pay. Later in the day, he brings in a few more workers and makes them the same promise. Near the end of the day, another crew is brought in with promise of a day's pay as well. At the end of the day, when all the workers gathered to receive their pay, each received the same amount. Obviously, those starting early in the work cycle were upset. But the parable goes on to say that all the workers were given what they were promised.

And sometimes, as workers we need to pay attention to our work agreement. What starts out as OK can sometimes regress into an unacceptable situation. But perhaps the employer is consistent, fair, and true to his word. It's just that now the worker has a change of heart, and sees his or her situation through a different set of glasses than when she started the job. As workers, we need to always be aware under what conditions we've agreed to work. That awareness can save a lot of grief down the line.

On the other hand, organizations must understand that they are in the "people business" first and the "product business" second. People make things happen. So how one treats workers is critical to the success of an organization. By maximizing employees' natural skills, talents, knowledge of the job, creativity, and leadership abilities, employers develop a momentum that propels productivity, profits, and service. Leaders must assess what workers bring to the table, and do all they can to surface that package of abilities and apply them to their job responsibilities. The better the match, the better the results.

At the same time, workers have a personal obligation to contribute as best they can to the bottom line. Business is not a benevolent society. There must be a profit for a business to stay open. Workers should feel the obligation to earn more for their employer than the cost of their employment. Not doing so makes what you do a liability rather than an asset. While this may not be possible with every position within an organization, approaching work with this mindset assures that you will make the maximum contribution you can, and lend support to the salary and benefits you receive.

Within the ranks of government agencies and some service organizations, profit is not the motivator for their existence. To keep taxpayers and contributors happy, and willingly supporting their work, there must be a perception that a sincere effort to control costs is in place. Any sign of waste or inefficiency in government or non-profits seems less tolerable by taxpayers and contributors than it might be in the private sector. Any effort to build confidence in the quality and quantity of work performed by government or non-profit workers goes a long way towards maintaining public confidence in such entities.

When workers find their calling, no matter their career choice, they become more passionate about their work, and productivity is a natural outcome from this feeling. We all have a calling, and reaching that destination is the motivation for the search. God has a purpose designed explicitly for each one of us. His will is what we must strive to achieve. And we start this journey with God by claiming the "possessions" that He has gifted each of us to use for His glory and the benefit of mankind.

Jim and Naomi Rhode have built a multi-million dollar business through hard work and dedication to meeting client needs. They contend that, "People should choose a career that they are 'passionate about,' pour themselves into that passion, go the extra mile, and help others succeed at the same time you are succeeding." They are proof that following this pattern can produce outstanding results.

We glorify God by properly using our gifts. That is the expectation God has of each and every one of us. The more closely a worker can align gifts to job skills, the happier and more productive he or she will be. It's not too complicated and rather straightforward in its simplicity. God wants us to be happy with our work. He gives us a leg up by providing abilities to sufficiently master skills and talents that can bring happiness while we work. Properly choosing makes all this happen.

Jodi's daughter Alicia is a very intelligent young lady who graduated from LSU with a degree in psychology. Following graduation, she came to the realization that she would not be happy working in that field. After some deep reflection, and an assessment of where her career focus should be, she concluded that she really wanted to work in a beauty salon. When she mentioned this to Jodi and his wife Darlene, Alicia did not know what to expect. Some parents might have the reaction that because so much money was spent on her education, it should be used. But that was not the reaction Alicia got from her parents. Instead, they encouraged her to look into the possibilities of this new career. Alicia found an apprenticeship program and now is a budding superstar in the world of hair design.

Certainly no education is lost. Alicia will likely use her psychology education in the many hours of talking she does as she works on women's hair. Part of her success comes from listening to how women want their hair styled. And clients will often bring their life stories to the salon chair. As an aside, many years ago the Baton Rouge Crisis Intervention Center solicited barber and beauty shops, as well as bartenders, for help in spreading the news about their services! This story shows that skills can be used for different jobs. It also exemplifies that it is important to find a career that will be more than just a job. Our search must be for work that we can become fully dedicated to perform without reservation.

"I have no confidence in our management."

Who you work for, and how you react to that leadership style, can be a major reason for unhappiness on the job. Corporate and public sector leaders that fail to lead in the best interest of workers will ultimately lose and pay the price for their incompetence. Suffice to say here that poor management can impact worker attitudes and their happiness on the job, and everyone who leads should be very clear about that fact. We understand that people choose their attitude, but we also know that environmental factors do influence the choices people make.

We are of the opinion that leadership within the organizational structure is everything. As the leader goes, so goes the organization. Sometimes a company can survive with weak leaders, but that is the rare exception. It is up to the corporate leadership to establish, within the minds of workers, its credibility and confidence to get the job done. Leaders who "walk the talk" are best able to grow dedicated workers. Truthfulness, integrity, honesty—no matter how it is labeled, workers must sense that their leaders will not lead them down the wrong path. Jim and Naomi share that they hire "attitude and ethics before knowledge," an important validation of these points.

Keeping everyone informed in a manner that is cloaked with integrity, truthfulness, and honesty helps workers believe in their leaders, no matter the news shared. When workers feel they understand what is happening in a company, they always have a feeling of hope. It's when workers lose hope that unhappiness, and a loss of confidence in the management team, spreads like a wildfire.

One work environment where we strongly believe confidence in the leadership is critical is in the field of education. School leaders are charged with providing a sound educational opportunity for all students. In this case, the school principal is the key component for getting that done. When teachers lose confidence in the leadership potential of their principal, the results can domino throughout a school. Sometimes this can be overcome by a strong teaching staff. But too often poor principals paralyze pupil progress. The accomplishments of schools impact the future of our country. Teachers are the preparers of the workforce of tomorrow and getting the job done properly is one of the most important tasks in our society. Getting this incredibly important job done truly hinges on competent leadership and management skills on the part of all individuals in such roles.

There is a wonderful book entitled *God is my CEO* written by Larry Julian. It's impossible to think of anyone who could provide a better leadership model than God. As Julian notes, God exemplifies patience. He is tolerant and forgiving of His creation much as a good CEO is. He shows us how to be courageous and committed to a goal through the life and example of His Son, Jesus. He is the ultimate manager in whom we truly can have faith and confidence.

If you want a valuable lesson on leadership, and the loss of confidence of followers in their leader, read Exodus, which details the forty-year journey Moses and his followers took. Could you have persisted under such conditions, or would you have abandoned the management team? Just something to think about.

Almost everyone is aware of the situation that existed in Louisiana as the result of hurricane Katrina. The storm devastated the southern portions of the state, particularly the city of New Orleans and its surrounding areas. While the pictures told the story of the devastation, and the actual impact the catastrophe had on the lives of the people who lived in the areas most affected, what people didn't see was the minute-by-minute, hour-by-hour, day-by-day efforts of the local, state, and federal governments to react to what is now considered the most devastating natural disaster to ever hit the United States. The Governor of Louisiana, Kathleen Blanco, was based at the Office of Emergency Preparedness. She was in charge of the staff that was reacting to one failure after another. First the levee failed, then the pumps failed, then the reinforcements were delayed. The entire time, she watched as the staff became more and more fatigued and frustrated. There are plenty of stories of heroes in action saving people from rooftops and boating people out of flooded areas. But what people don't realize is the heroic work of the people manning the Office of Emergency Preparedness.

The storm first hit the Louisiana coast on Monday, August 29 at 6:10 a.m. near Buras-Triumph, small communities southeast of New Orleans. As the storm moved inland, by 8:00 a.m., there was flooding in New Orleans on both sides of the Industrial Canal. More levees began to breach and soon about 85 percent of the city was under water. And despite the efforts of local, state, and federal officials to pull resources together, by Wednesday, while Katrina had been downgraded to a tropical depression, it was painfully obvious that the worst was still to come. Governor Blanco, sensing the frustration, did something that might appear a little strange to some. She told Jodi during his interview with the Governor, "All I knew was to call for prayer!" The Governor then described how she pulled together two ministers, one Protestant and one Catholic, and on Wednesday morning the entire staff of the Office of Emergency Preparedness stopped long enough to ask the Lord for divine intervention.

After the prayer meeting, it appeared that the stress level went way down and people appeared to be re-energized and more strongly committed to the work ahead. "I can't tell you how many of the staff came up to me and thanked me for calling the prayer service," the Governor relayed to Jodi one Sunday after Mass. The Governor told Jodi that she was convinced that things began to take a turn for the better after that prayer service. This is an example of a leader taking a risk for her employees. We all know of the supposed "Separation of Church and State," but Governor Blanco, sensing a need in her staff, took a risk and put her employees above any possible backlash that might have come from having such a religious service.

Leadership at the management level can be improved in many circumstances. However, if a person finds himself or herself in a bad situation under poor management, then it might be time for a job or career change. Change takes courage and faith; however, many who have made career changes have excelled. We know a gentleman who works at a chemical plant. He is very successful, but knew he didn't want to work there forever. In his off time from his job, he started a company that built decks and fences. His decks are now considered some of the best in the greater Baton Rouge area. We met with him recently, and he is just on the verge of expanding this business and leaving his job at the plant.

If you are in a bad work environment and need some direction, there are many places to get education and help. With the internet, for example, you might look to find online seminars and conference calls on a specific subject matter. There are night classes at universities, vocational colleges, and job-training centers. These are usually inexpensive ways to get very valuable advice regarding success in work and business, and re-training for a new career. Sometimes it might be wise to take a career assessment test using a properly trained counselor. These data can be very revealing and help point the way to a new career. One of Billy's daughters used this process to open an entirely new career opportunity. Her test data showed a strong tendency to counsel others. Using this information, she entered graduate school and completed her Masters in Marriage and Family Counseling. Today, she is a well-respected and successful counselor working with addiction rehabilitation, marital relations, and parenting issues.

If your career is moving in an unsatisfactory direction, it's important that you also pray about it. Pray for guidance, and listen to the answer. Divine intervention can occur through prayer. God can reveal insights that will help you set a new course on your journey. Prayer is a wonderful tool to carry in your career toolbox.

"I don't see any opportunity to grow my career."

If workers feel like they are up against a brick wall with no escape potential, they become very uncomfortable with their work. Most workers want opportunity for advancement and personal growth in their career. Once work is perceived as a dead-end street, some employees will begin to update their resumé.

Research by behavioral scientists has shown that we may have as much as 75 percent of our abilities that go unused in our lifetime. We have this magnificent mass of intellect within our brain that is available to help, yet we fail to tap this reservoir of resources. Organizations that recognize this gift that comes packaged with their employees will offer training opportunities to grow skills. The Rhodes felt they should spend time and money on training and empowering employees for creativity, accomplishment, and a self-starting work ethic. That mindset is at the core of their phenomenal business growth. Good organizations follow this rule when it comes to helping employees grow their career because they understand that, as employees grow, so will the organization.

Too often companies see training as a needless expense and, when things get tight, it's one of the first cost centers to get cut. That is a major mistake. To the contrary, when things are tough, that is truly the time to target employees for training. Workers, who grow their skills on the job, help to improve the bottom line. Workers who are properly trained can become the next generation to lead the organization to greater heights. Keep employees growing, and you perpetuate profits.

Those who lead must be perpetual teachers and help workers gain a little knowledge every day. Encourage training within the organization. Encourage initiatives that produce new information to help maintain a competitive edge. There is always a risk that you train and they leave. That may be true, but a truer truth is that if you don't train, and help those who want to grow their career, they positively will leave, or will become a burden to the business.

It's not good enough to offer training. Such offerings should directly support the overall strategy of the organization. For example, when Billy speaks to school board members in a training session, he will emphasize the need to tie training within the school district to the strategic plans of the district. With sometimes limited resources, a school district should be judicious with monies allocated for training purposes. Sending a teacher, principal, or district staff member to a conference that does not provide information to help achieve the district's strategic initiative is a waste of monies. And it's no different in the for-profit sectors. Congruency of training and strategy is the wisest investment of resources. In short, if any learning opportunity does not make achievement of the organization's overall strategic initiative more of a reality, don't spend time and money doing it.

Workers who have personal ambition, and seek growth opportunities, can follow this simple approach: Look around the organization for some work that needs to be done that is not being done by anyone. Assess your ability to carry out this new function and, if you have such abilities, ask permission to assume that responsibility. You may not always get what you want, but we promise you that your management will appreciate your initiative and remove some barriers for your future advancement later on.

If we take a look at the life of Jesus, we will certainly note that He was a perpetual teacher. He constantly shared lessons on how to live, and was the consummate role model. He was patient and forgiving. He constantly reinforced His message on self-management. He established a clear path of growth for the apostles and the many disciples that followed. He opened eyes to the potential to grow spiritually, much as you can do with employee skills in the workplace. Again, the character exhibited by Jesus, God made man, to encourage and motivate His followers to grow their spiritual career, is a great model of success.

Jodi worked as Associate General Counsel for a major corporation for fifteen years. When the General Counsel retired, he expected to be promoted. Instead, a person from the outside was promoted to that position and became Jodi's boss. Jodi could have reacted emotionally and quit, but he did not. Instead, he dedicated himself to re-inventing his position, and stayed at the company for several more years. When the opportunity came to move on, he was hired by a large law firm with an increase in salary. He often tells the story that he could not have even gotten an interview with this firm out of law school, but later in life found himself a shareholder in the firm.

There are two points here: perseverance pays off, and it is never too late to succeed by changing and re-focusing your career.

"If any man builds on this foundation using gold, silver, costly stones, wood, hay or straw, his work will be shown for what it is, because the Day will bring it

to light. It will be revealed with fire, and the fire will test the quality of each man's work. If what he has built survives, he will receive his reward. If it is burned up, he will suffer loss; he himself will be saved, but only as one escaping through the flames." —1 Corinthians 3:12-15 (NIV®)

"I'm just not motivated."

There are workers who expect someone else to motivate them to find happiness and opportunity on the job. These folks have it all wrong. Motivation is a personal self-improvement process. We are responsible for our motivation. It's a task we must assume. It is an "inside job." We must have that winning feeling before we can become winners. Likewise, we must inculcate a feeling of happiness within ourselves before we can find happiness. We do understand that some work environments can be de-motivating. In such circumstances, a worker must make a choice to live with things as they are, work to change the situation or leave. None of these options can be done without internal motivation and courage. If you find yourself in such a situation, weigh your options and make the appropriate choice. However, never make the choice to stay de-motivated. Psychologists will tell you that you often cannot control the circumstance you find yourself in, but you can always control your reaction to those circumstances.

This is a tricky issue. Company leaders mistakenly believe they are in charge of building motivation. While that may be technically true, the reality is that all motivation is self-motivation. The responsibility of an organization is to provide a culture that supports flourishing self-motivation. Such a culture:

- Provides positive, yet truthful feedback on performance
- Has a consistent discipline policy that cuts across the organization
- Sets challenging but realistically achievable objectives
- Provides resources to get the job done well
- Offers fair pay for a day's work
- Allows employees to experience achievement and personal growth
- Creates opportunities for increasing responsibility on the job
- Offers flexibility in structuring job functions
- Listens to the needs of workers and makes satisfying these needs an important leadership philosophy
- Recognizes and rewards achievement at every level

Again, let's look at the internal motivation Jesus provided His followers. He inspired hope and a vision within His apostles and disciples. No one understands motivation better than Jesus. He promised eternity with Him in Heaven, and the joy of that possibility motivated His followers to endure martyrdom rather than renounce their beliefs and teachings.

While we humans are not God or Jesus, we certainly can offer a brand of hope to employees that will surface the momentum of self-motivation and happiness with work assignments. If you are a leader, you have an obligation to create an environment that keeps the self-motivation of workers at its peak.

There is a perception by taxpayers that far too many government workers are not motivated to do a good job. While there are certainly "slackers" in the government, the reality is that they also exist within corporate America. Worker motivation is a personal choice, not a corporate or government thing. As an employee of any entity, one has the obligation to keep the motors of motivation running. Those who take such an attitude will often find great pleasure with their work.

James L. Nolan, in his book, *Doing the Right Things at Work*, says this: "Our actions are the results of the fires that drive us and the habits and disciplines we have developed over time to challenge and direct our desire for completeness and wholeness." These are great words for those seeking how to self-motivate. Read them again if you are struggling with your interest in your career. This is very sound advice.

Another thing you can do is read the New Testament for accounts of how Jesus lived His message as He journeyed during His public life. If these lessons don't motivate you, check your pulse. You might be dead!

"I'll never find the right job for me."

People who feel they are not working at their ideal job experience dissatisfaction and unhappiness with their current situation. A feeling of helplessness permeates their mind, and they feel trapped in a situation with no escape route. That can be a terrible feeling. Unfortunately, what happens is that workers remain dissatisfied and seldom take the initiative to produce change. They forsake security for sanity. Life is too short to work at a job we hate.

Discovering what we want to be when we grow up can be a daunting task. Those individuals who find the perfect job setting early in their careers are fortunate. People have a natural desire to work at a job that makes a difference and to experience happiness with their work. What we must understand is that it is up to us as individuals to manage our career. We need to get in touch with our passion—the thing we would do for free, and see how we can integrate it into our career choice. (Remember the deep gladness and deep hunger goal.) But we also need to understand that, over time, passions change. As we mature and grow in knowledge, so might our true focus in life. Therefore, where you are now will probably not be where you will be later in your life.

Billy decided that he wanted to teach when he was in the seventh grade. He didn't know what subjects he wanted to teach, only that he wanted to be a teacher. Was it the wrong choice? Fortunately he followed the path where his passion called. Unfortunately, what he didn't realize was that the pay was substandard. Eventually he was forced to leave his career choice in order to better support his family. (Remember the pecking order—God, Family, Career.)

But here is where passion can still prevail even when you make a career change. Billy used his skill as a teacher while serving as a manager for his company. He had to train workers under his supervision how to carry out their job responsibilities. He constantly nurtured employees and supported building the workers' knowledge of their jobs. He really never stopped being a "teacher."

Today, he constantly uses his teaching skills when he speaks to audiences. This career actually began as a "second job." He crafted these new teaching skills by speaking to clients in the evenings, after work, or on weekends. He took vacation time to travel out-of-state. He began to write as part of this new teaching opportunity he was developing, and here is where his passion began to change again. Rather than being a speaker who writes, today he is beginning to view himself as a writer who speaks. What was once a very painful process (writing), has now become one of the great joys of his life. That is what we meant when we said earlier that as we mature and grow in knowledge, we can experience a change of focus regarding our passion in life. That is exactly what happened to Billy, and certainly, a similar change can occur within you as well.

Recently, Billy was returning from a business trip to Chicago when he met Hansel Cunningham. Hansel was the cab driver who drove him from his hotel to O'Hare airport. As the trip began, he asked Hansel how long he had been driving a cab. Hansel told him that he had driven seventeen years in the city but recently moved to the suburbs. This area was less stressful to drive through than downtown Chicago. At 63, Hansel was ready for a more relaxing work atmosphere.

As the conversation continued, he learned that Hansel had spent twenty years working in the insurance business. Hansel enjoyed his work and had worked his way to a nice management position. But he wanted more. He wanted to operate his own business, and he capitalized on his dream by buying his own cab. Seventeen years later, he owns five cabs, and has a business that appreciates in value each year. Hansel told Billy that getting a medallion to drive a cab in downtown Chicago now costs $90,000. You can do the math and see that Hansel's decision was a good one.

Billy asked Hansel if he liked driving cabs. His reply, "I like it more than I dislike it." What Hansel had learned as a business owner was that he controlled his successes, and he preferred that to being dependent upon someone else to provide him that opportunity. Owning his own business allows him to control the amount of time he works and, to a large degree, the amount of money he earns. He is a classic example of someone who found the right job and did something with it.

It is never too late to move into a job or career that is more satisfying. Jodi's dad, Joe Moscona, worked for nearly forty years in the automobile business, spending most of those years in the finance and insurance part of the business. A few years ago, Joe had the opportunity to help start a business with a friend. The business offered warranties for pre-owned cars and sold them through dealerships. The change gave him more independence and a greater income potential. He now has time to play golf at least once per week, and although he has a large territory, he has more control of his life.

We have found these words from *Psalm 139: 1-12* to be especially poignant regarding this point on God knowing our heart.

"*O Lord, you have probed me and you know me; you know when I sit and when I stand; you understand my thoughts from afar. My journeys and my rest you scrutinize, with all my ways you are familiar.*

Even before a word is on my tongue, behold, O Lord, you know the whole of it. Behind me and before, you hem me in and rest your hand upon me. Such knowledge is too wonderful for me; too lofty for me to attain.

Where can I go from your Spirit? From your presence where can I flee? If I go up to the heavens, you are there. If I sink to the nether world, you are present there.

If I take the wings of the dawn, if I settle at the farthest limits of the sea, even there your hand shall guide me, and your right hand hold me fast.

If I say, "Surely the darkness shall hide me, and night shall be my light," . . . For the darkness itself is not dark, and night shines as the day. (Darkness and light are the same.)

"I have a life outside of this company and I want to use it."

More and more companies are demanding greater productivity with fewer and fewer employees. Downsizing, certainly a source of unhappiness and low morale in the marketplace, is now the norm rather than the exception. Because of this trend, workers are feeling forced to work longer hours. Promotions are tied to this commitment, and staying employed is often threatened if workers don't comply with this new mandate. Thus the normal forty-hour week has grown into a fifty- or sixty-hour burden. Workers are feeling out of control, and that becomes a major source of dissatisfaction with their work.

With the increased pressure from state and federal legislators to bring more accountability to the classroom, teachers are finding increased responsibilities placed on their performance. Accountability is the buzzword in the world of education. The increased accountability and responsibility are taking their toll on the time and life of teachers.

Likewise, we sense a downsizing of staff in hospitals and nursing homes in order to keep such facilities in operation. This causes more overtime and stress on nurses and support staff. Long hours in the workplace are eating away at time away from work, and that sometimes leads to mistakes affecting the quality of patient care. It's another sign of today's work environment that is expecting more from fewer workers.

There is a real "Catch 22" going on in today's workplace. Global competition is feeding this frenzy. To compete with rising cost and lower pricing from global competition, American companies are increasingly shifting to technology to save on human capital. This has resulted in a smaller workforce with more demands for their skills and time. This situation has also fueled a drop in loyalty to employers. Today's workers are much quicker to change jobs than at any other time in the past. They sense that companies too often use workers without regard for their personal feelings or needs, and for them, this is an intolerable situation.

Keeping a climate of dignity and respect for people and their needs, goes a long ways towards diminishing the feeling of disloyalty workers can acquire. Leaders must raise their antenna, and do all they can to pick up worker signals of unhappiness. Striving to bring a balance between work and home life is critical to overcoming this dilemma. One way leaders can do this is by providing back-up so that, when people travel for business, take personal vacations, or are sick, some of their work gets done. It can be discouraging to face a backlog of projects when one returns to the workplace from such situations.

People at the top of the organization must support family values while balancing the needs of the organization. Workers don't mind some exceptions to this practice. They just don't want complete abandonment while the company expounds on the virtue of family. That inconsistency is deadly to employee happiness and morale.

We'd like to suggest that you build your life away from work around a strong spiritual base. Getting that part of life right transcends itself into your work habits. Bringing spirituality into your workplace makes you a better worker, and grows a strong sense of ethics within the decision-making process. We are not suggesting that you bring "religion" to the workplace, just a "joint venture" between you and God to establish how you should approach your work and relationships with your fellow employees. In the words of St. Francis of Assisi, "Preach the Gospel at all times, and, when necessary, use words." Let the way that you live be your witness! Keep it personal and don't insist others follow you. Show them goodness and effectiveness by your example. Your attitude about this is critical because you don't want to turn off people with your preaching and teaching. Turn them on by your shining example.

Jodi is an ordained Permanent Deacon in the Catholic Church. Permanent Deacons receive the same sacramental ordination as priests, except they are not ordained to celebrate mass or hear confessions. Permanent Deacons preach, officiate at funerals, baptisms, weddings, attend to the sick and dying, and also participate in any other administrative or teaching functions assigned.

One of Jodi's classmates in diaconate formation is an insurance agent. He owns his own agency and is very successful. He, like almost all Permanent Deacons, participates in his ministry activities in addition to holding a full time job. This falls in line with our suggestion above to use your own time to build a life outside of work around a strong spiritual base. It has been said that what you do from nine to five makes a living, but what you do from five to nine creates a life.

Many people use this philosophy to get ahead by participating in business activities in addition to their job (moonlighting) to provide a better lifestyle for their family. Perhaps they make the choice to go back to school. These are excellent ways to get ahead as long as it is kept in perspective.

Jodi's father-in-law, Bill Mumford, is nearing retirement. By all accounts, he has had a successful career. The reason he is successful now is because of what he did at the beginning of his career. Bill is now a manufacturer's rep, selling for many companies, but early in his career he worked for a large distribution company, eventually becoming vice president. On the way up, he also drove a cab at night to make extra money to provide for his family. It is that work ethic— the willingness to do whatever it takes— that sets successful people apart from those who just want to be employees. Everyone has the choice to succeed or not, and in large part, it is what you do with your time that matters. We must all keep in mind that we have to do it God's way. View your work as a spiritual journey, and you will find fulfillment both on and off the job.

Striking that right balance between work and life off the job can be a constant struggle. It becomes easier when we have our priorities clearly defined. That's why we have stressed from the beginning that keeping priorities of God, family, and career, in that sequence, is the key component of a successful life. Maintaining that balance is a critical choice.

"I feel isolated. No one likes me."

Truthfully, not all workers blend into the workforce. It's not so much that people are bad. It's just that some people are different. They are shy, lack confidence, and struggle building personal relationships. On the other hand, workers can be reluctant to bring new folks into their "cliques." They may have a personal bias towards an ethnicity or gender. In worst cases, harassment and bullying get in the way of a new employee's acclimating to the culture.

In this day of quick lawsuits, company leaders and HR professionals should educate their workforce on how to help new employees fit into the company. They must make sure that their current employees don't begin to exhibit bad habits that discriminate against a co-worker. The more the company culture supports teamwork, strong internal customer service between workers, and a warm appreciation for each other, the quicker feelings of isolation go away. This is an issue that cannot be ignored. Doing so can be very costly in more ways than money out of the company till.

New workers should make the effort to develop relationships with their peers and superiors. Get rid of that "timid" hat, and put on the hat of an outgoing, confident individual. Be cautious rather than caustic. Be friendly rather than fearful. Be enthusiastic rather than empty of energy. Be optimistic rather than open to negativity. Success lies in your hands, and you should take charge of your career. Yes, there may be tough moments of anxiety, but there is no place for fear in the hearts of the courageous. You are now a courageous individual venturing into new territory with an unstoppable attitude of persistence to succeed.

This feeling of isolation, and not being liked, was certainly experienced by pioneering women who ventured into what was previously a "male only" environment. One such woman is Sarah Lou Hill. When Jodi worked in the corporate world, the company moved from being a family-owned private company to one that is publicly traded. During the transition, Ms. Hill was asked to participate in much of the due diligence process. She was often involved in meetings where she was the only female. While this might have intimidated some women, Sarah rose to the occasion, becoming one of the main participants in the expansion of the company. She had the respect of everyone she worked with, not because she was a woman, but because she contributed substantially to the success of transaction after transaction. She was admired for her business skills, but even more so for her people skills. When she retired from the company—you guessed it, they replaced her with another woman.

Remember, even Jesus went through periods of isolation and abandonment. In the garden, He prayed to have the burden He was about to undergo lifted.

" . . . *My Father, if it is possible, let this cup pass me by.*"

—Matthew 26:39

But His faithfulness to the Father allowed Him to accept His will and experience crucifixion and death. By fulfilling His assignment, Jesus brought victory to the human race over sin when He rose from the dead on Easter Sunday. While certainly not as daunting an achievement, your faithfulness to being successful nevertheless will remove your periods of isolation and abandonment, and turn them into a victory party as well.

"I'm not paid what I'm worth and these benefits stink."

Staying competitive within an industry is a necessity today. With the growing lack of loyalty towards an employer, workers don't hesitate to go to work for the competition. In our area, we are seeing teachers shifting to different school districts because of pay. Within the chemical industry (very large in Louisiana) companies must remain competitive. We believe this will be more and more of an issue in the coming years. Money paid for services and long-term benefits workers receive become more important as the cost of living increases, retirement plans are cut back, the payment to Social Security goes up as the benefit potential goes down, and workers want more discretionary income to fund after-work pleasures.

In truth, unless you compensate top performers, they will leave. Younger workers are more mobile than their parents or grandparents. They acclimate to a variety of environments, and are far less loyal than past generations. While pay is not the most important factor, it is nonetheless important. What companies need to do is strive to pay competitively while raising the level of other factors that make work satisfying.

An important element to consider here is honesty. If you control pay, you should keep workers informed regarding the ability of the company to compensate. Look for ways, other than monetary compensation, to display your feelings about an employee's worth. Sometimes those acts can be equally as effective as money. Be sure everyone understands that every effort is being made to remain competitive with benefits in the industry.

As we write this paragraph, the Louisiana legislature has just approved a teacher pay raise equivalent to the average salary within the Southern Region. That promise is old as the hills. There has never been a serious effort to make this salary structure a reality in the past. From our viewpoint, teachers will still be underpaid, but at least the effort has been made, and there will be richer paydays ahead for them. This is a classic case of a prevailing attitude that, because most teachers are women, as a second income for a household, the salary structure is fine. The real value an outstanding teacher brings to the lives of children is never part of the equation, and thus the struggle for decent pay must always be active.

This is a tricky and often complicated situation. For employers, there has to be profit in operating a business, and for workers there has to be benefit in working for that particular business. Workers need to understand that in business there is risk, and the owner absorbs all of the risk. If employees demand too much, the company can fail, and the result will be fewer jobs or no jobs at all.

We have witnessed this phenomenon for many years in the automobile industry. Worker benefits have burdened the cash flow to such a degree that a "black hole" has been created that manufacturers are finding very difficult to overcome. Certainly other factors, such as a slowness to adapt to the changing consumer needs, are at play in this industry, but salary and benefit demands are key components of the cash flow crunch the Big Three automakers are experiencing.

We also know that at virtually every level of government, there are unfunded retirement liabilities that must be paid to their retirees. At the federal level, social security has been expanded and borrowed to the point that the future burden may be more than workers and taxpayers can afford. Many state retirement systems are in similar shape. Payments to the system are behind schedule, causing investments to experience a shortfall and monies available to pay retirees in danger of not being there in the future. If the private sector was equally irresponsible, there would be a hue and cry from these legislators who have not mastered the law of sowing and reaping.

On the other hand, employees are not forced to work at any particular place. As an employee, one must realize the power of being able to walk away to a better job with more opportunity.

We know someone who got fed up with the pay he received for his job and started cutting grass on the side to supplement his income. His landscaping business became so profitable that he quit his job. Now he has employees and has to deal with the dilemma that his former boss faced regarding how much to pay workers.

For years, Jodi has spoken to groups of individuals looking to learn how to start their own businesses. There are many business models. However, the first step is always setting the proper goal. What he found in meeting with many of these individuals is that they are unhappy with their job, but they don't know why. In counseling them, it becomes evident that they have not set goals, and don't even know why they are working at the job they have. Many have let the employer set the goals for them. This can be a source of frustration. We believe goal setting is crucial because you can't reach a goal you haven't set. Goals can be used to explore options that might bring greater satisfaction with your work, or increased pay for the job you are doing.

An important part of the goal setting process is that goals should come from within, not from without. Goals created from within, when reached, bring self-satisfaction and add value to your spiritual nature. Goals from without are more about the acquisition of things. Certainly, as you travel down your success road, you will accumulate things along the way. But the things alone don't bring satisfaction. Reaching the goal is what raises the true feelings of accomplishment and satisfaction. Scripture refers to goals as "visions." And in *Habakkuk 2:2* it says:

"Write down the vision on a tablet."

Many theologians have interpreted this to mean that we should write down our goals. We highly recommend that practice.

We've discussed low wages in the non-profit and government sectors earlier in this chapter. The reality is that wages are not always reflective of the importance of a job. One can argue that teachers, the clergy, office workers, and laborers are underpaid. We suspect most individuals reading this book feel they should be earning more money for what they do. In Ralph Waldo Emerson's Essay on Compensation, he says, "For everything you have missed, you have gained something else; and for everything you gain, you lose something else." Emerson went on to say, "The whole of what we know is a system of compensations. Every defect in one manner is made up in another. Every suffering is rewarded; every sacrifice is made up; every debt is paid."

As you reflect on the compensation the world and your employer have provided, are you in agreement with Emerson that "we reap what we sow"? We wish to have you understand and appreciate that this is not God's way of punishing you but simply a law of natural consequences. It's only when we have a true appreciation of the unfailing consequences of this natural law that we can avoid pain and unhappiness and replace them with pleasure and happiness.

"I don't know what's going on in this company."

Company leaders can ill afford to treat people like mushrooms—keeping them in the dark. They do not keep workers informed on important issues for which they should have awareness. Today's workers want to know what is going on with the company. And they want an honest message. We understand there are some facts that must be kept under wraps, but those events are few in number in light of all the potential information that can be shared with employees. Painting an honest picture in hard times can be a critical contribution to future survival.

We see stock prices drop the minute a major corporation disseminates bad news to the world. Certainly this is a cause for some of the great secrecy within corporate America. But the shift in the late 1990's from placing employees and customers first to building shareholder equity has had dramatic consequences. The entire complexity of the workplace in corporate America is now different. The past failures of companies like Enron, Tyco, Arthur Anderson, and WorldCom have worsened this situation. However, we still maintain that telling employees the truth will motivate them to help in times of need, and possibly help reverse some of the potential stock value dropping that may occur.

Billy's former employer experienced a severe drop in cash flow at a time when the demand for its' product declined. The company experienced very hard times, and survival was shaky. Employees were told the real facts that, if things did not take a positive turn, their survival was in jeopardy. By being honest, every employee understood the situation. Thus, no one resented not receiving a pay raise for two years. No one resented doing whatever job needed to be done in order to control costs. No one quit to look for more stable ground. Instead, everyone worked to help the company survive. No one minded this commitment, if doing so kept jobs intact. The result of this unbelievable two years of teamwork did pay off. Not only did the company survive troubled times, recovery came back with a vengeance. Through dedication and commitment from every employee, the red ink stopped flowing. Everyone stayed employed and the company actually was able to make a very small profit in those two years. Once things began to swing upward, employees were given a pay raise and increased benefits, and the company ultimately regained its global presence and went on to many more years of profitable existence.

When employees understand how significant their contribution is to the survival of a company, amazing things can happen. It's when corporate leaders think only they can bring profitability back that this ego trip results in a disaster. By keeping an open dialog regarding the state of the organization, workers are better able to contribute and maintain the potential for profits and growth.

A similar situation occurs when one does not have an intimate knowledge of what God offers each of us. When you don't know what you must do to get to know, love, and serve God, you are living in darkness rather than receiving radiance from the light of God. Just like workers need to know what is going on in the company, we need to know what is going on in our relationship with God in order to bring the proper balance and priorities to our life. Too often, that is the missing link in the happiness chain.

We bring God back into the discussion to remind you that one cannot put spiritual life in a separate compartment from the rest of life. Thus spirituality should, and must, exist in the workplace. That is an important element in keeping an organization viable.

"I've got the boss from hell, what can I do?"

We are not all fortunate to work only for great people. Sometimes, we land an individual that makes the work environment most unpleasant. Some people reach what is called the "Peter Principle." They rise to their level of incompetence. Whether they received a promotion for longevity on the job, their workaholic tendencies, or vast knowledge of the job, it really doesn't matter. What you must concern yourself with is how you can make the best of the situation. Here are some ideas on how to possibly turn your lemon into lemonade.

In Chapter 12, we share a lot of advice, including how to work with your boss. We believe the ideas shared in this entire chapter can go a long way towards making your job environment a comfortable one. If you have a bad boss, start by really studying the ideas shared in this chapter and applying them to your workday activities.

On the other hand, sometimes we do find a boss who is sarcastic, not trustworthy, manipulates and bullies people, is never wrong (in his or her mind), and takes credit for everything you do. Such people are far from pleasant to work with and can make your work life miserable. How do you cope?

- Give your boss the benefit of the doubt. Just because he may have a bad reputation doesn't mean he will behave the same with you. Starting on a positive note just might work for you.
- Don't try to change her. Adjust your behavior. Make every effort to understand her personality and quirks. It sometimes requires that you become like a rubber ball and bounce around a bit. Learning how to take the unacceptable "punches" you receive and striving to understand the behaviors exhibited can make it easier to work with this person.
- Get a clear understanding of the expectations of your boss, and strive to be an advocate, not an adversary. Cooperation diminishes controversy while resistance can raise the wrath. So long as the expected behavior is not illegal, immoral, or unethical, do your best to get the expectations done. The better you know the boundaries,

the better you can stay in bounds and play the game.
- Keep notes on his or her unacceptable behavior that is threatening to you. Protect yourself with evidence of the bad behavior as a safety-net should things get out-of-hand. When all is said and done, the person with the best notes usually wins the argument.
- A risky choice is to speak to the HR Department or the manager over your boss. These options should be a last resort, unless you feel either party will keep your conversation in confidence, and act on those things that are clearly improper behavior. However, you can get stung, and perhaps even get fired for taking this bold step. You've got to carefully weigh the situation and the people involved. We also suggest you pray about the situation for insight. God listens, even when it comes to helping you understand how to work with a horrible boss. Once you've done these things, go with your instincts.
- You may find this suggestion rather strange. We suggest that you thoroughly study the messages found in Dale Carnegie's classic book, *How to Win Friends and Influence People*. Even if it doesn't help with your current situation, we guarantee it will be a very positive factor in your future.
- When left with no other option, quit! As we often say, life is too short to work at a bad job or for a bad boss.

"I'm over fifty and I've lost my job."

While we are both over fifty, we are also both fortunate to have work before us. For workers who have lost their job to a younger workforce or to downsizing, there is clearly unhappiness present in their life. There is even some evidence that workers in this category of the unemployed increase their risk of a heart attack due to the stress of having no job. Clearly this is a traumatic situation. So what can one do? Here are a few facts we uncovered on this subject that we hope will provide you with some insights and directions to pursue.

The over-fifty workforce is a growing trend. Very soon, they will be the greatest number in the workforce. But here is the good news. Most people over fifty have a reasonable amount of experience. The bad news is that they want to be paid accordingly. Today many companies prefer hiring entry level personnel at lower salaries. They feel if they make the right hire, they can train these new hires into their system from the start of their employment. These companies are willing to risk a knowledge deficiency rather than pay the higher priced knowledge worker. Certainly, this is a huge disadvantage for older unemployed workers.

A second obstacle is that companies are increasingly pinched with higher health care costs. The wise investment in their eyes is to bring in a younger, cheaper priced, and healthier employee, rather than risk the potential health issues and nearing retirement age of older workers.

Some HR specialist say if you are over fifty, and lack senior management experience, jobs are not plentiful for you. Again, the younger, cheaper employee wins. It's a silent game far too many companies play.

Here are the best suggestions we could find to help you with this transition. We've put ourselves in the picture to help us understand options to pursue.

It's most important that you be flexible and willing to take some chances that might normally be highly resistant to you. Become someone who will do whatever it takes to get a job. This is not the time to be picky, choosy, or just stubborn. What this really means is that you must be ready to re-invent yourself. Turn a hobby into a career. Look in areas you would never have dreamed to pursue thirty years earlier. Ask yourself such questions as:

- What am I good at doing that was not part of my previous employment skills?
- What skills from my previous work experiences can I carry over into a new career field?
- Am I willing to begin studying an entirely new field?
- What emerging trends can I hitch a ride on and find that exciting new career?
- Do I have the persistence to keep looking for work until I find employment?
- Can I ask for help or will I let my pride get in the way?
- Am I willing to work for a much younger person?

Another way to bring job possibilities into reality is to work on the network of people you established during your career. Sit down and make a list of everyone you know who might help you. Attack that list with a vengeance, determined to find that right person who can open doors for you. If you are now fully employed, begin to build that list of people. You never know when you will need them.

Dress for success when you seek employment. That makes you look younger, more energetic, and attractive as a candidate. Clothes do make the difference, and under these circumstances, the difference may result in a paycheck.

It's important that you maintain the proper attitude throughout this process. Avoid negative thinking, and when something negative occurs, look for the positive spin. An optimist will always overcome the pessimist. Your attitude is probably the single most important attribute you can use. Make it work for you and it just might make you work.

If you are over fifty and now unemployed, why not take time to answer these additional questions. Be brutally honest with yourself. This is no time to be lazy or dishonest. There is too much at stake. Heck, if you are employed, these might not be bad questions to ponder as you look into where you wish your life to go.

1. What strengths do I bring to prospective employers that would enhance their effectiveness?
2. Do I have a flexible attitude regarding change of career or am I stuck on rigid?
3. Do I want to go in business for myself or do I need to work for someone else?
4. What do I truly enjoy doing and what fields offer me job opportunities where I would be doing what I truly enjoy? (This can be an entirely new direction.)
5. Examine every facet of your career. List every position you've held and what you did in those positions. Search through the list for the most viable skills used during each phase of your career. What industries, businesses, or fields do I qualify to work in? What positions might I hold?
6. Develop a narrative stating why you would make the ideal employee because you possess those skills. If you wish to become self-employed, why would someone hire a person with your skills?
7. Can I take my experience and skills to the competition?
8. How much do I need to work to survive financially? Forty hours per week? Twenty?
9. Do I have other business experiences, hobbies, skills that would be useful in an entirely new career? What fields would that be?
10. Is there someone with whom I might partner in a business venture?

Chapter 11 — Some Thoughts about Work   157

11. Ask a trusted friend what they think you might do.
12. Do I have the tenacity to make things happen in my life? What is my attitude about myself and the possibilities of finding just the right job at my age?

Finally, we'd be remiss if we did not include the importance of connecting with God in this part of your journey. We remind you again what it says in Matthew 7:7:

"Ask and it will be given to you; seek and you will find; knock and the door will be opened to you." (NIV®)

We believe God does not play tricks on us. In this pit of despair, we must raise ourselves to a level of trust that God will respond to our prayers. That is part of the optimism we suggested earlier in this chapter. It is an integral part of keeping God first in our life.

Early in his corporate career, Jodi found himself out of a job. The company laid off five top executives to save money and to prove to the banks that they were serious about cutting expenses. It was a tough time. He had given up his client base to move into the corporate legal environment, so he was not an attractive hire to a law firm wanting to bring in lawyers that had clients. And he had not worked in the corporate world long enough to be an attractive hire to other corporations.

During this period, the early 1990s, grocery stores did not accept credit cards. He did manage to find one. Their prices were expensive. Jodi and his family had no choice but to charge groceries on credit cards while he searched for work. They built up debt. It was very difficult. Eventually, he was hired by the FDIC as a staff attorney. It was a good job. The important part of this story is that he and his wife never gave up on God. They knew He had a plan. They just didn't know what it was. The ordeal taught them a great deal, and they grew from it. While Jodi was not over fifty when this occurred, he was in a similar situation that unemployed workers over fifty are now experiencing. It is important to note that these seven months were only a blip on the radar screen. Whatever you go through, it is incredibly important to rely on family, friends, and God to pull you through with the confidence that, when it is over, you will be stronger and better.

If you find yourself without a job and over fifty, please know that you have a lot to offer the marketplace. You have so much wisdom and experience that is valuable to organizations. Examine every experience you've had in the workplace. Experience is never lost. Verify the value you offer. Value is always a strong commodity. Now examine the potential jobs available, and seek out employers that can profit from your wisdom and experience. The stories of people who succeeded, even after their sixtieth birthday, are endless. Henry Ford, Colonel Sanders, Thomas Edison, and Grandma Moses are but a few who overcame tremendous obstacles to move on to great success.

We believe you always have abilities available to offer the marketplace. One may have to start over, and that can be discouraging. But starting is what you must do. Feeling sorry, or simply giving up, is not an option for you. Create confidence, build belief, and push persistence. Failure is not an option.

At this point you may be saying, well it's easy for you to be optimistic. You've got work. That's true today, but in our careers, we've both been without work. In those circumstances, the one thing that we never gave up on was our trust that God is there to help. Our belief and trust is supported by many passages of scripture that speak to having hope. In *Isaiah 43:1-2*, it says,

"Fear not, for I have redeemed you; I have called you by name; you are mine. When you pass through the water, I will be with you in the rivers; you will not drown. When you walk through fire, you shall not be burned; the flames shall not consume you."

Jeremiah 29:11-12 has a great reminder that God is a God of hope. It says,

"For I know well the plans I have in mind for you says the Lord, plans for your welfare, not for woe! Plans to give you a future full of hope. When you call me, when you go to pray to me, I will listen."

These are such encouraging words that emphasize the power of prayer, trust in God and hope.

Armed with our knowledge, persistence, and confidence in God and His goodness, we can overcome great odds and prosper. God always has a plan for us. We just have to commit to listening to the message He provides and working His plan.

Chapter 12

Develop Personal Leadership Skills to Enhance Your Career

If we look at the journey Moses took for 40 years, it was ultimately leadership skills that made the journey successful. Yes, few would have had this persistence. But Moses believed in the promise God made to his people and, in spite of many low moments, he was able to muster sufficient leadership skills to lead his people to the Promised Land. And, for most people today, their 40-year journey will be the years they spend in the workplace. To make this journey work in our favor, we must develop our personal leadership skills. We share ideas to help with that portion of your journey in this chapter.

Lessons on Failure

*"I have missed more than 9000 shots in my career.
I have lost almost 300 games.
On 26 occasions I have been entrusted to take
the game winning shot—and missed!
And, I have failed over and over again in my life.
And that is why I succeed."*

—Michael Jordan

If you believe you will go through your working years without failure, someone needs to nudge you because you're dreaming. If you live, you fail. It's that simple. And Michael Jordan, perhaps the most successful professional basketball player ever, provides his testimony that personal failure is part of becoming successful. Jordan understands that it was his drive to be successful that made his achievements so amazing. He understood that it was his failures that helped to develop his ability to continue to press on, and improve. He understood that major success is often found one tiny step past a major failure. He did not understand how to be a quitter.

In one of his recent seminars, Billy was talking to a group of managers about overcoming failure. Everyone in that room had experienced some type of failure in his lifetime. As we discussed these events, we were unanimous in our thinking that those who profited from the failure were able to learn the lesson it taught them. Please understand there is always good in every adversity. Sometimes we just have to look a bit harder to find it. Never forget that within every adversity is the seed for a great accomplishment. We just have to plant that seed.

Here are four ideas Billy shared with this audience. Hopefully they will help you get a better handle on future failures you might face as you strive to build your own personal leadership on the job.

   1. Understand that to fail does not make you a failure. A failure is but a temporary inconvenience in the path of life. Put failures in perspective, and don't cast a dark shadow over your life because of a small obstacle. Life is made up of many years. Failures are only a heartbeat by comparison. When Peter denied Christ, he failed. It was a dark moment for Peter, but his love and devotion to Jesus helped him realize the error of his judgment. And the forgiving nature of Jesus enabled Peter to overcome his failure, and ultimately be picked by Jesus to assume the reins of the church as the first Pope.

"And I tell you that you are Peter, and on this rock I will build my church" —Matthew 16:18 (NIV®)

   2. Learn from your failures; then forget them. Dwelling forever on your mistakes will not change what was. All we can do is commit ourselves to avoid repeating the mistake. Forgive and forget is good advice. Life is not a boxing match. You don't have to walk away with scars and bruises to show you've lived. There are a number of stories where Jesus forgot past failures, and encouraged individuals to move on with their lives. His apostles abandoned Jesus as His captors arrived. Yet, Jesus forgave His captors who crucified Him, forgave His apostles, and ultimately sent them out to spread the word of His resurrection and His teachings. The apostles learned from their failures and Jesus forgot their failures.

"*Father forgive them, they know not what they are doing.*"—Luke 23:34

3. You are never a failure as long as you keep on trying. Persistence has a way of neutralizing obstacles and diminishing the impact of failures. Never give up, and failures will become history. There is nothing in your life you cannot overcome if you persist long enough. The road to success is not straight. There is a curve called Failure, a loop called Confusion, speed bumps called Friends, red lights called Enemies, caution lights called Family. You will have flats called Jobs. But, if you have a spare called Determination, an engine called Perseverance, insurance called Faith, a driver called Jesus, you will make it to a place called Success. In the end, we should never forget this great passage from scripture:

"*I can do all things through Christ who strengthens me.*"—Philippians 4:13

4. Failure is never final unless you let it be final. Our attitude is the single most important factor for effectively dealing with failures. Remind yourself that recovery is always potentially possible. Giving up is for losers. Make adjustments and move on. Life is too valuable to give up enjoying it. What about you? Have you ventured forward only to quit one step from the door of success? Don't be a quitter when you have the option to be a winner. You will never have a desire without the ability to fulfill that desire. We are not talking about a "wishful" thought, but rather one that is so powerful, nothing can stop its creation. When you think like that, it's just a matter of time when your wish will be fulfilled. God doesn't make us have a deep seated desire without providing the talents to get the job done. We must never lose faith in God to help us on our journey, and we must never view failure as finality.

Understanding the Power of Our Habits and Choices

Making the right choices and forming the right habits drive your successes. Those who truly understand the dynamics of how to bring success to their careers know that their habits and choices will either propel them over career obstacles or push them into the wall of failure.

If we took a survey of the world, few, if any, would say they want to be failures. We all want to succeed. Why is it, with all of us well intended, we have so many who simply don't make it?

Success is not guaranteed, nor is failure an inevitable end of our journey through life. Both happen for the same reason—the choices we make. Our daily habits (choices) are the drivers of success or failure. We make "little habitual choices" each day that don't seem to have a great impact on our life, so we don't give them a second thought. Cumulatively, like a massive weight, these choices eventually can bring devastation to our career or chaos in our personal life.

For example, missing that day of exercise yesterday doesn't hurt us tomorrow, but a few years of this type of neglect may bring on very serious health issues. We don't keep up with the trends and new insights relating to our career, and that promotion we wanted doesn't become reality. We don't ever seem to have time to really bond with our children; then one day they are grown, and our relationship is distant. The same can be said of our relationship with God. We need to inculcate the habit of conversation with God (prayer) into our daily routine. There is no more powerful habit or better choice to make. Get straight with God, and it is much easier to get the rest of your life straight.

The good news is that, by changing the quality of your choices (habits), you can improve any situation. Watch the foods you ingest, exercise regularly, and you dramatically increase the odds of a longer life. Establish a daily reading habit to broaden your mind and inoculate your brain with new ideas, and soon you will be recognized for your insights, and offered better job opportunities. Talk to your children every day as they are growing up. Establish that unbreakable bond of love and support early and equally with every child. Support them in their school activities. Be their parent, willing to sternly steer them in the right direction when needed, but also be their friend when they need someone to talk to.

Develop your personal philosophy of life, and make the choices to bring that philosophy to your life. Small choices each day create a strong future. Think about where you want to be and do today what is necessary to get there tomorrow. It's a discipline worth the effort. These small tips will assist you in maintaining the vertical alignment that we spoke of earlier. They will maintain the integrity of your spiritual life and will ultimately help you succeed in all areas of your life, especially in your career. Besides the river that watered the Garden of Eden, God offered the first couple the choice between obedient love and self-seeking death. The choice remains ours to make each day.

Tips to Improve Your Career Opportunities and Build Leadership Skills

In today's work environment, moving up the ladder of success is becoming more and more competitive. Interested in a promotion? Try these ideas to move your career into high gear.

Become more visible

It's important that management see you as an "action" person who responds when there are corporate needs. Responding when help beckons can separate you from your peers. By becoming a "take charge" employee, management will view you as someone who can and does lead.

Look through your organization and visualize where you might fit. By keeping your eyes on future positions, you are less likely to miss an opportunity. Anticipation and preparation go hand in hand towards grasping that promotion. And success comes when preparedness and opportunity meet. Constantly reflect on your personal effectiveness, and review how you do things. Create a plan and work your plan.

Each day, we should strive to be more valuable. Each day we should also strive to be more attentive and more responsive to God. That is the invitation given to us, and it is God's hope for us. Just like we work to build our career, we must work to build our desire to include God in every aspect of our life. When that is the deepest desire in your heart, you are opening yourself to greater insights and opportunities. God can help with our careers if we willingly open our mind and hearts to His messages. He wants us to be successful. All it takes is for us to trust in His power, and to respond to His unconditional love.

"If you believe in God and focus on the best in yourself, nothing can defeat you—nothing!" —Mark Link

Complete all work assigned in the time prescribed.

Leaders complete what they start. They get things done, and they do them in an efficient and effective manner. They set deadlines and stay on track. Consistency with this approach to your work assignments can be a major boost to your value and opportunities to grow your career. Likewise, don't fall behind on your assignments; don't make excuses why things aren't done, and keep all work scheduled on one calendar. Each day, prioritize by the highest need to complete, and always know the tasks that lie ahead. This allows better scheduling and proficiency of tasks. Having a detailed schedule also gives you insights regarding the number of people needed to keep projects on target, and when it might be necessary to speed up activities. The last thing managers want is not getting work out on time, and a litany of excuses why the work was not done.

When discussing an assignment from your manager, don't leave until you are very clear on the outcome desired. When the discussion is done, get started. Completing projects as requested increases your credibility, and greatly enhances the trust level your management team will have in you.

No matter if you dig ditches or run a billion-dollar corporation, give every action the best you have to offer. Don't accept second-rate performance from yourself. Doing your best is a prideful act. Knowing you've done your best is a prideful feeling. So, be proud! (This is one of the rare exceptions where we support pride over humility.)

And let's not forget the work God has assigned each of us to do with our timeline (our time on earth) for completion—to follow His will for us. This is perhaps the most significant "work" assignment you will ever get.

Be proactive.

Keep your eyes on the big picture, and look for ways to improve how things are done. Be aggressive in anticipating events before they surface. Such actions can bring about huge cost savings. A Quality Circle team that Billy worked with researched reasons why a particular type of process pump was experiencing a large number of failures each year. By simply changing the type of seal used for this pump, an annual savings of over $200,000 was realized. That's real proactive thinking.

Then there is the story of the employee who worked for an underwear company. She suggested replacing the tags in the back of undershirts with information stamped on the shirt. The suggestion helped the company realize millions of dollars of savings, and the employee was also handsomely rewarded.

In our relationship with God, we should also seek a proactive posture.

God is waiting for us to take actions that move us closer to Him. Doing so is our choice. He is eternal love, and we should be His lover. We don't believe you can be too proactive in your journey towards God's love and the eternal reward He promises in heaven. In the end, being proactive has its potential rewards both on Earth and in Heaven.

Accountable is awesome.

True leaders do their tasks but also require those who undertake assignments for them to complete their work. Accountability is a key characteristic all great leaders practice and expect from those they lead. Be accountable for actions under your responsibility and expect accountability from those to whom you've assigned responsibility.

As we strive to build our relationship with God, we should never forget that our Beloved Companion holds us accountable to complete our earthly tasks of loving, serving, and following Him. That is a truly awesome accountability none of us can afford to ignore.

Be a team player and a professional.

Build the reputation of being a cooperative and cordial player. You don't have to like all your co-workers, but you have a professional obligation to work well with them. If you cannot do this, you don't deserve to lead . . . *Period!* Team players place the greater good of the organization over personal desires. They understand that there is power in many that far exceeds any single effort.

What better example of teamwork can we have than what is demonstrated by the activities of the apostles and disciples of Jesus. They lived the message and worked for the common good—helping others reach the kingdom. They were like a well-oiled machine: precise in defining the outcome and committed to carrying out the mission. The movement started with one person, Jesus. But it was the team effort that put the mission into action, and started the message momentum that is still being carried by teams of millions of followers today. Here is the assignment of the team Jesus assembled:

"Full authority has been given to me both in heaven and on earth; go therefore, and make disciples of all the nations. Baptize them in the name of the Father and of the Son, and of the Holy Spirit. Teach them to carry out everything I have commanded you. And know that I am with you always, until the end of the world." —Matthew 28:18-20

Communicate! Communicate! Communicate!

As you work through projects, keep your management team informed regarding progress. Short emails, memos, phone calls, meetings—use the best communication media for the situation. Document those contact periods in your day planner, computer calendar, or in a notebook so you can chronicle your activities, should anyone question your efforts or communications. Find out exactly how your supervisor wants to be updated on progress, and do it as he or she expects. It's better to be told you don't need to feed as much information to your boss then to be questioned why you failed to keep everyone informed.

As you study the life of Christ during His public ministry, we get a sense of how much and how often He communicated His message to all He encountered. In parables, Jesus communicated how to reach the kingdom. He was patient, and thorough in His explanation of the "how to's" needed to reach the glory of heaven.

Raise your enthusiasm level.

The Greeks bequeathed to us one of the most beautiful words in our language—the word 'enthusiasm'—*en theos*—a god within. Louis Pasteur said it like this:

"The grandeur of human actions is measured by the inspiration from which they spring. Happy is he who bears a god within, and who obeys it."

Being enthusiastic about undertaking a task will make the activity a pleasure to perform. To be perceived as enthusiastic, you must be enthusiastic. Don't be fooled by this seemingly simple approach. It works.

The power of enthusiasm is even amplified in *Romans 12:11*. It says,

"Never be lacking in zeal, but keep your spiritual fervor, serving the Lord." (NIV®)

Your enthusiasm is determined by your attitude, and you control your attitude. Now some of you may be thinking, "I can't be enthusiastic about a boring job." While there may be some truth in that statement, the reality is that you can build enthusiasm for virtually anything by acting enthusiastic. Doing so makes you a more pleasant person to be around, and this behavior will also build your credibility and reputation. Enthusiasm is an energy builder. Enthusiasm is contagious. So make sure you spread this "disease of success." Warning! This may change your life and your career for the better.

Minimize socializing.
When you come to work, be prepared to work. Earn your pay by your productivity. Yes, it's important to take an occasional break. But you are not paid to socialize. You are paid to produce. It's perfectly acceptable to visit co-workers, but be constantly aware when visiting becomes a time wasting activity. Busy people get more done, and people who get more done gain a higher level of respect. People with a higher level of respect usually have a greater opportunity to rise on the ladder of responsibility. It's actually a relatively straightforward process.

Become a student and turn into an expert.
You must continually build your learning curve. Network with fellow professionals; read magazines and books in your field and on leadership and management topics. Attend conferences. Research the Internet. Keep learning. There is always something new on the horizon. The better informed you are, the wiser you will become. Being a person who possesses wisdom places you on the apex of the respectability pyramid.

Begin to build a library of books on leadership and personal success strategies. Read the books with a highlighter and pen. When you read a passage that you find significant, highlight it. Write notes on pages when personal thoughts or ideas are generated. Then the book becomes a living document to which you can refer over and over again. Serious students never stop looking for the next great idea that might help build their career, or add to their success components.

Earl Nightingale shared this thought with the world many years ago in his *Lead the Field* audio program. He said that by studying our job for one hour a day while making permanent notes, in a five-year period we could become an expert in that discipline. Strong concentration in a specialty niche is a great way to build your expertise. Commit to this process, and you open multiple opportunities for advancement on your job. You will also build enthusiasm for the subject matter because, the more you learn about a subject, the higher your interest becomes. It's a self-feeding process that can bring outstanding results to your career possibilities.

Westaff CEO Lisa Coleman echoes what Nightingale says. This former high school teacher and guidance counselor feels one can never learn enough. She relates that when her daughters were born, she and her husband bought every parenting journal and magazine they could find.

They've now taken the knowledge gained from this study to mentor others by teaching a parenting class at their church.

Respect your time and the time of others.

If you are asked to participate in a meeting, arrive a few minutes early. Be punctual. There is no benefit to being the last one to enter the room. Come to work a few minutes early. Avoid the label of a "late arriver." It does nothing to enhance your reputation.

When you call someone on the telephone, always ask if that person has time to talk now, or would it be better to call back later? It's a courtesy that might seem trivial, but if you don't ask and you've called at a bad time, you may not get the same attention or answer you would if you called at a different time.

The bottom line? In all you do, respect other people's time, and they will respect yours.

Act like you want the job.

To be considered for a leadership position, you must display an ability to lead. Acting indifferent or in an inefficient manner does not endear one to managers. Let people know by your actions that you are the best candidate for the next management opening. Think about this: you never saw Jesus acting like He didn't want to complete His mission. He faced His task with a commitment to do it right. He acted like He wanted the job.

Never forget that management is looking at your performance. Your behavior, demeanor, and attitude are in a constant evaluation mode. Let everyone see what they need to see in order to build confidence in your leadership ability. Become the person managers are talking about with a positive tone.

As one looks at the lives of the first disciples Jesus commissioned to spread the good news, we clearly sense the commitment and desire these individuals had for getting the job done. Their commitment was so great, they willingly died for Christ and His teachings rather than abandoning their job. Are we suggesting that you become a martyr for your career? Certainly not! But we think this point helps you get the idea about commitment to your work.

Be easy to work with.

Individuals who strive to provide top-quality service to those they work with and to those they work under will separate themselves from the average crowd. Be generous with your knowledge. Help others. A mentality of service will result in greater rewards and recognition of your leadership abilities. Be accommodating. Don't "cop an attitude" as kids say.

Be comfortable with who you are.

Individuals with self-confidence are willing to take some risks. They undertake difficult assignments to prove their worth. Don't be arrogant, but don't be a wall flower either. Act confidently even when your knees are knocking and your legs are wobbly. Believe in your worth. Remind yourself that God loves you, warts and all. And what greater support mechanism could you want?

Well, how are you doing so far? Have the previous points challenged you to think differently about your career, and the opportunities it offers? But we're not done yet with our career challenge. Here are a series of questions that need answers if you are to really move ahead of the curve, and take on the leadership potential in your chosen career. These questions will test your brain a bit, but we believe taking the time to assess your true position and thoughts on each can be a life changing, if not a career changing, exercise. Don't treat this exercise lightly. The answers can be difference-makers.

1. Face the things you fear: What events are creating inertia in your career development? What fear is holding you back from taking career-changing risks? What perceptions do you have about your abilities that don't accurately reflect your actual skill level? What action steps are you willing to implement within the next week that will help you overcome your fears?

2. There's more than one way: What did you avoid doing because the one way you thought it had to be done was not possible? What activities, if changed, will make a dramatic difference in your future? Do you often say, "We've always done it this way?"

3. Make a public commitment: What activity should you rekindle? What new techniques should you employ to expand your career options? Who are your cheerleaders? Are you willing to share your career dreams with those who can help support you?

4. Try giving up instead of holding on: What habits are you unwilling to give up that, once abandoned, might move you up the career ladder? Are you willing to alter your tactics? What activities are creating clutter in your life thus preventing time to concentrate on building your career?

5. Share your message with the world: Are you keeping secret skills and talents that could advance your career? What business activities have you ignored because you did not recognize that you had the talent to pursue? What is your passion? How often do you tell the world about your passion? What message is still inside you because you've made the choice to be mute rather than being the master of your fate?

6. Follow your heart: You remember that we said earlier, "The place God calls you is where your deep gladness meets the deep hunger of the world." What is your deep gladness? Is your business satisfying your own deep hunger? Is your business satisfying the deep hunger of your clients or potential clients?

7. Ground yourself: Where is the central focus of your life? Is it focused on career, family or spiritual development? Do you believe spiritual grounding brings relief to your life? Do you have balance between career and family obligations? Do you exercise? Are you aware of the effects your diet is having on your lifestyle? How much balance do you have in your life?

We hope you've found the suggestions on how to find success in your work environment valuable. We are now ready to move to another critically important element in the workplace—the relationship you establish with your immediate supervisor. He or she plays a significant role in your on-the-job happiness, and your future potential to grow and advance. Implement the following eight ideas as you build that all-important relationship with your boss. Successfully doing so can propel your career into high gear.

How to Work Successfully with Your Boss

Everyone has a boss! Whether you work for shareholders, corporate management, or department supervisors, you are working under someone's supervision. For the self-employed, you know that your customer is "boss."

If your job is to be an enjoyable experience, you have to be able to work well with the boss. Realistically, your supervisor sets the direction for your professional development. You have to make him or her happy or set a new course for your career under a new boss.

Why is this important? It's important because a good working relationship with your boss lengthens your stay with your employer. Just as important, though, is that working relationship can make the difference between a growing, rewarding work experience, and an eight-to-five purgatory. If she is happy, the odds favor you being happy.

How can you develop a more effective working relationship with your boss? Answering the following questions might help build that type of relationship, and help you survive in today's volatile work environment.

   1. *How well do you know the responsibilities assigned to your boss?* To whom does she report? What is his authority? How is she evaluated? What is his chief on-the-job success? All these things, and more, are important considerations. In short, the more you know, the more you can grow.

   2. *How clear are you about the expectations of your job?* You may feel you clearly understand what your boss wants from you. On the other hand, your understanding of responsibilities may differ from your boss. If you're not exactly sure what it is that he or she expects of you, make a list of your responsibilities. Then sit down with him or her to review the list. If he agrees, you're on the right track. If she doesn't, ask for direction. It's a win-win conversation few people take the time to clarify.

   3. *Do you have respect and admiration for your boss's position?* If you don't respect her position, you will not be able to work for her. It's probably best that you look for another job.

   4. *Do you by-pass your boss?* If you do this regularly, it's impossible to maintain an effective relationship. Keep your boss involved regarding what is going on in your areas of responsibility. Communication between you and your boss is a critical and essential process. Never go over his or her head to their manager without asking permission. We realize that sometimes managers might not ever let you speak to their boss. But we also believe, that if your immediate supervisor cannot solve a pressing problem, you should ask permission to find someone who can. Just don't make this practice a habit. One last tip on this point—be prepared to answer the "why do you want to do this" question. If you don't know or can't say why, don't make this move.

   5. *What type of temperament do you bring to your workplace?* Keep control of your moods and don't take your personal troubles to work. Exercise self-control when pressures mount. Be predictable in your behavior, and be positive about the way you handle your work and your working relationships. It's important that you keep your cool and display a consistently even emotional state most of the time. We don't believe it's wrong to raise your emotional level a bit on occasion. But those situations should be rare and warranted. Stay pleasant and easy to work with, and you will be appreci-

ated, not alienated by your boss.

6. Are you an independent problem solver? Be dependable as a source of information. Act as a problem solver to become a key asset for your boss. Never complain about a problem unless you can offer a possible solution. Independence is in. Incompetence is not.

7. Can you admit when you "screwed up?" No one is perfect and everyone makes mistakes. If you goof, let your boss know. There is no better time to be gut-level honest. Don't try to cover up mistakes or offer excuses why your performance was under par. Your credibility is enhanced if you take full responsibility for your mistakes. The only mistake to avoid is repeating a mistake. Learn your lessons well, and an occasional screw-up will be tolerated.

8. Are you strong enough for the truth about your performance? Feedback is the best way to learn. Accepting constructive criticism allows you to acknowledge your professional deficiencies and to improve or eliminate them.

I hope these questions start you on your way to asking more questions about your working relationships with your boss. Life is too short to work at a miserable job. Working effectively with your supervisor is one way to add happiness to your career. And it always helps to remember this saying, "I may not always be right, but I'm always the boss!"

A Little Action, Please

We'd like to propose a follow-up exercise using the previous eight questions to conduct a personal evaluation of how each affects your relationship with God. *Warning*—this is an exercise that demands impeccable honesty before meaningful results can occur. And we want to remind you that the *ultimate performance review* will take place following our last breath on earth. Start now to prepare yourself for that judgment day so that the truth will set you free to enter the kingdom.

Positioning Yourself to Build Strong Relationships

To get the most and the best out of life, we need the help of others. There is no better way to get help and support when we are in need than to build a strong relationship with people. Lisa Coleman, Westaff CEO says, "Understanding the needs and wants of others, and building on that relationship, are keys to creating business success." In the past, you may have called this networking. Why not change that term to relationship building? If you want to get that extra edge, build strong relationships with individuals that represent resources of value to you. Then treat them like gold.

As you build your business relationships, you must first position yourself in your mind as a person of value. You must first believe that you are worthy and actually deserve help. This is having the confidence in your abilities sufficiently high enough that you won't quit before you start. Understand that as your attitude goes, so will your success ratios

Once you've built your own self-confidence, you must position yourself as someone of value with whom others would willingly partner. This process is not a one-way street of help. Relationships are strongest when both parties are mutually beneficial to each other. Seek to give first, and you will receive.

Creating that All-Important First Impression

Let's start off with what you wear. The impression you make on people with the types of clothes you wear can be an important first step towards their willingness to even talk to you. Many young people are wearing low-cut pants or blouses cut so low that their undergarment shows. In a majority of business relationship-building events, this will limit your success potential. You can seldom go wrong with clean, conservatively styled clothes. If you look like a pro, you will get treated like a pro. We want you to dress well because you may not get a second chance to make that all-important first impression.

Whenever you will be with people, be sure that you *have plenty of business cards handy*. Keep some in your wallet, purse, day planner, pockets—anywhere you can quickly get to them. You never want to miss an opportunity to give away a business card, and more importantly, collect those cards. Place all your contacts in a database. There are a number of good software programs that you can use. We like ACT, but there are certainly others just as good.

When you are entering an opportunity to build contacts, *take time to pre-plan the outcome you desire*. Is there a particular business leader you want to meet? Position yourself to talk to that individual. Don't be shy about asking for a minute or two, but don't dominate their time or make a pest of yourself. However, be sure that you don't leave without their card so you can follow-up and, over time, build that important trust relationship. You want to use this time to meet new people. You can always visit with your friends later. Remember your purpose for being there—meeting new people to build your contact list.

Another very strong strategy that makes a great first impression is to listen to what the other person has to say. Great listeners are considered by most to be great conversationalists. You can further your first impression by educating yourself with information from books, articles, and other resources in your area of expertise. Learning how to be an effective communicator, and saying the proper things in conversation, separate you from the masses. Be a smart talker, and people will notice. One caution—we are not suggesting that you be devious or deceptive. We believe honest talk has longer effectiveness than BS. People appreciate business associations with individuals who can express themselves well, articulate their concerns, and suggest strong solutions in a confident, correct manner. Staying current on worldly events is a great opener when conversations stall a bit. We believe that if you learn, you earn not only respect but potentially greater income.

How do you answer the "What do you do?" question? It's important that you be able, in thirty seconds or less, to tell people what you do. Make it interesting, enticing, and a bit vague so people will be compelled to ask, "Tell me more," or "How do you do that?" For example, when Billy is in a crowd of people in the education field and someone asks what he does, his standard reply is, "I work with education leaders to keep children first." That statement never fails to elicit a positive response and opens the door to further dialog.

After a business event where you meet people for the first time, why not send a handwritten thank-you note to them expressing your genuine appreciation for their time and the opportunity to have met them. This small act goes a very long way. If the relationship is one you'd like to see grow, find a way to bring value to them as a way to stay in touch. Billy and Jodi will often put such individuals (after getting their permission) on their subscriber list for their e-zines. Jodi writes his *Monthly Memo on Ethics, Spirituality and Success* that touches on one or all three of those topics. (You can read past issues on his website, www.deaconjodi.com.) Billy writes two e-zines, *News from the Swamp*, containing personal and organizational leadership tips and *Children First*, containing tips on effective parental leadership. (Check out past issues of both e-zines plus interesting articles on his website, www.SearchingForSuccess.com.) Other actions you might take would be to clip an article of value from magazines or the newspaper and send it to them. Perhaps you've read a great book. Buy a copy, or send them a note about how the book might be of value to them. The approach is simple—follow-up, follow-up, follow-up. We can't stress this enough.

Strive to get referrals from the people with whom you establish your value and credibility. People are comfortable recommending your services or products to someone else if they are comfortable with you. Leave no room for doubt that you are a great resource, and you will be happily recommended. Billy has often referred his speaker friends to business associates. Because he has been in their audience and knows the skill level they possess, he knows they will do an outstanding job. Likewise, he has been recommended by these same individuals. Helping each other and passing on business opportunities is a great relationship builder and a great business strategy.

If you possess writing and speaking skills, use them to your advantage. One of the best ways is to write articles or give speeches before groups to establish your expertise and credibility. Obviously, this has worked well for both Jodi and Billy, but there is no reason it cannot work well for you. Write articles for your local newspaper. People read them, and that gives you name recognition. Speak to your local Rotary on your business subject. Every opportunity, done well, builds your relationship ability and supports your expertise and credibility.

In the business world, action still speaks louder than words, and results only come once you overcome your own inertia. Make the actions you take count. Engage in activities that make you stronger in the eyes of those with whom you are forging business connections.

You need to make a concerted effort to find the time to build those important relationships. This won't happen by chance. Develop a plan and use your time effectively in order to maximize the results you get. Make the effort to be available and around people that are important to your success. This positioning idea requires that you take deliberate and calculated steps to meet these individuals. Develop your plan, and work your plan. It's really that simple. One last thought. Want to meet someone? Call him and ask for time. However, make your time together beneficial to the other person, not you. Be creative and think what benefit you can offer first. Then you've earned the right to ask him to be a part of your business affiliates.

Position yourself with your brand power. Billy brands himself as *"The Leadership Strategist."* That is a clear identifier of what his services represent. And whenever he can offer help to someone on this topic, he does. Jodi, in his roles as an ordained Deacon and an attorney, often counsels individuals privately on spiritual matters and can certainly in his practice provide legal guidance. But when we both share our knowledge outside of the workplace and can help provide insights in casual conversation, this establishes our credibility as well as making us givers first. We'd rather be owed to than owe. That's our personal feeling on this matter. We are not stingy with helping solve issues in our areas of expertise. Identify your brand, use it to your advantage, and watch your value grow.

Let's Summarize

Positioning demands that you first be credible. People must trust that you bring something of value to the table. The stronger the credibility you build, the easier it is to develop relationships. Credible people are also trustworthy, and trust is the cornerstone of relationship building.

Secondly, be a source of knowledge. When people perceive you as someone who is wise and able to provide solutions, people will come to your door, and the opportunities will grow dramatically.

Third, learn all you can about the market in which you work and the clients you can serve in this market. The more you know, the more you can grow. Knowledge is truly power in this situation. Being seen as the expert raises your status and helps to grow your list of business friends.

Lastly, having rock-solid information at your fingertips that is relevant and cutting edge will make you stand out in the crowd. These four steps, along with the specific position ideas we shared, are a sure-fire way to make you a relationship-building king or queen. So go for the crown!

A Little Satisfaction, Please

It doesn't matter what type of work you do. You owe it to yourself to find satisfaction with your work. As we said earlier, if you are unhappy on the job, that unhappiness will spread to all parts of your life. Unhappy workers make unhappy spouses, parents, and friends. Here are tips on how you can make your job a more satisfying experience, and remove stress, unhappiness, and frustration from your job environment forever.

1. Look beyond the routine parts of your job—Examine your daily activities to see if you can come up with ways to make the activities more fun, exciting, and rewarding. Be creative. Think hard. You will surprise yourself with the number of possibilities that can surface with just a little creative thinking. Can you add more to what you do? What can you do that no one else is doing? What is needed that is not now being done? Can I do these activities? Answering these questions will open an endless array of opportunities to grow and build job satisfaction.

2. Avoid self-limitations—The way we think can sometimes limit our possibilities. With our personally constructed "glass ceiling," we box ourselves into a lesser posture because of our own self-limiting thoughts. We have far more abilities than we give ourselves credit for having, and we seldom challenge ourselves to stretch beyond the routine and break the glass ceiling we've created. Working with pride, enthusiasm, and a high degree of expertise, can break the bondage of self-limitations and shatter that glass restrainer. What limits are holding you back? What limitations are building dissatisfaction with your work?

3. Look in your own pastures first—Cows are always trying to eat the grass on the other side of the fence. They, like us, often think that the grass is greener and tastier in the other pasture. Avoid "cow thinking" by grasping the opportunities under our feet. By implementing the ideas previously discussed in this section, we make our own pastures green and reduce the need for looking over the fence.

"Look upon your work as the lever by which you can rise in the world. To get the best and most out of life, put the best and most of yourself into it. Eventually, each of use gets the reward we merit." —B. C. Forbes

Author Pat McHenry Sullivan in his book, *Work with Meaning Work with Joy*, says, "It's important to treat your workspace as sacred space so that when you enter it, you can connect to the deepest truth within and outside yourself as you commit to serving the highest good." That makes, as James L. Nolan says in his book, *Doing the Right Thing at Work*, your workplace truly where one can team up with God. What great thoughts to help you find that deep gladness and great satisfaction with your work.

Chapter 13

Develop Your Ability to Lead Others for Greater Career Opportunities

Those individuals who, throughout their journey of life, master the art of leading others, will rank among the most successful in any society. The world has a tendency to step aside for those who exhibit an outstanding ability to lead. For us, leadership is where the rubber meets the road. We feel learning how to be an effective leader is one of the most important skills that you can master. Leadership skills open the doors of opportunity. And if one can couple leadership skills with great wisdom, that becomes the ultimate combination we can attain. Learn about leadership at every opportunity. Study successful leaders and those who fail. Don't miss one minute of learning that comes your way, and you will find your journey enjoyable, memorable, productive, and impactful.

> *"Moses followed the advice of his father-in-law and did all that he had suggested. He picked out able men from all Israel and put them in charge of the people . . . "*
>
> —Exodus 18:24-25

Understanding what Leadership Means

If you've ever seen raw milk, you know that after a brief refrigeration period, there will be a layer of rich cream on top of the milk. The workplace is like raw milk in that those workers who are rich in abilities and potential eventually rise to the top. We understand that sometimes it's who you know, not what you know, that gets individuals promoted. But those types of promotions most often end in a flare of failure. Unless you are prepared to lead, you greatly diminish your changes of successfully leading others for any extended period of time. Your flaws eventually catch up with you.

We've written a considerable amount in this part of our book on how you can lead yourself to a more successful level of achievement. Now we'd like to share a few ideas that will help you grow your leadership potential and personal effectiveness and emerge as a successful leader.

From our viewpoint, leaders are individuals who understand where they are going and have the ability to persuade others to follow them. In simple terms, if you don't have followers, you are not leading. We want you to think in terms of possibilities. Do you want to grow into becoming a leader? What can you lead? Are you ready to assume a leadership role? Have you demonstrated your leadership abilities on the job? Do workers have confidence in your abilities? Do you work well with your peers? These are some of the questions we want you to ponder as you plan on assuming a leadership role.

Use Your Life Experiences to Build Your Leadership Arsenal

Billy has had a number of opportunities to test his leadership potential in his career. Even today, the skills learned during the years he taught and coached prove valuable. Virtually all sports-minded individuals feel great coaches are great leaders. One such coach-leader example is the legendary, former UCLA basketball coach, John Wooden, in our opinion, the greatest basketball coach ever. Wooden, with the help of one of his former players, Steve Jamison, wrote a great book on leadership entitled, *Wooden on Leadership*.

John Wooden won an unprecedented ten national championships in twelve years. That is a record that will probably never be broken. As a former basketball coach, Billy stands in awe of that accomplishment.

Without doubt, Wooden is the consummate leader. He truly understood how to maximize the potential of every player and how to blend those skills into an impregnable wall. He dominated by teaching and demanding that his players be industrious, loyal, cooperative, and enthusiastic about the game and how it is played. He stressed initiative, built skills, instilled confidence, and fostered an unmatched competitive greatness. We highly recommend you study, not just read, Wooden's words of wisdom on leadership. His lessons have universal application and are very needed in today's business environment.

Women get their fair share of glory on the court as well. And there is a John Wooden "equal" in the women's basketball game—Pat Summit, coach of the Tennessee Women's 2007 National Champions. Summit has won seven titles in her tenure at Tennessee. As we write this book, Summit has compiled the most wins of any basketball coach in the history of men and women's basketball. And, unlike Wooden, she still has a few years of coaching left. (That's a scary thought for two LSU fans and the rest of the SEC schools). But without doubt, Pat Summit is one of the greatest ever to have coached women's basketball. It'll be a long time before her record is broken, if it ever is.

Here are three points important to successfully leading others that Wooden and Summit have used to build their teams, and so have many other great coaches mentioned here.

1. Bring out the best in those you lead. Summit understands that leaders must look at the heart and soul of those they lead, and seek to bring out every ounce of their abilities. Too often, people shortchange themselves and vastly underestimate their potential. Strong leaders do all in their power to prevent this from happening. They are not intimidated or reluctant to develop talents and abilities because they understand that the more they can get from those under their leadership, the greater the potential of the organization or team. *Question:* Are you leaving abilities inside those you lead, and shortchanging their potential and the greatness of your organization?

2. When problems surface, your first step is to examine how your performance contributed to the problem. Bear Bryant, legendary football coach of the Alabama Crimson Tide, always blamed himself when his team lost a game. He never criticized a player. He just took the blame for the team failure. Summit and Wooden are also legendary for taking the same position with their basketball programs. Strong leaders have broad shoulders and they willingly place the weight of failure squarely on them. *Question:* Are you willing to face your deficiencies and how they contribute to lackluster performance of the team you lead?

3. Leaders clearly articulate the purpose for which the organization exists, and the plan to get there. Vince Lombardi, former coach of the Green Bay Packers, while holding a football in his hands, once started his practice with these words: "Gentlemen, this is a football." He started with the most basic instruction. Then, he moved on to the purpose and method of playing the game. He was clear on how the performance of players was supposed to be, and he never let up until he got that level of performance. He had a plan and a purpose—to create a great football team and win the Super Bowl. And he did both. *Question:* Does your team have a true appreciation of their purpose and function in the organization, and do you have a sound plan to reach that purpose?

While you may not be a famous or successful coach, you nonetheless have had many personal experiences that taught you lessons in leadership. Use these ideas as the foundation-building components to create your house of leadership principles. Add to those experiences these three components—*Faith*, *Truth*, and *Relationships*, and you have the beginning of greatness.

Faith: Scripture tells us that if we have faith as large as a mustard seed, we can command the great mulberry tree to move into the sea. Faith helps us move towards a better life. We must have an unshakable faith in ourselves and our abilities to get the job done. But faith without works is meaningless. Faith may be able to move mountains, but it takes a bit of sweat and muscle power to pull it off. Thus, we must do something to get something because faith without *action* achieves nothing. Want to improve your leadership skills—take action to get things done.

Truth: Our faith must be based upon truth. We must understand the proper way to act as we take action on our faith. We need knowledge to help us make the right choices because all the action in the world can be meaningless if it is focused on a falsehood. It is truth that sets us free. It grows confidence, commitment, and clarity. When we act on truths, we can predict the results. Taking action on the right truths opens the pathway to success. So always be true to yourself. And likewise, use truth as an integral part of your leadership principles.

Scripture tells us that Jesus is the truth, the way, and the light. He dealt in truths. Jesus never uttered a falsehood, nor led others in the wrong direction. Base all your actions on truth, and you will prevail just as the lessons Jesus taught still prevail today.

Relationships: As we demonstrate faith in our abilities, and use truth to help with our decision process, people around us begin to sense our commitment and passion for improving our situation in life. And when possible, they will lend their support. Having the encouragement of supporters is sometimes the critical component in our search for success. Therefore, building strong relationships with people who can help us reach our life's destination is a critical strategic move. We have limited achievement if we are the only force making advances. But when we couple our energy with the energy of others, our force becomes exponentially powerful. That is the core of becoming a leader—using the power of many through strong, loyal relationships.

Let's examine how Jesus fulfilled His mission. We know that He used a band of simple-living men rather than "the rich and famous" to form His core group. He could have waved His magic wand to make it happen, but His method was to bring others into the process. He created an unwavering bond with His apostles, who in turn developed disciples to help spread the message Jesus delivered to them. And, from that point on, the circle of influence broadened until today we have millions upon millions spreading the gospel of Jesus Christ. And it all started with the right relationship and one man with a vision.

Build faith in your leadership abilities based upon truth, and couple these with the energy of others, and you have a process that virtually has no limitations.

Some Ideas on Leadership Strategies

If you are assigned leadership duties in the future, or if you currently lead others, these ideas will help propel the value of your skills. Examine each point and seek ways to begin to apply these ideas now. These are a sampling of strategies/techniques successful leaders apply in their leadership situations. Having a cadre of strategies at your fingertips, and taking the time to fully appreciate and understand the power of each, can make a difference between success and failure in your career and life.

Make integrity your core value.

We cannot overemphasize the significance and importance of possessing integrity in all that you do throughout your life. The cynicism that now exists about corporate and political leaders has its basis in the lack of integrity these individuals all too often demonstrate. It's probably not stretching the idea too much to say that integrity has lost its foothold in our culture. It's as if the moral code of society has gone underground.

But the irony of this situation for us is that we believe people know when they are doing wrong. With few exceptions, humans have this internal radar that senses when we are driving on the wrong side of life. Ignoring that signal is where we go wrong. We know better, but things like greed, a lust for power and control, plod us on the crooked path. Each second of our life we have the option to be a person of integrity or one who forsakes it. It truly comes down to the choices we make.

Integrity makes us genuine, scented with truth. Integrity allows us to stay connected to God as we move through our life. Integrity provides courage to face up to those who would bend the rules, break the laws, or exude evil. Integrity also helps with our memory and energy level. If truth is our cornerstone, then we don't have to remember what we say, or have to waste energy trying to cover up lies. We will be consistent, predictable, and genuine at all times.

"I know, my God, that you test the heart and are pleased with integrity."
—1 Chronicles 29:17 (NIV®)

Be professionally competent.

It goes without saying that you should possess the knowledge to do your job. But how often do we find situations where this is not the case? Painfully, too often! Organizations move a good salesperson into management but don't provide the education to help with the transition. If you feel you are on the short end of the stick on this point, start studying your craft. Seek ways your employer can help grow your skills. Be constantly vigilant for opportunities to gain knowledge about your career and specific job responsibilities. You can never be too competent or professional in the way you go about doing your work.

Remove obstacles for teamwork.

We all need help along the way. With the complexities and competitiveness of the 21st century workplace, cooperation from workers makes the job a lot easier. Obstructions can destroy progress. Build your team well, and you will build your future at the same time. Study techniques that foster teamwork and, more importantly, put into practice the ideas you learn. When you are observed as being a team player, your future options grow. No one likes a selfish, self-centered, and self-serving leader.

Grow employees.

Don't be selfish with your knowledge, and don't strive to be "king or queen of the hill." Take pride in making employees better. Spend time and monies developing the skills and talents of your employees. It's a sound investment that pays dividends for many years. Workers appreciate a leader who is a great teacher and unselfish with their support. Common sense should tell you, unless you've prepared someone in your department to take your position, it's difficult to advance above your current job. Don't view your team as a threat. See them as a springboard for better opportunities for your career. It's a classic case of giving first and receiving later.

Looking through the public life of Jesus, we see a leader growing His "employees." Jesus constantly instructed all who came in contact with Him. His message was one of spiritual growth to help all who practiced and implemented His teachings. The Ultimate Leader grew His disciples into individuals who in turn grew His church—an institution that still flourishes today.

Be an encourager.

You are the cheerleader. Upbeat thinking, genuine concern for employees, and a willing spirit comprise the character of the encourager. Push and prod timid employees. Encourage risks. Support innovation. Be the role model others willingly follow.

And what an encourager Jesus was to His followers. His entire message was one of encouragement to live life in such a way that would be pleasing to His Father, and ensure a place for them in the heavenly kingdom.

Keep learning.

As leaders, we must read, take courses, observe other successful leaders—do whatever it takes to keep getting smarter each day. File the lessons of the day into your memory bank to avoid future mistakes and to be able to replicate past successes. Learning keeps you stimulated towards greatness and wisdom. Each day ask, "What did I learn today that I did not know yesterday?" If the most frequent answer is "Nothing," perhaps it's time you re-think how you are approaching your career.

Rose Hudson built her career by not saying "No" to job opportunities. She always trusted that the right career opportunity would eventually come if she kept learning and building job skills by working at the various jobs she willingly undertook. In the end, the Louisiana Lottery Corporation sought her services as Senior Vice-President. She didn't even have to apply for the job. That recruitment allowed her to seek and get her current position as President and CEO.

Be trustful.

If you commit to something, do it. Make what you say be the ultimate truth. Never lie to employees, or do anything to lose their trust. Once lost, trust is very difficult to regain. However, once employees trust you, it is next to impossible to stop the momentum you can build. We can't think of a more important quality to practice or one that can be more devastating if not practiced.

The path Jesus offers us is filled with trust. No one living today has seen Jesus, yet millions trust in His words. Perhaps we should seek to build the trust level Jesus established during His journey on earth over 2000 years ago. Not a bad role model!

In *John 14:1*, Jesus comforts his disciples with these words:

"*Do not let your hearts be troubled. Trust in God; trust also in me.*"

People listen to your words but watch your actions.

Leaders are in the limelight, and their actions are constantly scrutinized by followers. They will begin to question your motives if you speak with a forked tongue. This is a case where you cannot fake it until you make it. Walk the talk, and all will remain well. Walk one way and talk another and you're done as a leader.

Jesus never wavered from the path He started in His public journey. He was consistent in every way. He truly walked the talk, and lived the message.

Be open to new ideas.

Some of the best suggestions for improvements in your leadership skills can come from people who work for you. Closed minds stifle creativity and innovation. Encourage the flow of thoughts between team members and you. Give credit to the originator of an idea that gets implemented. That's a great trust-building technique as well. Never steal another's idea and take the credit yourself. That's a great trust buster. In our careers we have found that people on the front line have much to contribute to the profitability and success of an organization.

At Toyota, workers offer an average of one suggestion per week and, in the past forty years, have provided Toyota management over 20 million suggestions to improve their manufacturing process. Is it any wonder that they are probably the most successful auto manufacturer in the world?

Be a straight shooter.

Give honest feedback on performance. Nobody enjoys being lied to. Your job as a leader is to bring reality to your employees so that the proper growth plan can be developed. And nowhere is this more truthful than in performance reviews. In this situation, it is imperative that you give factual feedback backed with a plan to improve performance. In the long run, your employees will appreciate your candor, and actually will begin to view performance review as a growth opportunity.

Part of being professionally competent is making the hard decisions regarding personnel under your leadership. Louisiana Lottery CEO, Rose Hudson, shared that when she assumed her position, there was someone on staff that just didn't fit the team she was trying to assemble. She related that, "There was no place I could go to figure out the right decision to make than to God." She prayerfully said, "Help me." In the end, being a straight shooter with this employee has made her team stronger and more effective.

Be accessible.

People you lead need to occasionally catch your ear. Be there for them when there is a need for conversation. Setting up "walls" with subordinates at times is necessary, but when the need is right, you should be a person they can reach. An open-door policy and immediate accessibility to employee says you care. And, when employees see how much you care, they will follow.

Roger Thomas was the first President of Melamine Chemicals in Donaldsonville, LA. One of the endearing qualities that made Roger a very popular leader among his employees was his accessibility. Roger had an open-door policy, and was never too busy to listen to employee concerns. He not only listened, but he acted on many of the concerns or suggestions offered by employees. His accessibility and genuine concern for the welfare of employees earned him employee loyalty, and helped to provide many years of profitability and growth for this melamine-producing facility.

Teach your employees to understand the bottom line.

When everyone pulls together to watch the cash flow, there can be tremendous cost savings. Get the focus on minimizing waste and you can ultimately maximize your return on investment (ROI). Reward suggestions that save money. That can be a great incentive. It can be as simple as a public "thank you" or as substantial as a monetary reward. Unless and until employees can see how the way they work impacts the bottom line, saving dollars is still a pipe dream. But, once you've educated them, and they buy into the process of continuous improvement, you will see a tremendous increase in both productivity and profits.

Know how to solve process and people problems.

Address concerns quickly. Utilize experiences of your employees to help solve process issues. Don't let people problems grow out of control. Stress teamwork, cooperation, and a professional relationship at all times. Great leaders are great problem solvers. Great leaders turn every problem into an opportunity to grow.

Practice visionary thinking.

Create possibilities. Leaders take the long-term view. They anticipate problems and clearly think through the goals of the future. This type of thinking opens the doors of opportunity and promotes longevity and growth for the organization. On the other hand, those with myopic vision can only see what is directly in front of their eyes, thus they miss all the opportunities in the periphery. Broaden your vision, and you broaden your possibilities.

What a vision Jesus offered his followers. You've got to admit that "eternity" is all about the long-term view. And His message clearly offered a way to achieve the vision. Yes, Jesus was the ultimate visionary leader. What an example for you to follow on your journey.

Make people feel important.

This is the strongest non-biological urge of humans. Do all you can to make people feel valued, and you will have loyalty every step of the way. Leaders understand that people want to feel appreciated, and they never miss an opportunity to extend that appreciation. The appreciative comment is genuine, not contrived. It comes from the heart, not the brain. It's intended to build, not tear down. The unique thing about this practice is that not only will you make the receiver of your comment swell with pride, but your own confidence level will grow as well. That's just how it works.

There are a number of references in the Bible to the words *important* and *importance*. One that comes to mind is taken from Mark 12:33.

"To love him with all your heart, with all your understanding and with all your strength, and to love your neighbor as yourself is more important than all burnt offerings and sacrifices." (NIV®)

With these words, Mark lets us know that caring for others, not only in an intimate sense but in all our relationships, is God's wish for our behavior. Mark stresses that one must love God, but of equal importance is loving others. For us, this is a clear sign that making others feel important is also very important to God.

Be consistent.

This trait makes you very predictable and that is how it should be. Given a set of circumstances, the same decision should be made tomorrow that you made today. Inconsistency is probably one of the most potentially damaging practices in which a leader can engage. Inconsistency in your behavior or responses is stressful for those under your leadership. Keeping an even-keeled, predictable personality, is soothing and makes association with you a comfortable experience. Even if your followers don't like your decision, when you are predictable and they know how you will react, they become more accepting. It's amazing how it works. But it works.

Be passionate.

Passion creates belief, and belief is the first step in the accomplishment cycle. If you don't have passion for the cause you lead, let someone else do it. Passion evokes enthusiasm, enthusiasm produces energy, and energy is what you need to get things done. People can sense your level of passion. It's been our experience that those with passion get more done than those who lack that level of belief. Become a passionate leader and followship comes.

Improve the life of those you lead.

Your job as a leader is to help remove obstacles that hinder progress. Your job is to grow intellect and skills so efficiency can occur. Your job is to make things better for those you lead. Remember, they trust you; they see your passion; they sense your commitment to the organizational outcomes. Then, they become open to direction, and are better able to take the positive steps to improve themselves and the organization.

Dare to be different.

Being a leader offers you the opportunity to take risks and change the direction things are going. We're not asking for you to behave stupidly. We certainly understand the potential devastation of stupidity. We want to encourage you to step out in front, and lead in a new way if that is the only way to win. Be bold! Be courageous! Remember, no explorer ever found new lands by being timid. And no great leader was timid in his method to achieve better things for those he led. Any dead fish can float with the current, but it takes a strong one to swim upstream. Swim upstream, taking problems head on, considering them as challenges. Make a name for yourself with your actions.

Wow! Is there a better description of the message Jesus brought to the world? Jesus was different. He mixed with prostitutes, tax collectors, and Samaritans. He rebuked the Pharisees. He preached a "different" kind of message than the Jewish leaders did. And who can argue with the results of his "different" approach to living one's life?

Live a balanced life.

It's easy to get your life out of kilter if you develop a one-dimension life. There must be balance. Work is important, but family overrides any career obligation. There is always a job, but you have only one chance to get family right. Work hard but make time with your most important asset, otherwise you will lose it. This is truly the essence of this book. Balance means you have your priorities in order, and you tend to each one as you should. Tilting too much in any one direction will throw you off balance, and the resulting fall may be difficult to overcome. Remember, it's God, family, and career.

Use your time wisely.

Time moves on no matter how hard we try to stall its advance. When we have the right priorities, we can allot the proper amount of time to the many events that make up our life. With proper focus and time allocation, we get the most significant things done, and that is exactly what leaders are charged to do. Learn strategies for using time effectively. This can be your greatest ally as you carry out your leadership duties. Also, very good users of time are also held in high esteem by those who sense this quality.

Become a servant leader.

We cannot emphasize enough how important this mindset is. We are closing this section with one of the most important characteristics of great leaders. Robert Greenleaf is generally credited with popularizing the term "servant leader" in the 1970s. There are a number of good books on this subject as well. As we strive to learn how to put into practice the techniques and style of a servant leader, we should never forget that the greatest one to ever walk the face of the earth came to serve mankind. That fact in itself should tell us such a leadership style works. Those who serve are willing to put others first. Servant leadership was Jesus' way of serving, and the example every leader can use to bring success to their work place.

"I know your deeds, your love and faith, your service and perseverance, and that you are now doing more than you did at first." —Revelation 2:19 (NIV®)

Now you have a starting point upon which to begin your journey down the leadership trail. We've provided a short list of leadership traits. Many more exist, and we will turn the responsibility to do further research and study over to you. There are a number of references we recommend in our Reading List at the end of the book. We want you to understand that it's just as easy to lead as it is to follow. In fact, from our experiences, we both feel it's actually easier to assume a leadership position because most people don't want to lead. Find your comfort zone. Begin studying what makes great leaders great. Then, adapt what works for you in your particular situation. Leaders have existed since the beginning of time. And certainly, as we just said, the greatest leader of all was Jesus. Adapting His style should be a no-brainer, and the true position you seek to achieve in this lifetime.

Show Up at a 100 percent Level

If we are to take the true spiritual approach to our work, we have an obligation to show up to work when we show up at work. Individuals with a high moral code understand that they are paid to provide a good, solid performance at their jobs. In candid terms, if you slack on the job, you are not only hurting the profit potential of your employer, you are also developing very poor work habits that do not serve you well. Here are some interesting statistics regarding what constitutes a less than 100 percent commitment.

Jupiter Media Metrix and other research firms place the amount of lost productivity due to Internet abuse at 34 percent. According to the 2000

National Sleep Foundation (NSF) Poll, one-half of American employees report that sleepiness on the job interferes with the amount of work they get done. The NSF estimates the direct costs of sleepiness and lost productivity in the workplace at about $18 billion. The nation's first, oldest, and premier outplacement consulting organization, Challenger, Gray and Christmas, Inc., estimate that Corporate America *lost $1.2 billion in productivity* during the 2007 NCAA basketball tournament.

With this minimal list of events that show every worker does not show up at the 100 percent level, one can easily surmise that far too many people are costing businesses billions and billions each year. They come to work, but they are not ready to give a day's toil for a day's pay.

On the positive side, these statistics are a testimony to the strength and viability of the American economy. On the negative side, just think what we could accomplish as a nation if everyone showed up at a 100 percent level.

We challenge our readers to think deeply about their personal commitment to their career. Are you a slacker? Do you look for ways to coast during the day? Do you feel you are not paid enough to give it your all? How much does your unwillingness to give a maximum account of your time use cost your employer? If we've done nothing else, we hope we've helped you decide to improve in the future, and to be fair and honest to the people who provide your paycheck. We further encourage you to be the example to others, as Jesus is our example for how to live our life. Become a leader who demonstrates how to show up at the 100 percent level. We guarantee that you will ultimately be the benefactor of such a change in work habits.

If we examine the life of Jesus, we will find that He clearly showed up with a 100 percent contribution mentality. He suffered and died for our sins, yet was sinless Himself. His powerful message and purpose ignited a flame of enthusiasm that is still burning today. Jesus is our role model. He showed us the way we should live our life in the 100 percent mode. Are you ready to accept that challenge?

Success Challenges

1. What is your opinion of the career you've chosen to make your life's work? Do you truly enjoy what you do or is it a living hell? Please answer why you feel the way you do, regardless of your choice.

2. What activity gives you the feeling of "deep gladness?" Is this your career choice, a hobby, or an incidental activity in which you engage? Describe how you feel when you are engaged with this activity.
3. In my career, what are my honest feelings about my employer and career choice as it relates to the following statements:
    a. My employer treats me fairly
    b. Your attitude towards your management team
    c. The growth potential of your career
    d. Your personal motivation to carry out the responsibilities of your job
    e. The amount of time you spend each week performing your job
    f. Your professional relationships
    g. The salary and benefits provided by your employer
    h. How informed you feel about your company's activities
    i. The potential security you have for the long term

    Note: If the overwhelming responses are negative for these questions, perhaps it's time to look for another career opportunity.
4. Do you have regrets regarding your career choice? Have you experienced on-the-job failures that still plague your thinking? What lessons have you learned about either situation? What are you going to do about this?
5. In Chapter 12, we've listed tips to improve your career. Develop a game plan with detailed action steps to put these items in place.
6. How well do you work with your boss? If the relationship is rocky, how can you change to make the relationship work better?
7. Chapter 13 has a number of tips to build your leadership skills. Review the items and seek ways to incorporate those suggestions into all parts of your life. Continue studying leader characteristics, and, one-by-one, begin to incorporate those skills into your personal leadership arsenal.

PART IV

The Journey

to

Personal Success

Chapter 14

Do You Have a Little Stress in Your Life?

Life can present many obstacles that make our journey through this world a bit treacherous. If we're not prepared, the journey can produce a bumpy ride. How you learn to handle these bumps in the road will determine the quality of life you experience. We hope by now you've sensed that, no matter where you are with your life, it's most important that you maintain your connection with God. He is the great equalizer and source of peace when life becomes a bit hectic and stressful. So, use God to your advantage to help you cope in your hour of need. He is ever present in our midst, and created the holy ground upon which we walk through life. It's a blessing we all have. It's up to us to learn how to reap the blessings and graces God so willingly wants to give us.

> *"We do not want you to be uninformed, brothers, about the hardships we suffered in the province of Asia. We were under great pressure, far beyond our ability to endure, so that we despaired even of life. Indeed, in our hearts we felt the sentence of death. But this happened that we might not rely on ourselves but on God, who raises the dead."*
>
> —2 Corinthians 1:8-9 (NIV®)

We can look through Scripture and find examples of God's people who felt the pressures of life too much to bear. In the above quote from the letters of Paul to the Corinthians, we see Paul discussing the great pressure felt, as he and his followers spread the good news about God and the works of Jesus. It was a pressure almost unbearable except for the love of God helping them to cope. There is a lesson for us in this example.

In today's society, humans are still experiencing the same types of pressures brought on by life on earth. We find far too many people stressed out because of life's circumstances. Women working at their career, and having to care for the duties as moms, makes their day one big pressure cooker. Dads struggling in disappointing careers, and barely making enough to pay the bills, come home frustrated and fatigued. Add to that the challenges of just living in today's world, and there is little wonder why some folks are so filled with anxieties.

So what's happening as a result of this pressure-cooker existence? We feel one of the side-effects is that we've become a "pill popping" and medication-minded nation. Watch TV for an hour and you're likely to see at least one, if not several, commercials for some type of medication. We are being exposed to ailments that we never knew existed and just the right pill to cure it. Now, we understand that many medications today are producing miracle cures and serve humanity well. And we applaud these improvements that have extended our average lifespan and helped many to cope with depression, allergies, heart problems, cholesterol control, and other ailments. We clearly acknowledge being personally helped by the use of proper medication. But one might argue that pharmaceutical companies, via commercials on TV and print ads, do emphasize the use of their products and encourage patients to speak to physicians about possibly using them for their malady. While this is sound advertisement strategy, our concern is with individuals who might be influenced to needlessly seek and perhaps be given some medications that are not needed. Just think about the rising number of celebrities who have become addicted to prescription drugs. The mental and physical tensions of their celebrity lifestyle becomes overwhelming and they sadly turn to what they feel is a support mechanism that ultimately enslaves and destroys them. Our concern is that some individuals, like these celebrities, develop the mindset that a pill is the solution to all the pressures in their life.

Today, consumers spend more than $4 billion per year on prescription drugs. Add to that the billions spent on over-the-counter drugs, and you have a situation that is almost out of control. Remember that mild symptoms do not require any medication, and moderate symptoms often respond to home remedies. Drugs are not essential to recover from every illness nor is "popping a pill" always the best solution. Many experts argue we're an overmedicated society, kids included. For example, last year, doctors wrote more than 30 million prescriptions for ADHD meds alone. In many cases, the medication helps, but often these prescriptions are erroneously prescribed. And sadly, there are children who need the medication who never receive help. There is also another side to this abuse. A recent government survey, released by the Substance Abuse and Mental Health Services Administration, reported that slightly over three million people between the ages of twelve and twenty-five used cough and cold medicine to get high. Are we becoming an "out-of-control" society?

Are doctors just looking for a fast fix, when many pediatricians are booked to spend only five minutes on each child? We will not pretend to be authorities on medicine. But these facts and figures certainly should raise a red flag and question consumer consumption habits.

Jodi holds a Second Degree black belt in Tae Kwon Do. (Billy just has a black belt to hold up his pants. OK. It's time for a little humor). Although Jodi has just about given up on the fighting part of the sport, there was a time when sparring was a part of his regular routine. He also trained to be an instructor. His Master Instructor, Joel Neely, has many young students in his program that come because of their inability to sit still, focus, or pay attention. Some are having difficulty in school and are on medication. When they enter Neely's school, they agree to bring their report card every time it is issued. If the student does not maintain his grades, he will not be recommended to test for advancement to the next higher belt. Jodi has seen Neely's students get off their medication during this process. In such cases, all these children needed was to learn discipline, and earning their black belt is often enough incentive for them to maintain their discipline.

Certainly, medical advances have extended the life of humans. We don't want to take anything away from this success story. But in many cases, as we just noted, there are other options that can replace having to pop that pill. Let's take a look at a few ideas.

Exercise and Hobbies Can Work

"In the name of the Lord Jesus Christ, we command you, brothers, to keep away from every brother who is idle and does not live according to the teaching you received from us." —2 Thessalonians 3:6 (NIV®)

One excellent way to release stress is to engage in recreational activities. Staying busy can eliminate stress. For Jodi, Tae Kwon Do was a great stress buster. Like Jodi, others go to the gym to relieve stress by jogging, lifting weights, or engaging in some type of aerobic exercise. Sometimes the desire to exercise is carried out in some type of sporting activity. Here one must be very careful not to sustain an injury that can jeopardize the ability to perform work requirements—something that can bring big-time stress into life. This is a particularly common thing with men. One last aspect of engaging in these types of activities is the financial obligation. Men who are serious golfers, fishermen, hunters, drag racers, etc., will spend a fair amount of money to engage in these activities. Many women participate in Pilates, Jazzercise and other exercising activities. Some of the most ardent golfers are women, and of course many people play tennis to stay in shape and to relieve stress. We simply caution you to be diligent with your finances when it comes to hobbies, and not spend money that would be better spent on educating your children or reducing family debt.

Since he was a teenager, Billy has enjoyed woodworking as a hobby. Over the years, besides removing daily tensions, he has used this skill to build and repair many things in his home. Sometimes a hobby becomes more likeable than the job, and that can result in a complete career change. That's how Billy moved into his current career as a professional speaker. He built the business part-time over a twenty-year period and, when he retired from his corporate management position, the transition was smooth and quick.

Now technology has added its contribution to stress reduction. Recently, Robin Roberts, co-host of Good Morning America, endorsed a mini-biofeedback machine that helps to relax your body and calm your mind, just by changing your breathing and your focus. That in turn activates a part of the nervous system that quiets the body—reducing the unwanted tensions and anxieties.

A quick internet search will surface many websites that list numerous ways to remove stress. We bet you will find many things on those lists that you can start using to take that unneeded pressure out of your body. We encourage a little surfing on the web.

Those who don't take exercising so seriously, or do not want to try any other suggestions we have offered, may simply want to "chill" when they get home with a good dinner, and maybe a glass of wine or a cold beer. We promise not to be judgmental about such a decision. Just remember, moderation is best.

The common thread throughout this discussion is when we are full of apprehension and worry, we need a release. However, just releasing does not address the cause, nor does over-doing the relief make sense. Let us explain.

If relieving worry and tensions is the goal, then why not consider working to eliminate it altogether? Often the stress comes from people having the wrong priorities. The most flagrant violation we've noted occurs when people put their job as their #1 priority. We know people that are burning the candle at both ends trying to "make it" in their careers. We know many who work late every night, go into the office on Saturdays, and then work on Sunday afternoons. This obviously violates the priority scheme laid out in the first three parts of this book, and is an immense contributor to a stressful lifestyle.

Before we move on, we want to bring you back to our #1 priority—God. Don't overlook, as Paul did, the power of leaning on God as a stress-buster. Spending time in solitude, reflecting on your lifestyle and priorities, can be a very calming experience. Silence and solitude offer us the opportunity to listen to God speaking to us. In those moments, He can reveal insights that will help us cope or better still, remove the source of our stress. Remember, God is ever present (thus you are always standing on holy ground), and ever ready to shower us with His graces to strengthen our character and resolve to face life. This time investment costs no money but can pay very handsome dividends. It's quite a bargain!

When Stress and Wrong Priorities Can Be Deadly

Billy's younger brother was a sugarcane farmer who was truly in love with his profession. He started working on the farm as a partner with their father when he was nineteen. Both loved the land, and both were exceptional sugarcane farmers. Their reputation ranked high among their peers.

When their father retired, his brother bought his father's share and took over the operation.

Farming any crop is a risky business. But slowly, sugarcane farmers are becoming an endangered species. Constantly rising costs, erratic profits due to low market value of sugar, and potential damage caused by a variety of weather conditions contribute to the risk. These factors are out of the control of farmers, and those who manage to survive do so with their innate skills and lots of hard work. It can be a tough business.

Billy's brother had spent almost thirty years working the land when he was offered more land to farm, effectively doubling his total crop acreage. The future appeared bright because finally his dream of growing the size of his operation became a reality. Those who knew Billy's brother knew he never looked at the clock, or what day of the week it was. If work had to be done, he did it. In his younger days, he played hard. On the farm, he worked hard. It was this habit that he and Billy often discussed. Billy felt his brother spent too much time on the farm, and not enough time with his family. There was never a disagreement during the conversation. His standard reply to the lessons shared by his older brother often ended with, "Yeah, you right Bro." *But change was slow.*

In the fall of 2002, a few weeks before harvest time was to begin, Billy, his brother, and a cousin were talking about the upcoming "grinding season." Normally talkative, particularly on this subject, Billy noticed that his brother was unusually quiet, but shrugged off the observation. He knew that the stress of the upcoming grinding season was weighing heavily on his brother's mind. That wasn't unusual. He also knew that this meeting was probably the last time they would talk face-to-face until after the crop was completely harvested. About three weeks later, harvest time began. When the "grinding season" starts, farmers begin a non-stop work schedule that often extends three months without a day off.

As often happens in South Louisiana, it started raining. For about two weeks, the rains came down, creating a sea of mud in the fields. Ruts caused by the heavy equipment needed to harvest the sugarcane grew deeper by the day. Equipment failures were extending the work days even beyond the normal ten to twelve hours. Add to this worry factors about finances, labor difficulties, and the stress of long, hard days, and you've just created a recipe for a disaster.

As was his usual custom, Billy's brother went to the farm early on a rainy, October morning. But minutes after arriving, a family's worst nightmare became a grim reality. After apparently fighting a very deep depression for several weeks, Jody "Byrd" Arcement took his life. No one who knew him would ever have suspected he would take this journey. It was completely out of character. But the grimness of the moment could not be changed once the fatal decision was made. In an instant of poor decision-making, driven by the burdens and pressures life can cause, a father, husband, and brother was no longer physically here.

Today, as we write these words, Jody's family has made whatever adjustment can be made under such circumstances. His wife, always a great mother, with her faith and trust in God, has become the super mom. Her entire life since then has been 100 percent devoted to raising her two children and helping them return to normalcy. Without God in her life, her world would have quickly crumbled. With God, she has returned joy to her family and, in the long term, everyone will survive well because God remains in their heart, and is helping them journey through life. He is with them every step of the way. He is helping them walk the holy ground.

(*Billy's Note:* I'm sharing this story, as emotional as it still is in my mind, with the hope that it will help someone to recognize symptoms of depression within themselves or one of their family members. It's my hope that by sharing this personal and tragic story with our readers, I will bring value to the world from a most difficult moment in my life. If you are experiencing symptoms of depression or know someone who is, we encourage you to seek professional help from a counselor, physician, pastor, deacon or others who have been trained to handle such matters. It is literally a matter of life or death.)

"*I press on toward the goal to win the prize for which God has called me heavenward in Christ Jesus. All of us who are mature should take such a view of things. And if on some point you think differently, that too God will make clear to you.*" —Philippians 3:14-15 (NIV®)

What Are the Right Priorities?

Let's review. From the start of this book, we have said that God should be first. If you are among those who work excessively, ask yourself how the time you spend at the office compares to the time you spend in prayer, and with family. Your family concerns must supersede work. Few would challenge the statement that spending excessive time at the office, or engaging in hobbies, is good for establishing solid family relationships. In both cases, the result of this misalignment will produce stress. Stress can affect not only your health, but also your success. Although money is an indicator of success, it is not the only one. (But we do recognize that a lack of money can be a major factor in divorce, depression, and general dissatisfaction with life.) Just don't make money your "god." The Bible does not say that money is the root of all evil. Rather, in 1 *Timothy* 6:10, it says,

"*The love of money is the root of all evil.*"

True wealth is made up of more than money. Get your money and your relationships straight, and you are on your way towards building a successful life.

When you feel the stress coming on, remember that you often cannot change what happens to you, but you can control your reaction to every happening in your life. As a Deacon, some of Jodi's duties include assisting the priest at mass by reading scriptures, and assisting with other parts of the celebration. Once when he went into the sacristy to put on his vestments, his Alb was gone. (The Alb is a white robe-like garment that priests wear under their vestments and that deacons wear as an outer garment with a stole over it.) A visiting priest from France had mistakenly taken Jodi's Alb, a special gift from his ordination. Jodi relates that his initial reaction was to be upset at the visiting priest, but he caught himself and changed his attitude. He simply put on a different Alb, and went on to help with the mass. Jodi could have let his upset condition continue to fester and grow in magnitude. Doing so would have eventually stressed him out. But by controlling his reaction, he was able to avoid a stress buildup. This is a small example of how everyday events can affect our attitude and produce unwanted and unneeded stress. Our task is to take control, and not let such events affect us in a negative way.

When you do experience stress, there are many resources available to help you cope with it. Be smart. Educate yourself! Change habits! Get your priorities in order, and watch the stress melt away like a snowball on a warm day.

Chapter 15

The Final Leg of the Journey

The last leg of our journey on holy ground has to do specifically with you. We've discussed our relationship with God, family and our work. Now we want to focus directly on YOU! Yes, to put it all together, you've got to have good habits and a success plan to take full advantage of your gifts, talents, and desires. In this part of our book, we focus on several success principles that complement everything we've written about so far. From our vantage point, we believe that there is a spiritual connection with great success strategies. And that awakening is what we want you to experience. The most difficult part of the journey for us at this point was deciding what to leave out as we concluded our book. We pray that we've hit the target with you, and that, as you take this last step on your journey, you will come to appreciate the God-connection we always have and how to best use it to live a full and happy life. We wish you well on your journey. So let's continue.

> *"This is the confidence which we have before Him, that, if we ask anything according to His will, he hears us."*
>
> —1 John 5:14 (NIV®)

So far we've spent time sharing our thoughts on how you build relationships with God and family within the confines of your career. But we don't want to ignore the importance of your personal development and understanding of critical success principles. By that we mean the process by which you become comfortable with who you are. Understanding ourselves helps us to improve our relationship abilities with others. Some might argue that we should have begun this book with this section. Our feeling is that once we get our priorities in order, i.e., God, family, and career, we are stronger and more able to fully develop who we are. In some ways, it's a simultaneous journey with the focus for decision-making in the God, family, career alignment.

Where does this part of the journey begin? We asked that question as well. After much thought and discussion, we arrived at the following list of personal development activities to round off the journey.

It all Starts with Belief

It is hard to love others when you don't love yourself. Scripture says that we are made in the image and likeness of God.

"Then God said, 'Let us make man in our image, in our likeness' . . . "
—Genesis 1:26 (NIV®)

That being the case, developing a healthy confidence in our abilities begins with a healthy love of self. Each of us is a unique creation of God. No two people are exactly alike—even identical twins. Understanding that fact has to create in your mind the thoughts of how very special you are. If God has taken the time to create us in this special, unique way, it is important that we recognize how special each of us is in the eyes of God.

Inspirational and motivational speaker and author, Wanda Hope Carter, in her writings adds this commentary to this point when she encourages everyone to "Take control of your destiny. Believe in yourself. Ignore those who try to discourage you. Avoid negative sources, people, places, things and habits. Don't give up and don't give in."

Belief in self is the beginning of building confidence to take on life with vigor and vision. Belief sets the limits as high or low. Belief, no matter if it is right or wrong, becomes our reality.

Our entire Christian ideals are based upon belief. There are literally hundreds of passages in Scripture that talk about belief, faith, and trust, all terms with essentially the same meaning. Jesus recognized that belief becomes the momentum builder for action. This passage from *James 2:17* reinforces Jesus' position:

" . . . *faith by itself, if it is not accompanied by action, is dead."* (NIV®)

So while belief is a critical first step, listen to Jesus and let your faith lead you to take action.

Claude Bristol in his classic book, *The Magic of Believing*, says that belief is the motivating force that enables you to achieve your goals. Be a believer in the power of belief that God placed in your spirit to fulfill your destiny. Have confidence and trust in the Divine Power to be there when you need it along your journey. Then act so you can secure the destiny God has in mind for you. This is not the impossible dream!

Possess Integrity

"The integrity of the upright guides them, but the unfaithful are destroyed by their duplicity." —Proverbs 11:3 (NIV®)

It is important to display strong integrity in everything we do. One definition of principled characteristics is acting the same way when no one is around as we would act when we are in the company of very important or influential people. Possessing sound integrity gives you a sense of identity you can maintain at all times. This trait brings consistency and predictability into play, and ultimately will make you more respected and trustworthy

One of Jodi's good friends is Dr. Rudi Aguilar. Dr. Rudi is a remarkable person. He has achieved great success, despite the fact that he came to the United States as a young college student with no friends or English skills. Fast forward forty years or so, and he owns an engineering firm, a real estate development and appraisal firm, and is a clinical professor at Tulane University. Dr. Rudi explained to us one day that you can tell the character of an individual by what he does in the bathroom. We were a bit startled by that comment and asked him to explain. He said, 'If a person washes his or her hands only when someone else is in the rest room, and not when he or she is alone in the rest room, you know that the person is not genuine." Now, every time Jodi goes to the rest room, he washes his hands and tells himself that this is a sign of maintaining his integrity!

If you are consistent and predictable in all that you do, people will respect you even if they disagree with your position on a particular subject. It's individuals who waffle with the push of the wind that lack integrity of position and are inconsistent and unpredictable.

People don't like and, most often, can read through a fake. If you are a phony, others will know it. Such a characteristic will affect your level of success and derail your journey. This reminds us of a line from the cartoon character, Popeye. He would often say, "I am what I am." The question then becomes "Who are you?" Scripture tells us to be genuine in Revelation 3:15-16

"I know your deeds, that you are neither cold nor hot. I wish you were either one or the other! So, because you are lukewarm-neither hot nor cold-I am about to spit you out of my mouth."

The Daily Review Process

In an earlier part of this book, we discussed the "Daily Examine." This habit is so critical to your success journey that we want to again spend time reviewing the steps.

How you start your day impacts the type of day you will have. That's why the habit of starting your day with prayer—establishing your connection with God—can be energizing, and get you off to a great start. This should be your quiet time. Spending time in prayer and quiet helps crystallize your thoughts and clarify your day's journey.

Next, give thanks for the privilege of another day, and for the wonderful gifts God will shower you with this day (because He will if you just look for them). In the book, *The Science of Getting Rich*, by Wallace Wattles, the longest chapter in the book is on "gratitude." It is incredibly important to maintain an attitude of gratitude if you are to maintain proper balance in your personal mental, spiritual, and physical life. In *Ephesians 5:20*, we read that we are to give thanks always, in all things.

"*Give thanks to God the Father always and for everything in the name of our Lord Jesus Christ.*"

Additionally, it is important to spend a few moments throughout the day examining what you've accomplished, making course corrections, and again expressing your gratitude. These actions keep you moving towards your desired destination.

How you end your day to a large extent determines how you will live tomorrow. Review the entire events of the day, and identify where you were successful and where you could have done better. This act alone will help your success ratio go way up. In the areas you felt you were not successful, use your imagination to reconstruct the scenes to determine what you should have done differently. Focusing on the positive is powerful.

We'd like to add a new wrinkle to complete your Daily Examine that we've not previously discussed. This suggestion is to close your day by writing in a journal. When some of you read that sentence, you'll say, "No Way. I'm not about to write my personal feelings for someone else to read." That's a natural reaction. But write nonetheless. Doing so is a cleansing activity. Pray to get over the stigma of writing intimate thoughts about your feelings and/or actions. Just write because taking a few moments to write down your thoughts about your day is a very powerful and therapeutic activity. Writing helps you "dump" negativity and reinforce the positive events. And don't worry about spelling or grammar. Let the words flow from your heart to the paper. One day you will see what a treasure you've created.

A journal can also be a place where you park your dreams, so you have written evidence of what you wish to accomplish. Having your ideas on paper also allows you to occasionally re-read what you've written. Then, you can gauge the progress you've made, if you've made adjustments from events you committed to change, and, in general, recall your thoughts in those moments of time. Review and evaluation are how we improve. Having a journal is the perfect tool to help with your self-improvement program.

Two individuals come to mind that exemplify the power of journaling. Jim Rohn, American's foremost business philosopher and world renowned speaker, is a compulsive writer of his thoughts. Mark Victor Hansen, co-author of the extremely successful *Chicken Soup for the Soul* books, is another. Both are the epitome of personal and business success. And, by the way, both have a deep faith and don't hesitate to tell the world how they feel about God.

The last suggestion is to include, as part of your daily journal, three to five things for which you are thankful or grateful. Those entries can be events of that day, or anything in your lifetime that comes to mind for which you are grateful. It's that "attitude of gratitude" that helps you go to bed thinking and believing that tomorrow will be better. Focusing last on the good in your life will help you rest better, and wake up refreshed ready to begin another successful day. And don't forget to express your thanks to God for the greatness of the day and for guidance to improve tomorrow in areas that need an adjustment. Remember, God is always present, and always wants to help. We just have to ask. We believe this entire process is better than sleeping pills or any valium type medications you can take.

Time Use

We do not have space enough to provide you with a time-management seminar. But we will share with you what we believe are the three key elements for effective use of our time.

- **Priorities:** To get a handle on making your time and life more productive, you must have a deep appreciation for your life's priorities. This book is about what we believe they should be. But, let's go a bit further. Setting priorities means that we know and carry out each day activities that will help us achieve our most important desires. If actions that you take don't advance you towards the achievement of those desires, then chances are it's not an activity worth doing. The simple test is to examine your actions and ask, "Is this advancing me towards the most important things in my life"? If the answer is a resounding "No," don't do it. Simple! Sweet! Effective!
- **Planning:** Most people think that taking time to plan is a complete waste of good time. Nothing could be further from the truth. Research has shown, and results have validated, that those who plan will outperform those who don't. During the time Billy was a high school coach, whenever he had a sporting event to coach, he always took time to study his opponent's weaknesses and determine what strategies could be used to exploit them. Then he looked at what strengths his team possessed, and identified strategies that could be used to gain an advantage over his opponent. Without planning, his won-lost record would have been dismal. With planning, his coaching years were quite successful. And, if you study the working style of the most successful coaches ever, you will find the common thread to be extensive planning. Planning works if you work the plan. So get busy.
- **Procrastination:** This deadly habit of putting off what we should be doing can be a killer. Yes, there may be times when procrastination pays. But in a vast majority of cases, procrastination becomes punitive. One technique to help get you off your duff and moving, is to say to yourself whenever you know you are procrastinating, (and you do know this) "Do it now!" Create a neon sign in your brain that flashes these words repeatedly. Let this be the stimulus that moves you to take action and complete or begin working on a task. We understand that it is sometimes easier to do nothing, but if you want achievement in your life, you must become a doer. Only action produces results. Procrastination pins you down.

Let's briefly recall how Jesus used these three ideas. He clearly had His priorities.

> *"For the Son of Man came to seek and to save what was lost."*
> —Luke 19:10 (NIV®)

He had His plan early in life and never wavered from His purpose. Along the way, He taught us many lessons and helped us formulate our plan to reach the kingdom. And certainly, there was no procrastination. He followed through until His ascension into Heaven fulfilling the purpose and plan for His journey on Earth.

Awareness of Habits

Habits are created by constant repetition of a certain pattern of behavior. Habitual patterns are "grooved" into our mind in such a way that they become almost instinctive. We follow the path we've created, and eventually our habit groove becomes a deep rut that controls our actions. We recognize that some habits can be good—like the habit of establishing a specific time each day to pray and converse with God. But other habits can be destructive—using drugs, excessive alcohol consumption, etc. Somewhere in-between are hundreds, if not thousands, of other habits that are both good and bad for us.

The good news is that habits can be changed, and we're here to offer a few ideas for you to use. Try these techniques to remove a bad habit and groove in a good one. First, and most importantly, you must make the decision to change your habit. Nothing will ever change in your life until you've made this decision. Change begins with a willingness to try something different. It begins with the strong desire to take a different path. If you have no desire for change, no change will take place.

Replace the poor or bad habit with a good one. Substitution in a fast-paced sporting activity brings in fresh energy. Substituting poor habits accomplishes the same thing. Trying something new and getting better results is energizing. But be cautioned. You will need to practice this new habit for at least thirty days before it can stick. And, even then, you must be constantly aware of any slippage into past habitual patterns. Our experiences have shown us that good habits are hard to come by, but bad habits are easy to acquire. Good habits are easy to lose, while bad habits are difficult to lose. Keep this thought in mind as you strive to change your habits, and you should experience much better success.

Before you go to bed, encourage yourself to stay with the new habit. Think positively about the good results this new habit brings. Sell yourself on the benefits. Do this before bedtime, and throughout the night your subconscious mind will take the command and start helping you make the transition. Your mind is powerful, and can even help when you are sleeping. Doubt us? Read the classic by Joseph Murphy entitled, *The Power of the Subconscious Mind* to learn what a magnificent gift your subconscious can be when properly used. Don't let the power of this magnificent gift go under utilized.

Try "Prayer Power." Never underestimate the power of a conversation with God. He is always listening and always waiting to help. Pray, rely, and trust that God will help. And He will because He has such intense love for you. Don't we go to friends when we need help? Is there a better friend than God?

Look at your life and ask yourself if things are going like you want them to go. If you are struggling, or having difficulties, examine the habits that now rule your life, and consider the benefits of changing them. That's a decision you will never regret making.

Here are a few ideas expressed by others on the power of habits that hopefully will help you create just the right habits on your life's journey.

"Habit is habit and not to be flung out of the window by any man, but coaxed downstairs a step at a time." —Mark Twain

"First we make our habits, then our habits make us."—Charles C. Noble

"All human actions have one or more of these seven causes: chance, nature, compulsions, habit, reason, passion, desire." —Aristotle

"Sow a thought, and you reap an act; Sow an act, and you reap a habit; Sow a habit, and you reap a character; Sow a character, and you reap a destiny."

—Charles Reade

The Power of your Mind

If you look at your surroundings as you read these words, everything in your sight was created from the seed of a thought. In *Hebrews* 11:3, Paul writes,

"By faith we understand that the universe was ordered by the word of God so that what is visible came into being from the invisible."

Every invention began with a thought. Thoughts are powerful in that they are the initiators of action. Since thoughts initiate action, it is our thinking that will ultimately determine our future. What we think about today determines the kind of life we will live tomorrow. Therefore, getting control of your thought process is probably the single most critically important thing you can do. By focusing on the results you want as the core of your life achievements, and keeping those thoughts in the forefront of your mind, you literally create your life the way you want it to be.

Each of us is endowed with a brain that is more powerful than the fastest, smartest, or most effective computer ever created by man. And the beauty of it all is that this unbelievable gift was given to us free of charge by our Creator. We come gifted for greatness. We come gifted for personal success. How much greatness and/or success we achieve is really up to us. The most successful people have always been able to focus on the successes they want to achieve, and to keep that focus in the forefront of their thoughts. Don't shortchange yourself by not capitalizing on the power you have between your ears. We have found *Thinking for a Change* by John Maxwell to be a wonderful book on the power of thought and a great resource to understand the thinking process.

What dominates your thought process? Is it ideas on success or failure? Is your mind filled with focused thinking, or is it filled with ideas that are as scattered like dust in the wind? Think right and use your mind to its fullest, and your success potential will soar. Use your mind incorrectly, and you will end up as John Milton so eloquently said,

"*The mind is its own place, and in itself, can make heaven of Hell, and a hell of Heaven.*"

Keep Check on your Attitude

In one simple, short sentence—*attitude is everything*. In the previous point, we discussed the powerful mind we all possess and how thoughts drive our actions. Now we begin a building process. Our thoughts help create our attitudes. And, it is your attitude that determines the altitude you achieve. Your attitude controls the way you react to the events of your life, and how well you maintain a positive outlook. If someone is laying a bunch of negative thoughts on you, change the subject. If that does not work, stay away from that person. Negative people have a way of draining the life out of you. You are better off with no friends than to have nothing but nay-sayers around you.

It is important to create a good positive environment. To a large extent what we read, and who we associate with, impacts our attitude. Reading books, listening to CD's or iPod downloads, with positive messages, and hanging around positive people are some of the best ways to keep your attitude right.

We want to remind you that attitudes are chosen and learned. What we often forget is that with an attitude comes the result of practicing and adopting the attitude as part of our character.

In his book, *The Relaxation Response*, Dr. Herbert Benson says that 80 percent of angina pain can be relieved by positive belief. Many doctors now use positive thinking as part of their cure for ailments, including cancer. Without doubt, the optimist wins over the pessimist every time.

How can you change an attitude? Here are several ideas for you to use.

- See yourself in possession of the new attitude. Use your thinking and powerful mind to release yourself from the prison of a bad attitude.
- Change the way you talk to yourself. Often, through our silent self-talk, we feed our brain negative ideas which in turn spurn negative attitudes. Control your conversation with yourself.
- Your desire to change must be greater than your desire to continue with your current attitude. Desire is the fuel for change and improvement. Use your mind and thought process to build desire and remove destructive attitudes from your character.
- Let failures that result from poor attitudes serve as your lessons on living differently. Learn from your failures, and turn your lemons into lemonade.
- Build personal pride to help you change into the "new you."

Whenever you start letting your negative side take over and affect your outlook on life, think about this ancient Persian saying. It's one of our favorites.

"*I had the blues because I had no shoes until upon the street I met a man who had no feet.*"

And who could have a bad attitude when thinking about the love and support God offers us as we take our daily journey on His holy ground. That thought alone should be sufficient to motivate and inspire us. God wants our love. That's His attitude toward us. The important question to ponder is what's our attitude towards Him?

Following your Passion

It's difficult, if not impossible to, reach maximum success in an area that lacks personal passion. We are energized by passion, and we should capitalize on that energy by keeping our focus on activities that bring out our passion. For Billy, it's teaching and consulting on leadership topics. Jodi is passionate about his responsibilities as a Deacon. We're both excited about the messages in this book. What excites you? If you can become enthusiastic about something, you will find added energy in all aspects of your life. You will find that your mind will stay stimulated. You will find that your spiritual life will bring peace, and your body will provide you with energy. Draw from your inner strength, and this will allow you to maintain focus, maintain the proper energy level, and to realize and identify opportunities that will assist you in accomplishing the objectives that bring out the passion within you.

In December 2002, Billy received an email from a young twenty-seven-year-old Italian man who was living in Germany. Marco Bigornia was interested in learning about the speaking profession. As he had done on other occasions where similar requests were made, Billy addressed the questions Marco listed in his email. This email exchange began what has turned into a series of messages crossing the Atlantic and a long-distance friendship that endures today.

Marco enthusiastically responded to Billy's message. By February 2003, he had crystallized his vision of becoming a life coach and speaker. With Billy's encouragement, Marco joined a local Toastmaster group and very shortly gave his first speech, entitled, "What Matters Most to Me." That first speech rekindled the fires of ambition in Marco. He continued studying with Toastmaster, making French, German and English talks. A year later he founded the first Italian speaking Toastmasters club worldwide (Lasciatemi Parlare). Then he began studying Neuro-Linguistic Programming (NLP) and to further his commitment, Marco sought certification as a coach with the International Coaching Federation (ICF). Within two years, while still keeping his job in the banking industry, he had successfully climbed the ranks of Toastmaster achievement and received his NLP and ICF certifications. Additionally, Marco realized that feeding his mind was the key to maintaining his ambitions. He began to read books to stimulate his thoughts and build self-confidence. By now, the fires of ambition were roaring.

In the fall of 2003, Billy sent Marco a complimentary copy of his book, *Searching for Success*, to help him with the development of his dream profession. If every reader had approached the lessons from Billy's book as Marco did, *Searching for Success* would have been a million-seller. It's every author's dream to find such a student of his words.

A few months later the phone rang and from almost half way around the world, Billy and Marco spoke to each other for the first time. What a joy it was for Billy to receive this call of gratitude and listen to the many new adventures Marco had undertaken. It's hard to say who is more excited with the events that had transpired since their original email exchange.

Today Marco has left the banking profession and opened his own firm, *Bigornia-training*. He is on the cutting edge with his innovative ideas and has a very bright future as a life coach and trainer. Billy and his wife are working on plans to visit Italy to meet Marco and his family and savor a great Italian meal cooked by his grandmother, and drink a glass of his grandfather's wine. It would be difficult to write a better ending to this story of someone who took action and took charge of his dream and followed his passion

What does your passion meter read? Are you stuck on zero or busting 100 like Marco? Passionate people energize others. Individuals recognized as great leaders—Abe Lincoln, Gandhi, Martin Luther King, Jr., Pope John Paul II, Margaret Thatcher, and Jesus to name a few, were all passionate about their purpose in life. They displayed a commitment and resolve that could only be fueled by a perpetual passion for making the world a better place. Each of them garnered a tremendous following because we tend to flock to those who are truly passionate about a cause.

So follow your passion, and you will begin to view life as a wonderful journey that will bring a spring to your step, an enthusiasm to your nature, and a lesson to those who watch your actions.

Personal Discipline

The difference between winners and losers comes down to just one thing—*winners are willing to do the things that losers won't do*. How does that statement strike you? Did you feel a slight tinge of guilt when you read it? If you did, examine why you occasionally have resisted doing what you know deep in your heart you should be doing. Why do winners do the things that losers won't do? *They have the ability to use discipline as a weapon against a loser's mindset.*

Think about your past actions and achievements. What factors allowed you to achieve results? What factors got in the way of achievement? If one assesses the first case, the key factor that surfaces will be that you exercised self-discipline. You did what you had to do to achieve your task. In the latter case, you were undisciplined and therefore underachieved.

Life is about habits and being disciplined is a habit that successful people practice. Being disciplined opens doors to opportunities. By contrast, being undisciplined locks the doors to opportunity. How many opportunities have you let slip by because you were not disciplined enough to carry out the requirements of the task? We can certainly relate to many events in our life that have slipped through our fingers because we were not disciplined enough to grasp the opportunity. Writing this book has been an exercise in self-discipline. It has taken us one year from conception to completion of this book. Certainly, a bit more of self-discipline by both of us could have shortened our time line. (To make ourselves feel a bit better, we also understand that not too many people ever write a book)

The problem is people find being undisciplined much easier. Discipline can be hard work. But achievers do what is required, when it is required, for as long as is required. They finish what they start through the implementation of greater discipline. If you can do this, the initial pain of a little discipline will soon be replaced with the joy of accomplishment.

We like *Proverbs 12:1*. No need for further commentary. It says it all.

"*Whoever loves discipline loves knowledge, but he who hates correction is stupid.*" (NIV®)

Discipline and Dollars

Undisciplined people often struggle with their finances. They don't save for a rainy day, even though they walk through life drenched. There is no future planning for anything. They live for today, never thinking about future security or comfort in their old age. Please understand that everything we do carries a price. Success is costly, but failure is bankruptcy. No one in her right mind would choose to fail. Yet when it comes to money, too many live one paycheck from disaster. Starting with your next paycheck, be disciplined enough to put some money aside. Start slow if you are concerned about running out of money before you run out of month. Perhaps setting aside 1-3 percent is achievable now. When you get comfortable with your initial level of saving, try adding a little more. Continue raising the percentage in small increments until you reach at least 10 percent. Some people do much better, and you just might be one of those individuals. Examine your spending patterns. Enjoy the fruits of your labor, but don't be penny wise and pound foolish. Make sure you are not putting money in the black hole of debt, or wasting precious dollars on "stuff" you don't need. The discipline of this practice has gigantic financial rewards.

Got a 401K plan at your place of employment? Put all you can into this pot. With the match your employer makes, you get instant growth. In short order, the amount you are saving becomes substantial. If you don't have a 401K plan, open an IRA, a SIP if you are self-employed, or possibly a money market savings plan. It is critically important that you save a little each month. Be patient with your investment strategy. Don't try to get rich overnight. Most millionaires grew their money conservatively.

Now whatever you do, don't touch those savings. Let the money grow. Have the fortitude to resist using the money for any reason. Never forget that every dollar you take from these funds cannot grow other dollars. It would also be wise to seek the counsel of experts in the field of investing money. Screen this individual very carefully. There are scoundrels who will take your money. Get references, and check their track record. Be sure you monitor your account. Don't be afraid to ask questions and clarify any concerns you have. If your investor resents those queries, find someone else. It's your money, and you have every right to know what is going on. If you don't want to use outside advice, you must become very smart about saving and investing. This is too serious a process to leave to chance or dumb luck.

Exercise discipline with your dollars, and you will take away much stress and worry during your retirement years. More importantly, you might even be able to retire. Dollar discipline is a dandy duty that pays long term dividends. So put the big "D" to work for you. And it's sound advice to never forget the right priority when dealing with money. *Matthew 6:24* says is quite well.

"No one can serve two masters. Either he will hate the one and love the other, or he will be devoted to the one and despise the other. You cannot serve both God and money." (NIV®)

Discipline and Your Health

Medical costs are rising at an alarming rate. While we do not have much control over what medical practitioners charge, we do have some control over having to be treated medically. What is the best way we can avoid these rising costs for medical treatment? It's remaining as healthy as we can. And good health is also positively impacted by discipline.

For example, discipline with your diet means you choose to ingest foods that properly nourish your body. We are certainly not qualified to discuss what constitutes a proper diet, but there are experts who can do this for you. Our recommendation is to consult a Registered Dietitian, not a physician. Most doctors are not trained to understand the impact of food on the body. But that is what a dietitian can do for you. It would probably enhance medicine in this country if every doctor had a RD on staff to consult with his/her patients. Registered dietitians can put you on the right track with the proper diet that considers your health status, age and level of activity. By being disciplined with the quantity and quality of food you consume, you will not only be healthier, but you will save a dollar or two on your medical costs as well.

Exercise is another activity that has the ability to produce a healthier body and mind. And being disciplined about staying with an exercise program is a critical component to being successful getting and keeping your body in shape. The older you are the more important exercise becomes. Our body gets out of shape very rapidly as we age. Like a good machine, our body needs oiling, and exercise is that necessary lubricant. Be sure to seek advice from your doctor and a good trainer before starting a vigorous exercise regiment.

Americans have quickly gained the reputation of being one of the most overweight groups of people on earth. Obesity is almost epidemic with American youth. We over-eat and under-exercise—a lethal combination. Much of the maladies found in our society can be attributed to diet and a sedimentary lifestyle. Instead of expanding energy in the yard, children sit and play video games. Adults use, "I'm too busy," as the excuse for not having time to exercise. But they watch TV or sit at their computer for several hours each day.

Get with the program. Start eating right. Get your body back in shape. Being disciplined about maintaining this lifestyle offers one the opportunity to dramatically increase their life span. Now that is a benefit you should truly like.

"*The greatest wealth is health.*" —Virgil

Discipline and Desire

The last "D" we'll write about is desire. Possessing desire to achieve something builds our determination to accomplish. Desire helps to create laser beam focus—a universal trait of all successful people. Coupled with discipline, a strong desire will conquer obstacles others, with a weaker resolve, would find impossible to overcome. Having a strong desire for discipline enables you to be disciplined. Having a strong desire for good health enables you to diet and exercise properly. Having a strong desire for financial security enables you to save monies for your future.

Your dreams and destiny start with desire. It is desire that makes a difference. It is desire that provides momentum. It is desire that fuels ambition. Identify your strongest desires in life, and use the power of discipline to make them reality.

So, what are you waiting for?

Moving Towards Wisdom

Do you know anyone who doesn't appreciate a person of wisdom? There is something almost sanctimonious about being wise. Solomon is still revered as one of the wisest men to have ever lived. We generally admire those who we feel are able to somehow provide comfort and sensibility to the problems we face. The book of Proverbs is filled with words about wisdom. Among our favorites:

"*The discerning heart seeks knowledge, but the mouth of a fool feeds on folly.*"
—Proverbs 15:14 (NIV®)

"*How much better to get wisdom than gold, to choose understanding rather than silver.*"
—Proverbs 16:16 (NIV®)

"*Listen to advice and accept instruction, and in the end you will be wise.*"
—Proverbs 19:20 (NIV®)

"*Trust in the Lord with all your heart and lean not on your own understanding; in all your ways acknowledge him and he will make your paths straight.*"
—Proverbs 3:5-6 (NIV®)

If you truly wish to understand wisdom, seek the words of scripture and make them your way of life. The book of Proverbs is a good place to start. There are thirty-one chapters in the book of Proverbs. Get the habit of reading one chapter a day and repeat this month after month. You will be amazed at how wise Solomon really was. And the good news is that we can all benefit from that wisdom even centuries after his death.

Life Principles and Values

"If you don't stand for something, you'll probably fall for anything." This is a saying from an old wise friend of Jodi's great-grandmother. It was not meant to be insulting, but meant to emphasize having the courage to stand up for the things you believe in. If you have never made a list of values that guide your decision-making process, please take the time to do it now. Knowing your values, and standing firm on their application, creates consistency. Sound values based upon good Christian principles are probably the best attributes a person can have, and by making a list of them, you can create awareness within yourself of them. Get in tune with who you are and what you stand for, and you will find incredible peace in all you do.

Here's an exercise you can use to ingrain values. Make a list of your values and each week focus on one value. At every opportunity, incorporate the value in your decision process. Continue the practice until you've gone through each value several times. You can also use this same exercise when trying to change habits. Ben Franklin used this technique to literally change his personality and catapult himself to greatness.

We'd like to incorporate a brief commentary on ethics here because we are concerned that being ethical in every facet of one's life seems to be fading from our culture. Ethics are comprised of your moral code—the guiding principles and values you use to make daily decisions. In both our business and political leadership, we see increasing incidents of ethical lapses. Don't become one of those statistics. Ground yourself with sound principles and values blanketed with ethical practices. Doing so will make you very different, and help you stand out in a crowd.

And for Christians, our role model for all these ideals is Jesus. He is our shining example of how to live. With such a role model, we now have the template for how to make decisions with unwavering principles, values, and ethics.

Creating Wealth

Please let this statement sink in deeply—you will never be wealthy until you make up your mind to be wealthy. Creating wealth is not a spur of the moment process. It's a deliberate process that one undertakes. Unfortunately, most people never give serious thought to wealth accumulation. They plod through life living on every nickel of income they earn, and forfeiting their future by not saving a dime. If you're relying on Social Security to come to the rescue, we've got a wake-up call for you. Social Security will never make you wealthy and, in fact, with only this income, you will be living in poverty. Plan your own security by establishing a plan to create enough wealth to live comfortably until your last breath occurs. Minimize credit cards. They are like vacuum cleaners—except instead of sucking dust, they suck your money. Exercise that discipline we just discussed and get started on the right track. Remember, it's not income that makes you wealthy. It's the income you keep that does.

Being wealthy is not only money, but it starts with taking money out of your "problem areas." Make a decision to diversity your income portfolio. Use what you do well, and then do it well for profit. Think about what you know that someone else would pay to know. Then find a way to teach it to them for money. An example of this suggestion is used by a good friend of ours, Ted Chicola, owner of one of the most successful beauty salons in Baton Rouge, Technicuts. Ted has taught many individuals to be outstanding and profitable stylists through his apprenticeship program. Besides being a very successful stylist, Ted is also a certified golf professional. He does not accept pay for his golf lessons. Instead, he teaches clients from Technicuts as a sort of "payback" for their loyalty to Technicuts. Ted has found a way to profit from his skill. Wealth can be found and accumulated in many different ways.

The Power of a Mastermind Alliance

No man or woman is an island. We can choose to live in isolation, but it is virtually impossible that we will accomplish anything except being isolated. Success and achievement are more powerfully possible when we align ourselves with others of a similar mindset. Thus, a mastermind group is the perfect answer to that success process.

In his classic book, *Think and Grow Rich*, Napoleon Hill discusses the power of the mastermind alliance. Individuals in a mastermind group possess a synergy, energy, and a like mindset that is used to foster the goals and outcomes desired by each member of the group and outcomes desired by the entire group. It's an open, honest, and supportive endeavor that can produce bigger and better results than any one individual in the group could do alone.

In his speaking and consulting career, Billy has been associated with two types of mastermind groups. One group met periodically, and the other group carried on activities with regularly scheduled conference calls over the phone. In both previous groups, the power of many offered constructive ideas and helped him bring focus to his business outcomes. Mastermind with people more successful and more intelligent than you if you can, but be sure you can contribute to their success as well. There should be people that you learn from, and people that learn from you in the group. The ultimate outcome of a great mastermind group is that everyone receives benefits from the relationship. Mastermind associations are not built on a one-way street mentality. If you are fortunate enough to participate in such an endeavor, you have the perfect environment for exponential growth.

Steve Ridley is a good friend of Jodi's. He is a very successful attorney and entrepreneur who served as Ronald Reagan's finance chairman for Louisiana when Reagan ran for the presidency. Steve was teaching a group of young business men and women and told the group that what they would become would be influenced by the books they read and the people with whom they associated. Steve carried this idea further with Jodi by suggesting he get a legal pad, find the most successful person he knew, then sit down next to him and take notes. He told Jodi to find out how this person became successful, and then to imitate him.

You perhaps hadn't thought of masterminding as the process Jesus used with His apostles. Yes, there wasn't something Jesus could learn from them, but they certainly learned from each other as Jesus led the way.

If you are not in a mastermind group, make a commitment to join in the next ninety days. Don't procrastinate. Just do it. If the group doesn't work out, don't be shy about creating a stronger group. The idea is that everyone should experience growth, and information exchange becomes a two-way street.

Napoleon Hill in *Think and Grow Rich* carried the mastermind idea even further by encouraging the creation of a mastermind group made up of famous people who are no longer living. He recommends that you study these individuals so that you understand how they think. Then, "pick their brain" as you throw out your problems. You might ask Jesus how He would approach a situation on ethics and morality. You could pose a leadership question to George Washington. Don't laugh at this suggestion. It's powerful and effective. Engage in conversation with your "mentors," and you'll be amazed how your brain will process information as though these individuals were speaking directly to you. (And maybe they are?)

Being at Peace with Yourself

One of the greatest achievements in life is to feel peaceful with who you are and what you represent. When you arrive at this destination, it's okay to put on the brakes. Most of the stresses in life come when we are uncomfortable with our place. And becoming peaceful with ourselves begins with placing our trust in God. When we've established that ultimate relationship with God, there is incredible peace in our heart and soul.

"For he (Jesus) is our peace." —Ephesians 2:14

"The fruit of the Spirit is love, joy, peace, patience, kindness, goodness, faithfulness." —Galatians 5:22 (NIV®)

When you are able to incorporate the fruits of the Spirit listed in this passage from Galatians, wonderful things will begin to happen.

- When you build your relationships using **love** as the core component for greeting and appreciating family, friends, and business associates, life becomes more peaceful. And never forget that it's the love that God has for us that guards us and guides us today and every day of our life.
- Coating your outlook on life with a **joyous** mindset brightens your view, and creates less stress and more peaceful moments. When we follow God's plan, our life will be filled with joy—that's a guarantee.
- By keeping **peace** in our hearts, it becomes impossible to harbor ill feelings toward others. A peaceful heart can appease anger, halt hatred, and dissolve discrimination. A peaceful heart will prolong life.
- Exhibiting **patience** with everyone is not always the easiest thing to do. But how accepting you become to others when you can be patient. Proverbs 19:11 says it best,
"A man's wisdom gives him patience; it is to his glory to overlook an offense." (NIV®)
- We should extend **kindness** to those we encounter because it's God's kindness that leads us to repentance from our sins. We remind you what William Penn says about kindness, "If there is any kindness I can show, or any good thing I can do to any fellow being, let me do it now, and not deter or neglect it, as I shall not pass this way again."
- There is also so much truth to what Socrates said about **goodness**. He said, "A good man cannot be harmed either in life or in death." If we live our life in such a manner, God will bless us, not only in this life's journey, but also in the eternal bliss waiting for us when our time on earth is done. And, in the end, each of us will be judged

by the standards that comprised our life, by how much we gave to the world, and by the goodness we displayed towards others.
- Mother Teresa understood *faithfulness* well. She said, "I do not pray for success, I ask for faithfulness." Being faithful is being authentic. Who we are is clearly visible, and appreciated by those who depend upon our faithfulness.

Making Your Choice

God has gifted man with many things. Among the most powerful, yet sometimes most detrimental gift, is our ability to make choices. We want to close with four ideas that are powerful individually but collectively separate us from all other species on earth.

Here are the four most valuable and essentials things we bring to life that help to maximize our natural skills:

1. **Our ability to think.** No other living organism has the brain power we possess. No other living organism can think at our level. This trait alone places humans at the apex of life's triangle. However, most people are reluctant to practice this skill. They want everyone else to think for them. They just want to do and not think.
2. **Our ability to take action on our thoughts.** Step one is important. But, if you do nothing with the knowledge you gain by thinking, it's no different than not thinking at all. Take action on your knowledge the way you do business.
3. **Our ability to get results from our action.** If we choose the right actions, we will get the right results. Sounds simple? It really is. What we must do is utilize our thinking, take the correct action, and the results are automatic. How much better could God have set things up for us?
4. **Our free will.** The power to choose, like our ability to think, is a unique gift. We don't have to rely on instinct like other animals. We can think, and thus make choices. This wonderful ability is given to us free of charge yet, we often forget we can choose.

Lastly, we want to challenge you to make a choice. Why not spend time thinking and formulating goals you truly desire to achieve? *Write them down!* Make detailed plans and deadline action steps for their achievement. Become focused on your goals and make them a part of your daily activities.

Visualize yourself achieving the goals. *Feel it!* Don't quit until you reach your desired destination. If something gets in the way, use the experience as a learning tool, and use the good in it to help with the achievement of your goal. Overcome obstacles with persistence and determination, always remembering the words of Winston Churchill when he spoke to his countrymen during the bleak times of WW II, and encouraged them to *never give up!*

We encourage you to take the words of our book and create a list of goals that might have surfaced while you were reading. We've created a special place for you to write those goals on the Success Challenges page that follows.

Always remember that you have a free will, and you can make choices to adjust the journey and guarantee success. Sometimes we have to reset our goals because circumstances change. If this happens, focus on the new goal. Never replace a goal with *no goal.*

Finally, we remind you that success is not the destination, it is the journey. You now have the ticket for the journey free with this book. What a bargain!

Success Challenges

On this page, we've provided space to create up to ten goals that will help you improve your position in life and enhance the journey you are on. Don't limit your dreams, and don't limit yourself to writing just ten goals. Create a "Goal Book" and write as many goals as you can wish to write. Then it's a matter of prioritizing them and getting to work. God did not make you to fail. You have the gifts. It's up to you to use them for His greater glory and for your personal happiness.

1. _____

_____

_____

2. _____

_____

_____

3. _____

_____

_____

4. _____

_____

_____

5. _____

_____

_____

6. _____

_____

_____

7. _____

_____

_____

8. _____

_____

_____

9. _____

_____

_____

10. _____

_____

_____

PART V

A

Little

Lagniappe

The Journey Home

Lagniappe is a term we use in South Louisiana to designate "giving a little bit more." In the spirit of our tradition, we are pleased to share with you several additional ideas to help bring your journey to a successful close. We are pleased to start this part of the journey with an original work by our friend, John Preston Beck. We feel it's a fitting close to our message to help with your journey on holy ground.

The Journey Home
by John Preston Beck

Drawn as a magnet to a far away land,
for reasons unknown, and could not understand;
With a burning desire, and a thirst to fulfill,
the dream of my journey, was God's Holy Will.

With doubt in my mind, and fear in my soul,
the journey to be made was my destiny to control.
Seeking to understand, and yearning to find,
my journey began in the Soul of my Mind.

Visions of grandeur spilled forth from the past,
enlightening my Mind to origins of vast.

*Onward I pushed, as my Soul did retreat,
and in Mind, I returned to my Master's feet.*

*With tender Love and Mercy, He stretched forth his hand,
and said, "My child, Thou are more than a Man."
Oh Master, I asked, "From which land did I trod?"
and he Humbly responded . . .
"Is it not written in your Law, I said Ye are Gods."*

The Spirit of Manresa

Both Jodi and Billy are long-time attendees at the annual retreats held at Manresa House of Retreats in Convent, Louisiana. Because this annual spiritual renewal is so important and uplifting to us, we'd like to share a bit about the experience and the place. Some parts of the following story are included in Billy's book, *Searching for Success*.

One of the great joys of our life is the annual retreat we attend at Manresa Retreat House. Each year we drive the short distance from our home to the beautiful retreat setting along the banks of the Mississippi River. Manresa provides an inspirational setting with hundreds of stately oak trees on the grounds. It is an ideal environment for spiritual renewal. What is unique about the retreat is the vow of silence every participant practices. Here is how it works.

Each Thursday evening at 6:00 p.m. slightly over one hundred men arrive at Manresa to begin their retreat. After everyone checks in, and the evening meal is complete, the first of a series of thirty-minute sessions is conducted by a priest or deacon. He is known as the Retreat Master. Following his comments, the silence begins. Participants do not engage in conversation and continue the silence until the completion of the noon mass on Sunday.

Occasionally, there are those who cannot stand the quietness—they go home or they never return. For those who cherish the time to be alone with their thoughts, with no TV, telephone, radio, or person to interrupt, it can be a life-changing experience.

The retreat schedule involves a series of eleven lectures provided by the Retreat Master, daily mass, rosary recitation on Thursday afternoon, and a Way of the Cross on Friday afternoon. No activity is compulsory. Attendees are free to walk the grounds, stay in their room, or participate in the scheduled program. Each meal is a feast for the body, and every lecture contains powerful food for the soul. It is an experience like no other we've ever encountered.

Some personal time is allotted for those individuals who may wish to have a private session with a priest. These sessions are an opportunity to talk to someone about any issue. These are wonderfully educated and understanding priests who constantly amaze us with their ability to provide sensible and practical solutions to complex issues. Again, this is an option and not a mandatory practice. There is also private time that can be scheduled in one of the chapels where it's just you and God engaged in a direct conversation.

For individuals who like to speak as much as we do, we marvel at how much we enjoy the experience of silence. The time at Manresa is so precious that nothing but death or serious illness of a family member will ever stop us from completing this annual activity.

One final unique thing about the retreat is that there is no mandatory requirement to pay. Participants are told what the cost is to cover individual expenses, and are encouraged to make a contribution equal to that amount. Everyone receives an unmarked envelope in which to deposit their payment, whatever that is. No one but you and God knows how much you've contributed. Some are very generous. Others give what they can afford. The wonderful thing about this system of payment is that each week more than enough is paid to cover expenses and maintain this beautiful facility. To further demonstrate the generosity of the Men of Manresa, in one year a renovation balance of over eight million dollars was retired by the 6000 or so men that come annually to this magnificent spiritual environment. The Holy Spirit is truly at work in the hearts of these men.

The power of Manresa's silence gives attendees an opportunity to bring clarity and focus to their life. Reflecting on the past, and how the months ahead can be approached, is a much clearer process in the Manresa environment. We have learned how to be a better person and accept the challenges life brings. We have learned how to forgive our weaknesses and grow our strengths. We have learned how to become more tolerant of ourselves and others. Silence is a powerful stimulator.

If we were to choose a phrase to describe Manresa, we could not say it better than Louis Yarrut does in one of the booklets on Manresa. He described Manresa as, *"The house of silence and sacred sod, where nobody speaks to anybody and everybody speaks to God."*

Manresa Prayer

This is a prayer Billy composed at one of his retreats several years ago. It's intensely personal, but is shared in the hope that it will make a difference as you complete your spiritual search. May it bring a powerful message to your soul, peace to your heart and tranquility to your life as you move through your journey on holy ground.

Help me to have an open mind to receive Your daily gifts, and profit from the experience. Tear down my walls of resistance to Your love, and let me recognize the ways You are shaping and guiding my life. Help me to use all my talents, and to focus on Your love and the goodness and joy of Your kingdom.

Thank you for the many blessings You've bestowed upon me, for being there when I needed strength to get through the low moments of my day, for giving me courage to face tomorrow with confidence.

I'm sorry for the times I turned my back on You and fell into the grasp of sin. I ask for Your grace to repent and purify my heart so I would eliminate such actions from my life.

I love you and need Your love and guidance every moment of my life. I want all my actions to express my love for You. I am deeply grateful for Your patience, and humbly ask for Your forgiveness when I fail to acknowledge how important Your love is to me.

Be with me and help me develop the strength to always do Your will. Shape my mind to focus on the possibilities of what can be. Be with me so that all my actions are dedicated to fostering Your love within me, and every person I met. May I always remain Your servant.

Teach me to pray with an open heart so that I can receive Your message. Teach me to accept the things I cannot change or control. Give me the courage to act and change the things I can and should. Provide me with the wisdom to know the difference.

I ask all these things in Your name. *Amen.*

Personal Growth & Self-Improvement Reading List

The hardest thing about developing a reading list is deciding which books to leave out. We could have added many, many more. But this list does include our favorites. Some are old publications with a very solid message. Read with a highlighter in hand. Mark up your books. Write notes in the margins, and take action on the lessons learned. We promise that if you read and apply the lessons shared between the covers of these great books, your life will never be the same again.

1. *The Bible*—Contains all the "rules" we need for successful living techniques.
2. *How to Win Friends & Influence People*—Dale Carnegie
3. *Simple Steps To Impossible Dreams/The Richest Man Who Ever Lived/The Millionaire's Notebook*—Steven K. Scott
4. *Think and Grow Rich/Success Through A Positive Mental Attitude/Master Key to Riches*—Napoleon Hill
5. *The Secret*—Ronda Bryne
6. *Letting Go of What's Holding You Back*—Wayne Sotile, Ph.D. and Mary Sotile, M.A.
7. *The Magic of Thinking Big*—David Schwartz
8. *How Faith Works*—Dr. Fred Price
9. *Jesus, CEO*—Laurie Beth Jones
10. *Raising Respectful Children in a Disrespectful World*—Jill Rigby
11. *The Magic of Believing*—Claude Bristol
12. *The Richest Man in Babylon*—George Clason
13. *Life Strategies/Self Matters*—Phil McGraw
14. *Working Smart/The Millionaire In You*—Michael LeBoeuf
15. *Success: The Glen Bland Method*—Glen Bland
16. *Seeds of Greatness/The Joy of Work*—Dennis Waitley
17. *The Power of Positive Thinking*—Norman Vincent Peale
18. *Jesus of Nazareth*—Pope Benedict XVI
19. *Wooden on Leadership*—John Wooden
20. *The Five Temptations of A CEO*—Patrick Lencioni
21. *Being Your Own Best Friend/The Friendship Factor/Bringing Out the Best In People*—Allan Loy McGinnis
22. *The Hidden Value of Man*—Gary Smalley and John Trent, Ph.D.
23. *Happiness is an Inside Job*—John Powell, S.J.
24. *The Purpose Driven Life*—Rick Warren
25. *The Alchemist*—Paulo Coelho

26. *Don't Worry—Make Money/Don't Sweat the Small Stuff/You Can Be Happy No Matter What*—Richard Carlson
27. *The One-Minute Millionaire*—Robert Allen & Mark Victor Hansen
28. *The Leadership Challenge*—Kouzes & Posner
29. *Good to Great*—Jim Collins
30. *The Miracle of Motivation*—George Shinn
31. *Searching For Success*—Billy Arcement

We also highly recommend any books by Og Mandino, John Maxwell, Jack Canfield, Mark Victor Hanson and Stephen Covey as always having a powerful and useful message:

Spirituality/Religious Based Books:

Because this book has a strong spirituality intertwined in the messages, we wish to share this additional list of books that have lifted our spirit. We pray the words of these wonderful books will enhance your spiritual growth and move you closer to the Father as you travel on His Holy Ground.

1. *Spiritual Freedom*—John J. English, S.J.
2. *Business Through the Eyes of Faith*—Richard C. Chewning, John W. Eby and Shirley J. Roels
3. *Finding God in All Things/Paying Attention to God/What Do I Want in Prayer?/Who Do You Say I Am?*—William A. Barry, S.J.
4. *Who is Jesus? Why is He Important?*—Daniel J. Harrington, S.J.
5. *Discernment–the Art of Choosing Well*—Pierre Wolff
6. *The Lamb's Supper*—Scott Hahn
7. *Will the Real Me Stand Up?/Why Am I Afraid to Tell You Who I Am?/Through the Eyes of Faith/A Life-Giving Vision*—John Powell, S.J.
8. *Opening to God–a Guide to Prayer*—Thomas H. Green, S.J.
9. *The Ultimate Gift*—Jim Stovall
10. *Jesus of Nazareth*—Joseph Ratzinger, Pope Benedict XVI
11. *Traits of a Healthy Spirituality*—Melannie Svoboda, SND
12. *We Are the Beloved*—Ken Blanchard

A Personal Note from the Authors

We Want to Hear From You

Once you've spent time reading and interacting with the messages in our book, we encourage and welcome your comments. Let us know what you liked, what moved you, and what message we could have expanded a bit more. We don't bruise easily. We want your honest reaction to our work. This has been a labor of love and, from our view, a divinely inspired project. You can find contact information on our web sites, which are listed below, to write or email us.

Billy Arcement, MEd.

Billy is a Leadership Strategist who works with business and education leaders. His messages on leadership, management, and personal success strategies to his corporate clients are described as challenging, thought-provoking, yet fun to hear. He blends his unique style of Cajun humor with powerful messages that have proved to be a winning combination with every audience.

He is considered one of the premier consultants to work with school boards on roles and responsibilities, team building, and strategic planning retreats. He is passionate about his "Children First" advocacy as he speaks to school board association meetings around the country.

Billy is a former teacher, school board member, and corporate manager. He has been a member of the National Speakers Association since 1980 and is a member and past president of the New Orleans Chapter of NSA.

He received his BS in Physical Education and Science from Nicholls

State University, his MEd. in Administration and Supervision from Louisiana State University and completed post-graduate studies and certification as a Counselor from Nicholls State.

Billy writes nationally published articles on leadership, management, school board service and success strategies. He wrote the book, *Searching for Success*, now internationally published.

Learn more about his services at www.SearchingForSuccess.com.

Deacon Jodi Moscona, JD

An attorney, author, entrepreneur, motivator, and spiritual director, Deacon Jodi Moscona was born in New Orleans and holds a BA degree in Political Science from the University of New Orleans and a Juris Doctorate from Loyola University of the South. He also holds a certificate from the Religious Studies Institute and a Diaconate Certificate from St. Joseph's Seminary College at St. Benedict, Louisiana.

The founder of Moscona Ministries, Deacon Jodi, along with others, offers powerful retreat experiences for groups in various settings. Information about the opportunities provided by Moscona Ministries can be found at www.deaconjodi.com .

Jodi is also a teacher of success principles and has extensive experience training individuals and groups to "Reach their Goals and Achieve Success." Jodi's approach is entertaining but challenging. He is regularly invited to address groups as a keynote speaker. Information about Jodi's programs can be found at www.jodimoscona.com.

Jodi and his wife Darlene have two sons and a daughter. Brian, a graduate of the University of Notre Dame, lives in Atlanta and works at Holy Spirit Prep where he teaches and coaches. Matthew, a graduate of the Manship School of Mass Communication at Louisiana State University, is a radio personality in Baton Rouge, Louisiana. Their daughter Alicia is a graduate of LSU and is a stylist with "Technicuts" in Baton Rouge.

We Thank You for Purchasing and Reading Our Book

Lastly, we wish to thank you for purchasing our book. We also have CD's available on a variety of topics and will shortly have this book on CD. All our products can be purchased from our websites.

We hope your journey on holy ground is a blessed one.